THE HEALTH CARE EXECUTIVE SEARCH

A Guide to Recruiting and Job Seeking

Edited by

Earl A. Simendinger, PhD
Professor and Chairman
Department of Health Education
and Health Sciences
Central Michigan University
Mt. Pleasant, Michigan

Terence F. Moore
President
Mid-Michigan Health Care Systems, Inc.
Midland, Michigan

AN ASPEN PUBLICATION®
Aspen Publishers, Inc.

1989

Rockville, Maryland
Royal Tunbridge Wells

Library of Congress Cataloging-in-Publication Data

The Health care executive search: a guide to recruiting
and job seeking/edited by Earl A. Simendinger, Terence F. Moore.
p. cm.
"An Aspen publication."
Bibliography: p.
Includes index.
ISBN: 0-8342-0027-9
1. Health services administrators--Recruiting.
2. Health services administrators--Selection and appointment.
3. Job hunting. I. Simendinger, Earl A. II. Moore, Terence F..
RA971.H385   1989   362.1'0683--dc19   88-8101
CIP

Editorial Services: Ruth Bloom

Library of Congress Catalog Card Number: 88-8101
ISBN: 0-8342-0027-9

Printed in the United States of America

1 2 3 4 5

Contributors

Charlotte Beck

Joan Bourke

Michael D. Caver

Susan A. Cejka

John R. Clark

Mark M. Cox

J. Daniel Ford

James N. Heuerman

Michael C. Kieffer

John S. Lloyd

Terence F. Moore

Daniel M. Mulholland III

Terry Riedinger

Miceal C. Rooney

Mark B. Silber

Earl A. Simendinger

J. Larry Tyler

Peter A. Weil

Table of Contents

v

**Chapter 6— Effective Incentive Programs That Attract and
Retain Executive Talent 91**

Mark M. Cox, *Senior Vice President, Witt Associates
Inc., 724 Enterprise Drive, Oak Brook, IL 60521*

Joan Bourke, *Senior Associate, Executive
Compensation, Witt Associates Inc., 724 Enterprise
Drive, Oak Brook, IL 60521*

Chapter 7— Causes of Executive Failure in Health Care 105

Terence F. Moore, *President, Mid-Michigan Health
Care Systems, Inc., 4005 Orchard Drive, Midland, MI
48640*

Earl A. Simendinger, PhD, *Professor and Chairman,
Department of Health Education and Health Sciences,
Central Michigan University, Mt. Pleasant, MI 48859*

Chapter 11— Resumes: How To Write Them and How To
Evaluate Them 185

Earl A. Simendinger, PhD, Professor and Chairman,
Department of Health Education and Health Sciences,
Central Michigan University, Mt. Pleasant, MI 48859

Terence F. Moore, President, Mid-Michigan Health
Care Systems, Inc., 4005 Orchard Drive, Midland, MI
48640

Chapter 12— Attention to How You Are Perceived:
Appearance, Style, Body Language, and
Preparation 209

J. Larry Tyler, President, Tyler & Company,
9040 Roswell Road, Atlanta, GA 30350

Chapter 13— The Interview Process from the Hospital's and
the Candidate's Perspective 221

John R. Clark, PhD, Manager, Health Care Executive
Search Management Consulting Services, Coopers &
Lybrand, 203 N. LaSalle Street, Chicago, IL 60601

Preface

The turnover rate in health care facilities probably has never been greater than it is today. The reasons for voluntary and involuntary resignations of chief executive officers are numerous, but the results are the same—more health care executives are seeking positions and the velocity of executive turnover is high. Moreover, all of this turnover at the top has an unsettling effect throughout those organizations where it occurs and causes increased turnover at all levels.

This book has been produced to help organizations in their search for executive talent. More importantly, from our viewpoint, it has been written to assist our professional colleagues who are either in search of a position now or will be at some stage of their careers. Our estimate is that 90 to 95 percent of all practicing health care executives can benefit from the book, either now or in the future. It is our hope that the book will become an essential part of every health care executive's job search or career advancement folder, which also is sometimes referred to as a "parachute file."

The true experts in the field of job searches and executive recruitment are neither the academicians nor the health care practitioners. The true experts are the executive recruiters and outplacement directors who have handled hundreds of job placements and have heard stories from the governing bodies, medical staff, and practitioners. Unfortunately, these top professionals seldom are asked to document their thoughts about various aspects of job hunting and executive recruitment.

We asked executive recruiters and outplacement executives, who generally are acknowledged to be among the best known in the United States, if they would be willing to write a particular chapter for this book. Every one of these professionals readily accepted the challenge. A result—a handbook to help recruiters enhance their skills and health care executives prepare themselves for their next career move.

Terence F. Moore
Earl A. Simendinger, Ph.D.

xiii

Acknowledgments

We extend our deep appreciation to the authors of the various chapters. Each made a significant commitment in time and effort to make the necessary deadlines and develop the chapters in spite of the rigorous schedules. Peggy Oliver, Pat Wolfgram, and Phyllis de Lange provided invaluable assistance in the development of the project. The staff of Aspen Publishers, particularly Russell Pottle, Steven Mautner, Ruth Bloom, and all those who reviewed and revised the various drafts of this manuscript deserve special credit. We are grateful for their efforts and support and salute their professionalism.

Part I

The Hospital's Perspective

1

How To Evaluate Executive Staff: A Step-By-Step Approach*

James N. Heuerman, Managing Vice President/Senior Partner, Health Care Division, Korn/Ferry International, 600 Montgomery Street, San Francisco, CA 94111

The world is filled with bright people and good people, and people who work hard and think clearly. But for any given job, only a select few have that magical combination of qualities that make them ideal candidates. The most daunting task for anyone searching for a new executive is not to locate a pool of fine prospects, but to distinguish between people who are really right for the job and those who think they want it.

As the world's largest executive search firm, Korn/Ferry International's success and reputation rest on its recruiters' ability to make these distinctions accurately, and on the resources they have developed. In the field of executive search, quality and consistency are critical. As a top human resource officer recently said about the search business, "You're only as good as your last placement."

Of course, over many years a successful recruiter develops strong instincts about candidates and about the "fit" between the individual and the institution. In today's competitive environment, however, even a sixth sense is not enough. Professionals in the executive search field have developed rigorous techniques to ensure that they choose, from among a field of able, amiable candidates, those who will negotiate a smooth transition, work effectively with colleagues and the community, provide strong leadership, and move an organization toward its goals. This chapter describes those techniques, proven effective in any industry, and offers a sequence of steps that apply to any executive-level search.

The health care field has a unique climate and culture. Indeed, this is why some search firms and some recruiters—including Korn/Ferry International (a leading executive search firm)—have specialized in providing services to health care institutions. A brief glance at trends in the industry that decisively affect the search process follows.

UNIQUE CHALLENGES IN HEALTH CARE

The health care industry presents unique challenges to the executive recruiter. These are some of the considerations that color the search process from the outset.

- *High visibility.* Because most health care facilities operate as not-for-profit or public institutions, the search for a high-level executive is often a well publicized event that sparks interest among diverse segments of the community.
- *Sunshine laws.* In some cases, a community board or public body may do the hiring, and must open its deliberative sessions to the public in compliance with sunshine laws.
- *Search committee.* Typically, a search committee with anywhere from 2 to 12 members will already be in place when the executive recruiter steps in. (Facilitating deliberations is an important part of the recruiter's job.)
- *Staff participation.* Consultation with key medical personnel and other members of the executive team is often critical.
- *Sponsorship.* A shared set of values and the ability to support the sponsoring institution are often unwritten requirements.

All of these factors add up to front-end preparation that is more intense than in other industries.

NEW DEMANDS ON HEALTH CARE EXECUTIVES

Rapid technological change, a new entrepreneurial spirit, revised governmental strictures, and shifting insurance practices have reshaped the health care industry. Today's industry leaders must address effectively issues that had little relevance to health care a decade ago.

- *Intense competition.* Traditional hospital services such as emergency care, radiology, and elective surgery now are offered by smaller, diversified health care businesses run by innovative entrepreneurs in an unregulated, free-enterprise environment.

- *Corporate culture.* Many hospitals are banding together for economic security, forming multihospital corporations to offset losses from empty beds and from downtime caused by seasonal cycles or demographic shifts.
- *Managed care.* The proliferation of managed-care organizations has dramatically changed the face of health care financing and reimbursement.
- *Physician–hospital joint ventures.* New alignments in the health care field, and new kinds of contractual and financial arrangements between physicians and institutions are evident.

For health care executives, the task at hand is no longer simply to manage a hospital's daily operations. Instead, the executives must function as leaders and innovators—devising entrepreneurial strategies to create and maintain the institution's market share in the face of fierce competition, employing innovative financial techniques to structure internal cost-control mechanisms, and cultivating a knowledge of personnel incentives to help cement hospital–physician relationships.

The executive selection process is tied not only to industry conventions, and to an institution's present needs, but also to the future. The process is a dynamic one, linked to the unique characteristics of health care and responsive to change within the industry. The selection process also is rooted in established, proven techniques that allow professional recruiters to distinguish ideal candidates from those who would not serve the institution's best interests.

EXECUTIVE SELECTION—STEP-BY-STEP

Laying the Foundation

Anyone embarking on a search needs an accurate blueprint of the job to be filled and a clear picture of how that job fits into the organization's structure, that is, a solid, current job description. A working description, detailing what the job requires today, and what it is likely to require over the next 12 to 18 months is essential.

A job description encompasses five key elements:

1. title of job to be filled
2. organization's characteristics
3. reporting relationships

4. responsibilities
5. qualifications

Since it is a highly negotiable variable, compensation is best left out of the job description.

Creating a complete job description is not simply a fill-in-the-blank procedure, since the basic elements are rarely as straightforward as they appear.

Title

In today's fast-paced health care field, simply naming a position—whether existing or new—can cause complications. Also, public relations considerations sometimes make the title the biggest stumbling block in formulating a job description. Because of the open search process, the institution's visibility within the community, and the competitive marketplace, there may be strong feelings about what the title should represent. For example, chief executive officer (CEO) may sound too formal for a hospital that wants to market itself as a highly service-oriented community institution. It is important to monitor changing perceptions both from outside and inside the institution each time the position turns over.

The title must tie into the institution's legal structure. In a corporate setting, a single position may carry more than one title. For example, the chief administrator of a hospital may also be a vice president of the corporation that owns the hospital.

Organization Characteristics

The job description should include the name of the organization, including all subsidiary relationships, and its location. A brief statement describing its size, history, sponsorship, and legal governance will help pinpoint a candidate's parallel or relevant experience.

Reporting Relationships

The description is not complete without a summary of reporting and working relationships in all directions. This establishes the status and complexity of the position. Even replacing an individual in an existing job may affect the management structure if job requirements have changed. Therefore, review the organizational chart to ensure that it is consistent with the current institutional priorities, and that lines of authority are clearly defined up, down, and sideways from the vacated position.

Defining the management structure often takes far more than sketching an organizational chart. As institutions reorganize and join forces, new positions tend to blur traditional lines of authority. For example, six hospitals banding together need a corporate financial officer, but exactly how will this person relate to the present financial staff in each hospital?

Surprisingly, some important titles, as they are initially conceived, do not have enough substance to warrant a candidate with top-level qualifications, because management is reluctant to narrow its current employees' scope of authority or usurp decision-making power. It often is necessary to redefine other jobs and shift responsibilities in order to carve out a solid new position. Korn/Ferry recruiters often spend several days helping senior managers work out the required changes before launching a search.

Responsibilities

An inventory of job responsibilities can be organized effectively around basic management functions: planning, organizing, staffing, executing, and evaluating. The inventory must be a realistic working description with pragmatic goals. Specifications under each function should be stated as tasks for the first 12 to 18 months on the job. For example: create this program; recruit these staff positions; build this new wing; raise $1 million.

Qualifications

In specifying qualifications, you begin to create a screen, based on knowledge, skills, experience, and accomplishments. These terms have fairly specific meaning within the context of an executive search.

Knowledge generally covers academic background and training.

Skills are much more specific and more closely related to job requirements.

Experience, in concrete terms, indicates how the candidate gained those skills. What was the size, structure, and nature of the institutions or settings where he or she acquired the skills?

Finally, *accomplishments* give the candidate's track record, in quantifiable terms. Note that the job description usually will not require particular accomplishments, but it should be detailed enough to show whether the candidate's accomplishments will be a good predictor of success on the job.

Creating a Screen

Once the job description, including the organizational chart, is firmly in place, you can begin comparing real candidates—as they appear on paper—to the needs of the organization. For a key position such as CEO, you should be able to draw five or six critical variables from the job description. These variables form a primary screen that lets you rule out the least qualified candidates, and highlight the strongest. In addition, you should note a number of secondary qualifications or skills that are not mandatory, but would be highly desirable on the job. In the end, you will have to trade these off against one another, as no single candidate will possess every skill; including them in the screen will help you make comparisons.

Setting up the screen as a visual display matrix gives you an effective tool for presenting candidates to a hiring committee, as well as for quick reference, cross-checking, and review. The matrix lists candidates along with such basic information as current job title, institution, and age. Each of your five or six critical variables heads a column across from the names. Secondary skills can be listed on an extension of this matrix, with each skill at the head of another column.

Critical variables grow out of the job description, and should be fairly specific so you can work efficiently to narrow the field. Typical variables might include: management experience, physician–administrative relations, financial management skills, managed-care experience, or construction experience. Secondary variables might be even more specific skills such as experience settling labor disputes, raising a certain number of dollars for a specific purpose, upgrading services, or conducting a media campaign.

A matrix also may encompass personal characteristics that reflect the institutional culture and specific needs of the job. Does the position call for someone who identifies with the mission of the sponsoring organization? A charismatic public speaker? A "solid citizen" committed to community work?

This visual display is vital to the search process. It is the best safeguard against the recruiter's worst pitfall: recommending a candidate because he or she is an impressive, appealing person, rather than because the person has the right qualifications for the job. A well-constructed matrix will make a likable candidate's deficiencies obvious to all who view it; especially if the visual display is reviewed by a group.

During the initial stages of the search process, the candidate is only a name attached to a letter and resume.

As the search moves forward, however, and you begin talking with candidates in person, the matrix becomes less absolute and rigid. But it still serves an important review function, especially at search committee meetings. If committee members can see the advantages and disadvantages at a glance, less time will be spent at meetings debating strengths and weaknesses, and more time can be devoted to hammering out the compromises needed to reach a final decision.

Considering Internal Candidates

Nearly half of all top-level searches conducted for health care institutions give consideration to at least one strong internal candidate. It is not uncommon for internal candidates to land these jobs, but in too many instances, these candidates are mishandled or misled, sometimes with disastrous results. Like all bureaucracies, health care institutions are political bodies, and internal candidates must be treated with fairness and honesty throughout the search process to avoid rumors, factionalism, anger, and demoralization.

The rule of thumb is simple and straightforward: treat internal candidates as you would any other candidate. Every step that follows applies to them as well as to outside candidates. All communications about the job should be through the recruiter or an internal human resource person, who should screen and interview the candidates and keep them well-informed throughout the process.

Search committees sometimes are reluctant to apply an early screen and reject clearly underqualified internal candidates for fear that they will leave or disrupt the work environment. This caution often backfires. There is a better chance for retaining a good employee if he or she is dealt with honestly. If an employee is given false information, the person may quit or even wage a lawsuit that ties up valuable time, money, and energy.

In other instances, the committee may be tempted to dismiss an internal candidate, only to discover that by the final interview, this candidate has demonstrated a number of unexpected qualities that make him or her ideal for the job. In still other cases, committees may feel the internal candidate is well suited for the job, but conduct a full search anyway to make sure the individual measures up to national standards. This is a good strategy to ensure that colleagues will give the candidate proper respect and cooperation.

In short, the best policy for internal candidates is to stay as objective and apolitical as possible. This will ensure a fair search, a stable work environment, and a smooth transition when the new leader comes in.

Spotting a Winner

Based on the initial screening, you have eliminated unqualified candidates. In the early round, a resume provides all of the necessary factual information. If it is well constructed, a resume can also reveal important things about a candidate's past and even his attitude toward his career. To spot the winners, you have to read between the lines and then pursue your hunches face to face.

The first meeting, a subjective test, is critical. All too often, candidates who appear to be absolutely perfect on paper do not know how to present themselves in a polished way. Just as often, candidates who have presented their credentials in a low-key manner turn out to have a surprising degree of poise, intelligence, charm, and self-awareness.

Inevitably, this first encounter has its beauty-contest side: the recruiter certainly will be affected by how the candidate looks, dresses, speaks, and carries herself or himself. These factors often come into play during the final presentation to the search committee members, who may place great value on external characteristics. But even if the package looks perfect, it is important to probe beneath the surface, to get answers to the questions that came to mind as you read the resume. Through queries about the candidate's family, role models, education, and career goals, the recruiter will begin to see whether the candidate's knowledge, skills, attitude, and presentation add up to the right combination, and whether the person can fit into the culture of the organization.

It also is important to spend some time exploring the secondary qualifications noted on the matrix. Encourage the candidate to describe experiences, and continue to ask questions along the way so that you can gain insight into particular experiences that might bear on the new job responsibilities or operating environment.

During the interview, volunteer as many details as possible about the job to see which ones elicit a response or can be tied to relevant factors in the candidate's background. Initially, the candidate could only guess at what might be important to the search committee beyond its terse description of essential qualifications, so many details about the candidate might emerge that were edited out of the resume.

This is a good time to establish, in great detail, the candidate's compensation requirements, including cash compensation (salary plus bonuses); other pay vehicles, such as stock options; major benefits, including pension, medical and dental coverage, other insurance, and vacations; and other perks, such as cars, luncheon clubs, or spousal travel.

For the most part, health care resumes still address organizational responsibilities without mentioning quantifiable results. This is such an important area to investigate during the job interview that it warrants separate mention. After you absorb the details of a candidate's career, you must also find out what it all adds up to. In today's competitive environment, it is not enough merely to run things well; a CEO must run things better, more cost effectively, more imaginatively, and efficiently. The CEO must not be simply an administrator, but rather a change agent, a thought leader, a producer of favorable outcomes.

In the interview, a candidate should know and be prepared to discuss relevant aspects at length. If not, that is a good indication that the candidate views herself or himself as an overseer rather than an initiator of action in search of results. Generally speaking, if candidates have a realistic, responsible attitude toward fiscal and other measurable responsibilities, they will remember exactly what they set out to achieve, what they did (or are doing) to get there, and how close they have come to the original goal. This is the ultimate proof of an individual's capabilities, and even the most facile speaker will not be able to disguise an empty track record.

Do not forget to update the matrix at this point. As soon as the interview is over, add any new information. Committee members sometimes have a difficult time accepting the fact that no candidate meets every criterion they have set. The more information the committee has on the candidate's specific strengths and weaknesses, the easier members will find it to make trade-offs and discover unexpected strengths.

Evaluating and Gauging Leadership

The evaluation of candidates begins as soon as the search gets underway and continues until an offer is made and accepted. But the most critical evaluation phase comes now—after your prime candidates have been interviewed. At this point, you are in a position to assess not only the candidates' qualifications and accomplishments, but also their style and leadership ability.

Experience with thousands of job candidates has persuaded many at Korn/Ferry that people are not born leaders. As Lester Korn, Chairman of Korn/Ferry International, wrote, "Successful careers rarely happen by accident. To rise through the ranks you need not only talent, but courage. . . ." Most who make it to the top work extraordinarily hard to get there, following a disciplined path that almost invariably involves the same basic milestones. Some plan and follow these steps with great deliberation; others pursue them instinctively. Either way, the candidates' abilities to reflect on the ways they paved their career paths and to articulate how past decisions shaped their present capabilities, are important components of a leadership profile. Answers to the following eight questions give evidence of leadership milestones:

1. Has the candidate developed a strong work ethic? Leaders do this early on. Perhaps some are born with it, but more likely they acquire it

by observing hard-working parents or other role models, or by going to work at an early age to help the family or to gain a measure of independence. However it is acquired, this ethic—along with the drive and enthusiasm for the activities and rewards associated with work—is a basic requirement for success.

2. Has the candidate received a solid education? Some people are fortunate enough to be sent to top-notch schools at an early age, but others who must struggle every inch of the way end up with a superb education because they are highly motivated to learn and get ahead. In today's world, however, it is difficult to get an adequate education by reading books in front of the family hearth. A formal institution is where leaders acquire and hone skills, and often the better the institution, the better chance individuals have of acquiring superior skills.

3. Has the candidate found a mentor? Mentors play an important role in continuing a leader's education. Most successful people have the benefit of expert teaching, guidance, criticism, and encouragement from an older, more experienced person at an early stage in their careers. The mentor teaches by example, demonstrating successful behaviors, and steering clear of those that undermine success. Perceptive would-be leaders quickly learn how to adapt these behaviors to their own purposes and individual styles. Of course, it is important for the would-be leaders to separate from their mentors at some point and to begin functioning as independent decision makers.

4. Has the candidate worked for quality organizations? The only way to learn what excellence in an organization really means is to see it from the inside. Aspiring leaders make it their business to get jobs in organizations that are not necessarily big or prestigious, but that give them a chance to see how to make or deliver quality products or services, how to manage effectively, and how to treat employees decently and fairly.

5. Has the candidate actively sought "hands-on" experience? It has been said that there are two kinds of pay—experience and money, and that before age 30, you should always opt for experience. Budding leaders take on projects and staff work that afford the best opportunities to acquire skills they will need later on, often doing much more than is asked and creating opportunities for themselves where none exists.

6. Has the candidate developed and refined a personal philosophy and style? Over time, as leaders work and observe successful managers, leaders begin formulating definite ideas about how things should be done. This is not an unconscious process: it requires thought and deliberation, trial and error, and a great deal of flexibility. Those who are most successful constantly think about what they do, and try to

make it consistent and coherent to others. Perhaps more importantly, they try to learn from their mistakes, discarding approaches that do not work, and refining those that succeed.

7. Does the candidate accept responsibility for results? Leaders who want to maintain respect in the work place and community accept responsibility for profit and loss, employee productivity, and other quantifiable results. Leaders recognize that their credibility rests on these factors, not on grand strategies or future plans.

8. Is the candidate prepared to capitalize on opportunity? Many people appear to succeed simply by being in the right place at the right time. This, however, is never the whole story. As Lester Korn has said, "The life of any individual who makes it to the top is one of constant preparation. If you look closely, you will see someone who worked very hard, was a bit lucky, and then knew how to capitalize on opportunities at the right time."

Reading Danger Signals

After all of the time and effort that goes into the search process, nothing is more discouraging than to discover at the eleventh hour that an ideal candidate has some fatal flaw or circumstantial impediment that prevents her or him from accepting the job or performing it effectively. Although the problem may appear to have emerged "out of the blue," trouble has been lurking beneath the surface all along, and the recruiter simply did not probe deeply enough to uncover it, or failed to spot trouble when it first appeared. An awareness of danger signs throughout the search process can prevent the last-minute loss of a seemingly impeccable candidacy.

The resume can be a tip-off to certain problems, and during the first interview, the recruiter should have investigated suspicious items or patterns. If a candidate has made several job changes over a brief period, it is important to determine whether there were compelling or well-considered reasons. Generally speaking, it is acceptable in today's corporate world for top executives to move on after a few years at one job. In fact, many associate a long stint in a single company with lack of drive and ambition. Leaving a good job is not suspect; but it *is* unscrupulous to leave in the middle of a major initiative that is foundering, or to bolt after instituting policies that jack up short-term results at the expense of long-term achievement.

You may encounter fewer problems with the candidate's employment record than with a search committee's preconceptions. Committee members may associate long tenures with commitment and community involvement; their ideas may run counter to current thinking in the business world. It is important to know their views in advance so that you can present an excellent candidate to them in the best possible light.

Of course, one must be on the lookout for other red flags as well: a candidate who moves from one organization to another, or from one job area to another, may be impulsive, impatient, or unfocused. The person may get into power struggles with boards of directors or physicians. If explanations are vague, it is crucial to follow up with detailed accounts from references. If the candidate is reluctant or unwilling to supply references for a particular job or time period, or if there are gaps in the resume, something is probably amiss, and it is worth the time to investigate early on.

Academic background is another area that warrants close attention. Unfortunately, many candidates misrepresent their academic credentials. It is important to catch any misrepresentation early, as it can be extremely embarrassing if exposed when the candidate is already on the job.

In addition to the more obvious, verifiable details, there are other personal factors that may grind the hiring process to a halt at the last minute. Spouses are very important players in job changes, and the recruiter should find out about their work and their attitudes toward relocation, as well as the ages of all the candidate's children and where they go to school. Consider inviting a spouse along for the first on-site interview, to gauge his or her reaction to the setting and the prospect of a move.

The status of other dependents, such as aging parents, also may be relevant. Perhaps the candidate has more than one residence, ongoing commitments within the community, or some other special interest that would make relocating difficult. Moving into high-cost communities, like many of those in California, or out of depressed communities, like those found in parts of Texas, can pose very real economic problems. Although it is not necessary during the initial interview to make the candidate swear to move if he gets the job, try to get a sense of how eager the candidate and his or her family are for a change, and how many compromises the candidate might be willing to make.

Finally, you can head off problems by keeping strict counsel on the subjects of compensation and job responsibilities until quite late in the process. These highly volatile factors may change considerably during the search, and it is important that the candidate never feel that anything was misrepresented or taken away when the final offer is made.

Checking References

Once you have identified the best possible candidate, it is critical to make a careful check of all references. Ideally, you should contact the candidate's supervisors, colleagues and those he has supervised.

Today, many references offer only guarded comments, fearing that candid reactions may bring on legal action. Find ways to push past this fear, since forthright references are essential in an industry that so directly affects human lives, and that is, by nature, so personal. With patience and persistence, and a conversational style that involves and interests the reference, you can learn a great deal about the candidate.

Korn/Ferry recruiters ask candidates to provide references. Often, many of these hand-picked individuals do not give favorable accounts when the recruiters ask specific questions like: How did the candidate come to leave the job? How did he or she relate to subordinates? Was the candidate active in the life of the organization? How would you characterize this candidate's management style? Does the candidate make decisions easily?

Korn/Ferry recruiters also ask candidates whether there is anyone with whom they should not speak and then look into the circumstances behind this limitation. The recruiters prepare written summaries of conversations with references, and present them to the individuals who are directly responsible for making the offer of employment. Here again, confidentiality is a major consideration.

Using Psychological Tests

None of the leading executive search firms routinely use psychological testing to evaluate candidates. Although Korn/Ferry recruiters prefer to judge executive talent on the basis of past performance, it is not uncommon for Korn/Ferry clients to ask finalists to undergo psychological assessment. This entails a structured interview with a psychologist, and, in some cases, written testing as well.

In the 1940s and 1950s, American businesses made heavy use of psychological evaluation, sitting candidates down for hours of paper-and-pencil tests, and making hiring decisions based on the results. Today, industrial psychologists spend most of their time interviewing people, trying to project candidates not just into an organization's present, but also into its future. Will this person be able to survive as the organization moves forward, perhaps in new directions?

The industrial psychologists delve into personal history. They ask questions that other interviewers cannot pose, and construct a personality profile. What is the candidate's thinking style and motivation? How does she or he tackle problems? How well does the candidate listen? How does the candidate view herself or himself? Does this perception square with the psychologist's assessment?

"We don't see many unstable people," says Dr. Thaddeus O'Brien, a Cleveland-based specialist in the psychological assessment of business executives.

> Everyone we meet has gone through several filters, and is likely to be reasonable, personable, and bright. Nevertheless, we often see finalists who have no business on a short list. Usually, the people who put them there did not have a sufficiently firm grasp of the organization's strategic direction or unique culture.

Many psychologists routinely administer formal personality tests. O'Brien, for example, often gives candidates the *Sixteen PF* test. He considers this test particularly helpful when a candidate seems too good to be true—too polished, too consistent, and too much in control. "The test may tell you what [the person's] hiding," says O'Brien. "It helps distinguish between self-control and rigidity, and it has a built-in faking correction."

The psychologist adds one more dimension to the overall evaluation, and brings a measure of objectivity to the process. To make a real contribution to the selection process, however, the psychologist must have a clear understanding of the organization in order to address the critical question of "fit."

THE RIGHT CHOICE

If you follow the steps outlined above, you will probably end up with three or four candidates who truly are qualified for the position. But the one who is hired must be the person who most will enjoy having on the job. Personality, appearance, style, habits, hobbies, family, religion, moral values, and background all play a role in the committee's sense of how a person will fit into the organization, work as a new team member, and interact with key players.

From the outset, it is important to treat the selection process as a matchmaking process. There are real people on both sides, and if a key player has a strong feeling about not wanting to work with a smoker, or someone else is yearning for a tennis player to round out a weekly doubles game, these desires should not be dismissed.

Korn/Ferry recruiters, after checking and double checking all of the objective qualifications, go to great lengths to ensure that everyone concerned is comfortable with going with their "gut feelings." This kind of "taste test" only leads to trouble when committees bypass the steps previously outlined and go only for candidates who are personable.

Of course, the ultimate test for this match comes much later, when the selected candidate has been on the job for a year or more and has had a chance to convert talk into action. If, on the day the candidate receives and accepts the offer, everyone is confident that this person is objectively qualified and compatible with the environment the story very likely will have a happy ending.

2

Working with an Executive Search Firm

John S. Lloyd, President, Witt Associates Inc., 724 Enterprise Drive, Oak Brook, IL 60521

This topic is broad and has itself been the subject of entire books, so a single chapter can only touch on some of the key issues and topics. The reader will be given a brief history of the executive search as well as information on how to select, work with, and benefit from an executive search firm.

A BRIEF HISTORY OF THE EXECUTIVE SEARCH

Executive search became an industry in the United States after World War II, when the economy's tremendous growth required exceptional management and the traditional, "old-boy" network could no longer meet the demand. Companies could not develop their own management talent quickly enough. Along with rapid growth came rapid change and "business as usual" was no longer viable. At the same time, the positive effects from "cross-pollination" by executives from other companies and industries contributed to the rise of the executive search industry. Companies that exclusively promoted individuals from within often were not successful.

Health care fits easily into this general business scenario, once the 1966 Medicare legislation laid the groundwork for today's highly competitive environment. Before Medicare, health care had been essentially a charity operation; funding was continually doubtful and planning was more by crystal ball than by strategy. Especially after Medicare, forward-looking boards of health care organizations began to recognize the need for superb executives to lead in this new environment, and the way was clear for the emergence of the executive search as a necessary consulting service.

The first health care executive searches were conducted at the chief executive officer (CEO) level; only gradually did the realization dawn that the hospital would best be served by an excellent *team of executives*—chief operating officer, chief financial officer, chief nursing officer, chief information officer, and so on. With growing sophistication in these roles, it was no longer possible just to promote from within, or merely to reward long service.

The day of "kingmakers" doling out plum positions to hospital administration residents and the era of cigar-box accounting systems ended. Today, the hospital board and senior management have come to rely on the specialized services of consulting firms—in information systems, accounting, marketing, organizational design, construction engineering and in the executive search.

WHY YOU NEED A SEARCH FIRM

Today, health care organizations employ the services of executive search firms to assist in identifying and hiring only the top 1 percent or 2 percent of the organization—usually the senior management team, and occasionally a functional specialist in an area for which it is difficult to recruit. Typically clients use a search firm for one of seven reasons.

1. To define/refine the position. The search consultant helps the client define the role, and offers a perspective based on working with a wide variety of organizations.
2. To identify qualified candidates. Because the consultant is in the marketplace, talking with candidates every day, he or she knows what qualifications, experiences, and educational background are required to fit a given job.
3. To approach individuals directly. Sometimes, the client organization knows exactly who it wants, but cannot approach that person directly because of business or political constraints. The consultant can make the direct approach.
4. To save time. Search work entails hundreds of hours and often requires extensive travel to meet with candidates. The executive who already has a demanding job is not able to take on the search role—at least, not without sacrificing some quality in his or her primary job.
5. To deal with difficult "politics." Management guru Peter Drucker said, "Hospitals are the most complex social entities." Some situations simply cannot be handled by people on the scene—they require an outsider for resolution.
6. To objectively evaluate internal candidates. To determine how good even the best internal candidate is, he or she should be evaluated by the same criteria used for the best candidates from other organiza-

tions. If he or she is an exceptional candidate, that quality will be evident.

7. To broaden the organization's networks. When a search consultant tells an organization's story throughout the country, new contacts and friends are created. Perhaps the immediate payoff is negligible, but over the long run, an organization that is known nationally will be more attractive in the future to top candidates. In general, organizations can profit from broader horizons.

Even though these reasons justify the use of an executive search consultant, often senior health care executives do not perceive the need for such a consulting service. The reason is that the need that creates the search opportunity is often unpredictable. For example, executive turnover cannot be predicted clearly except in the case of planned retirement, when preparation of an internal incumbent (at least for the interim) should be expected from every senior manager. All other causes—death, resignation, dismissal, or reassignment of duties—seem to come unexpectedly.

In a 1986 survey conducted by the University of Dallas Graduate School of Management,[1] hospitals surveyed relegated management recruitment to the next-to-last position among identified management needs—far below marketing assessments, productivity improvements, cost accounting, strategic business planning, flexible staffing, alternate delivery systems, management information planning, financial planning, medical staff recruitment, and corporate structure and design. However, since the selection of executive officers is an important task, those organizations who want the best candidates should choose an executive search firm.

HOW TO DIFFERENTIATE AMONG FIRMS

Considering Key Characteristics of Search Firms

Some firms are solo practices, depending on the skills and knowledge of one person. Other firms operate almost as though they are solo practices, although they are companies with a number of employees. In these organizations, competition is fierce and there is little teamwork or information- and candidate-sharing possible. Outstanding candidates are guarded jealously. Although there is an appearance of group effort, in reality it is every person for himself or herself.

Some firms operate on a regional basis, while others are national in scope. Some firms specialize in a single position such as physician recruiting; others specialize in a single industry such as health care; still others conduct searches in a number of unrelated industries such as computer, transportation, automotive, entertainment, and manufacturing.

One method for differentiating among the different types of firms is to look for a variety of quality indicators. However, the firm's size, capability, limitations, style, process, and performance also should be considered.

Indicators were identified in a 1985 national survey of health care CEOs and COOs. The respondents rated important key characteristics in the selection of an executive search firm (Table 2-1).

A survey of organizations in a wide variety of businesses and industries, sponsored by the Association of Executive Search Consultants (AESC) in 1985, provided similar findings.[2] According to Dr. David H. Maister, who conducted the telephone interviews with executives, the following factors are considered in selecting a search firm or consultant: professionalism (53 percent); chemistry (51 percent); industry specialization (50 percent); recently handled a similar search (30 percent); speed (25 percent); and regular progress reports (10 percent).

In this study, professionalism was defined as: "The ability to present and deliver a set of behaviors that provide confidence in knowledge, industry, search experience, completion, problem-solving and a value-added service." Client company representatives told Maister they choose a search firm because of their trust and confidence in the firm or the individual consultant's ability. Also according to the survey results, clients said they want executive search firms to place more emphasis on reference checking (36 percent), research (34 percent) candidate evaluation (32 percent) and the introductory consultation (19 percent).

Table 2-1 Key Characteristics in Selecting an Executive Search Firm

Characteristics	Rated as important (percent)
Individual consultant's knowledge and understanding of the health care industry	96
The search firm's knowledge and understanding of the health care industry	95
The search firm's prior recruiting experience for a particular position	80
The reputation or industry image of the firm	76
Prior personal contact with the firm	72
Recommendation or referral by a colleague or professional association	66
Prior personal contact with a member of the firm	57

Source: "Survey of Health Executives," Market Opinion Research of Detroit, Michigan, September 1985 (unpublished data).

According to survey results, size and capability were not necessarily related. The number of offices or consultants an executive search consulting firm has does not determine the firm's ability to handle a search assignment successfully. More important is the firm's ability to research and identify the best possible candidates. It is essential for a client to know that an effective working relationship can be developed with the individual consultant who conducts the search assignment.

Any limitations affecting the search (such as clients or individuals considered "off limits") must be discussed fully and understood. Ethical firms accept the policy of holding client organizations off limits for a period of two years from the last completed search.

An executive search is a consulting engagement, not just recruitment activity. To do a quality job, the consultant meets with the client to assess the needs, prepares a written position specification that is mutually acceptable, provides a clear statement of fees and expenses, conducts extensive research to locate qualified individuals who may be interested in the job, reports on progress frequently, interviews candidates in person and in depth, facilitates interviews with the client, participates in the final negotiations and follows up with the client and new executive for some period of time.

Finally, performance is one of the key factors in selecting an executive search consulting firm. One can evaluate the firm's reputation, as well as that of the individual consultant handling the assignment, by checking references on past performance. A search consultant cannot guarantee to fill a position; however, the firm can guarantee performance quality. A filled position may not be the conclusion of an executive search consulting assignment. The client and consultant must establish an understanding about how unusual situations will be handled.

An executive search is complex, and a consultant should possess a wide variety of skills and abilities. In addition to the consultant gaining the trust of those who will make the final hiring decision, three skills are essential:

(1) excellent communications with the client organization and with candidates,
(2) extensive knowledge of the industry and the position, and
(3) sensitivity to the client's concerns and political realities.

Choosing a Firm

Table 2-2 is based on a list of firms that conduct executive searches in health care, taken from the September 25, 1987, issue of *Modern*

Table 2-2 Executive Search Firms in Health Care

Company Name*	AESC†	AAHC‡
Affiliated Hospital Consultants		
Barger & Sargent	x	
Boyden/Flynn, Campbell, Collins	x	
Brighton Consulting Group		
M.L. Carter & Associates		
Cejka & Co.		
CHI Systems		x
The Corson Group		
Dietary Management Advisory		x
Diversified Health Resources		
Sheldon I. Dorenfest Associates		
Druthers Agency		
Fulton, Longshore & Associates		
The Furst Group		
Garrett Associates		
George Ellen Associates		x
Goodman Group		
Malcolm W. Graham		
Guidry & East		
Health Search		
Healthtech		
Herman Smith Associates	x	x
Kieffer, Ford & Associates		x
Lamalie Associates		
Langlois & Associates		
Laventhol & Horwath		
R.E. Lowe Associates		
McGladrey, Hendrickson & Pullen		
MedEcon Services		
Bill Miller & Associates		
The Pace Group		
Peabody Group		
Price Waterhouse		
Premier Healthsearch		
Quigley Associates		
Don Rowe Associates		
Ryan Advisory		x
Arthur S. Shorr & Associates		
Theken Associates		x
Tyler & Co.		x
United Search Associates		
Weatherby Health Care		
Witt Associates Inc.	x	x
Wussow Consulting Group		
Arthur Young & Co.		

*Adapted with permission from *Modern Healthcare*. Copyright Crain Communications, Inc., 740 N. Rush Street, Chicago, IL 60611.
†Association of Executive Search Consultants, 1988 Directory.
‡American Association of Healthcare Consultants, 1988 Directory.

Healthcare, in which health care consulting firms were featured. The table indicates whether the firm is a member of AESC or the American Association of Healthcare Consultants. These two national organizations require adherence to codes of ethical practice for membership. For more information on each organization, you can write or call: Association of Executive Search Consultants Inc., 17 Sherwood Place, Greenwich, CT 06830, (203) 661-6606; or American Association of Healthcare Consultants, 1235 Jefferson Davis Highway, Suite 602, Arlington, VA 22202, (703) 979-3180.

HOW TO SELECT A SEARCH FIRM

The best technique in selecting a firm for any type of personal service is to meet and talk with a firm's key individuals *before* there is a specific need, when there is no urgency. In the calm atmosphere of pure research, it should be possible to learn about the firm's capabilities and services. This is especially important when a long-term relationship is sought that can be advantageous both to the client organization and to the firm. Be honest and explain that you are "shopping" with no particular project in mind. The best firms will be glad to have their consultants talk with you and to provide more information for your consideration.

Good times and places to make these contacts are during the major health care meetings held throughout the year, when scheduling some time for an informal meeting should not be difficult. The following checklist of questions to ask firm representatives will make the comparison of firms simpler.

Who will conduct the search? The best search consultant for your project may not be "the head barber." He or she may have had little recent experience in searching for your position, for example. The less-senior staff member who has more experience in your area may be the better choice. Talk frankly with the firm about this issue, and be sure to listen to what the firm's principals have to say as well. You may demand to have a partner do your search work but that will not guarantee you the highest quality search.

When does the search begin? When does the clock start running? Does the client control the process? How does the firm handle the unusual or difficult situations that can sometimes occur? Does the firm's sense of urgency and commitment match your own? Is the firm's pace compatible with your organization's?

When does the search assignment conclude? The actual *search* concludes when there is a signed offer of employment, an agreement between your organization and an individual to develop a working relationship at a certain salary and with certain benefits. But the *assignment* actually goes on, continuing from the first days of the new executive on the job through the first year's employment. There must be satisfaction on both sides for a successful match to occur.

What process does the firm follow? Asking a firm to describe its process will result in an interesting range of responses—some will detail an extensive list of activities and others will describe an operation that is much looser and less formal. The firm's process should accommodate to your organization's style and needs. For example, some firms interview all candidates in depth before they are presented; others bring a pile of resumes and ask you to select final candidates.

What are the reporting arrangements? How much communication does the firm offer; and how much do you want? Is there agreement on this basic item? To whom, and how often, will the search firm report on the status of the work? Some clients want to hear from a consultant every couple of days, while others are content with a written update every week or two. The range is wide, so ask questions to determine what each firm's style of communication will be.

What are the fee arrangements? Most quality search firms operate on a retainer basis—an agreed-upon fee (usually one-third of the first year's cash compensation) is paid, whether or not the firm actually identifies the individual who is ultimately hired. The fee can be discounted in some instances, but usually only by a few percentage points. For example, a discount may be given in the case of a preferred-provider arrangement within a system because a higher volume is presumed. *Note*: there is no cheap way to purchase a quality search effort.

Occasionally, a firm will work on a time-and-expense basis. But this may become more costly than a retained search, because of the nature of the work. The consultant agrees to find someone who will meet the specifications of the job. Note the obvious risk. A search takes as long as it takes, and while some simply race along, others are slower to conclude. The client may not save any money in a time-and-expense arrangement. What the fee is and how it will be charged is a negotiated point with any firm, and a client organization will need to ask what each one's policies are.

Who are the references? How comfortable is the firm in providing you with recent references from organizations that are similar in size and configuration to your own? Once you are given a list of references find out what people who have worked with the firms say about their abilities. Also, what are the positives and the negatives that former or current clients can discuss with you?

What are the firm's areas of expertise? Some firms specialize in a particular position such as chief financial officers or management information systems (MIS) executives. Others have a broader range of experience in a number of executive positions. But how do you measure expertise? It is not necessarily the same as experience.

One method is to review the firm's total involvement with an industry. Look at what organizations it has joined, and what is the level of its participation. Or consider what contributions the firm makes to its industry through such activities as surveys, speeches, and articles. Network-building devices such as these indicate that the firm is truly on the cutting edge of information and trends, both for the industry as a whole and for a particular position or specialty area.

What the client seeks is a consultant and firm that are constantly learning, continually open to new information, ideas, and challenges. Although they have no crystal ball, consultants should be fair predictors of the future because of the immense amount of information available to them.

If you ask consultants from several firms questions like those above, you will form a fairly precise picture of each one's strengths and weaknesses, and you will be in the best position to choose a firm swiftly when the need arises for a search. And you also will be a much more informed shopper for search services. You will know that a firm could be ideal for one search (for example, a marketing vice president), but may not be appropriate for a CEO search. As you become more knowledgeable, your own expectations will naturally rise until you expect and demand the very best in service from a firm.

HOW TO HAVE YOUR EXPECTATIONS MET

How will you know you have received a quality search? How can you build in to a search start-up the clear goals and direction that will give you what you really want? The key is in communications. Decide what you expect from the firm and communicate these expectations before and during the search. Here are a few key questions that you should ask and answer.

- Will the consultant indicate from the outset through a written set of position/specifications that he or she understands our organization and our specific needs for this project?
- Will we be involved in the process, from beginning to end? Will we know what the consultant is doing from week to week?
- Will the consultant do his or her work without our trying to second-guess him or her at every step? Will we contact individuals indepen-

dently, or will we feed every potential candidate into the process for the same type of evaluation?

- Will the initial specifications be maintained?
- Will we as a client be accessible for telephone and in-person meetings?
- Is all the necessary information available to the consultant?
- Will certain imperfections or thorny issues be hidden from the consultant?
- Will the consultant have constant feedback and guidance?
- Will the organization respond to memos and actually read all the materials that are sent?

To have your expectations met in an executive search process, you need to define your expectations and then communicate frequently and meaningfully. You will need to be flexible, and realize that you may not find the perfect person, but expect to come close.

THE EXECUTIVE'S PERSPECTIVE

Up to now, only the client's perspective has been explored. But the individual who is considering his or her career also will come into contact with search firms, and some of the phases of that relationship as well should be explored. A search firm obviously can be of great assistance in an executive's career development.

A clever executive will learn to play the game well, seeking to come to the attention of the search firm through "third-party endorsements." How are these achieved? Through involvement in professional organizations and societies, where an individual can shine in committee work or other types of leadership, or through speeches and articles, which tell the world the individual is an expert on a topic and is willing to share the information. If you are good at your work and you are known to have some expertise and leadership ability, you *will* be noticed by executive search consultants. It is not a question of whether, but of when.

Be aware also that this relationship with a search firm is not unlike a courtship—there is subtle pursuit on both sides, and honesty is the key to developing a meaningful relationship. As with any courtship, there are stages and levels of involvement—and each participant must understand the role he or she is playing.

Imagine this moment: You are sitting on a beach during your vacation, and you think about your career. You are probably not unhappy, but you may wonder if you could do better, if you should move now for some new experience, or you may wonder if you are indeed marketable in today's environment. You are not out of a job or panicked by sudden changes in your organization. You are simply thinking it all over.

When you return from that vacation would be an excellent time to make contact with an executive search firm. Send the firm a resume and a cover letter that describe your career and your goals in detail. In this instance, your resume will need to be more complete than in later, job-specific situations. Your goal here is to help the search consultant who receives it to learn a great deal about you, to make an impression that will last. In this, as in every communication with a search consultant, be honest. Do not overstate your qualifications or inflate your credentials. You may want to include information about your hobbies such as sailing, skiing, or golf, if they reflect your interest in a certain lifestyle or region of the country.

Sending a resume in this way is the equivalent of moving the first pawn forward in a game of chess. You indicate an interest in "playing" but you acknowledge that the entire game may take a good deal of time for completion. You cannot be in a hurry at this stage; that will only complicate the situation. Remember, the ethical search firm is working on behalf of its clients, looking for specific people to fill a specific job. The chances of your resume crossing the desk of a consultant just when he or she is looking for a person with your background are small. It does happen, but not often. Be content to know that your resume and letter are being reviewed; expect an acknowledgement letter, but not much else for a while.

If you wish to call the consultant to whom you sent your resume, do it with the expectation that you are unlikely to catch him or her in the office—about 80 percent of search work is done "on the road," and consultants are seldom sitting at a desk waiting for the phone to ring. Expect that a call back to you may take some time—remember, the consultant thinks of you as a *passive* candidate, not an *active* one. The difference is important, and it is a distinction that only you can make or change.

The passive candidate is one who is not looking, who is quite comfortable in his or her current situation, and who has no desire or need to change jobs in the immediate future. The active candidate, in contrast, is one who desires to look at new opportunities, who has gone through a certain amount of self-analysis and career planning and is ready to make a move.

But what does "readiness" really mean? It may mean many different things to each individual who seeks to become a candidate, but it usually only means one thing to the search consultant: This person can travel on short notice for interviews, and is open to considering new opportunities and challenges. Do not signal an active-candidate status to a search consultant unless you are willing to be taken up on it. The consultant always depends on the individual to communicate his or her intent clearly and honestly. If you know you will not be able to move because of your children's school arrangements, or your spouse's job, or your parents' poor health, do not give a search consultant the impression that you are an active candidate, or you and the consultant will be unhappy in a very short time.

The resume of the active candidate is different from the passive candidate's resume. It is much more job-centered, much more concerned with accomplishments in dollar terms, more finely tuned to the marketplace. It will have intensity and even urgency, and it will represent the individual primarily as a professional—not, perhaps, as the well-rounded person he or she may actually be.

Note that being even an active candidate may not net an immediate response. Once again, patience is required. The search consultant may not be prepared to respond to your needs as quickly as you would like. Here are a few key "don'ts" for the active candidate to keep in mind:

- Don't expect a call immediately about a dream job in your dream locale.
- Don't develop hurt feelings when you do not connect with a job at once.
- Don't call the consultant more than once a month to inquire about positions that you have heard of, no matter how qualified you may feel you are.
- Don't forget: This is business. The consultant can only present you if he or she feels you are a good match for an organization and a position. It does not matter how friendly you have become. If you are not the right person, the consultant will not discuss the job in detail with you.
- Don't be surprised, however, if the consultant calls about a specific position in a specific community. Be flexible and prepared to look at an opportunity that the consultant feels you should consider.

Ensuring a Successful Outcome

Suppose the consultant calls and asks you (the active candidate) to come to Crazy Woman, Wyoming, for an interview. What should you say? If you have clearly and honestly described your goals and interests to the consultant, he or she will know that you are interested in a position in a rural environment. If your family will not be able to move right now, can you decline the opportunity? If you want to work with the consultant again, you should not turn it down without further investigation. The consultant has reason to think you might be the right person for this job. You should consider it carefully. If you are called more than a couple of times and refuse even to look at the jobs the consultant wants to discuss with you, you may have shut the door on any future opportunities with that person. If the consultant has proposed what you consider to be unreasonable positions, it may be that you have not been clear enough about your career goals and needs, or it may just be that the consultant is sloppy or too casual a listener. One way or another, there is miscommunication going on.

Here are key points that you can rate a consultant on in the course of your working relationship:

- Professionalism
- Knowledge of the position
- Knowledge of the client institution
- Good listening skills
- Quick response to questions and concerns
- Courtesy
- Appropriate feedback given
- Confidentiality respected
- Personal concern
- Expectations met or exceeded
- You would work again with this individual
- You would recommend colleagues to the firm as potential candidates

These items are similar to the earlier checklist of factors to be considered in selection of a search firm, and they form the basis of any lasting relationship with an individual consultant or a company.

Your candidacy on a particular assignment will have a beginning and an end. It will begin when the consultant says something like, "I think you have the qualifications for this job. . ." or "You appear to meet the specifications the client has in mind. . ." or "I'm very interested in talking with you at greater length about this opportunity." At that point, you have become a true candidate in the eyes of the executive search consultant. Your candidacy ends when you receive a job offer in writing, or when you hear from the consultant that you are no longer being considered for a certain job. There are only two outcomes here—zero or one. You got a job or you did not. You will have to sort out how you feel about that situation, but it is a reality that you will ultimately have to accept.

Think of the Olympics—athletes spend much of their lives getting ready for an event, and then only one person gets the gold. The powerful consolation is that you ran with the best. And, unlike the athlete, you will most likely have another opportunity, because the search consultant will go on to other assignments and will consider your qualifications in the future. What can you legitimately ask a consultant if you did not receive the job offer? Is the consultant going to tell you why you did not get a job? It is perfectly acceptable to ask who got the position and something about the person's background. You may be told that it is not yet public information and that the name will be disclosed to you as soon as it is announced by the organization, but in most cases you can expect an answer immediately.

It also is acceptable to ask what differentiated you from the successful candidate. That allows the search consultant to give you some valuable advice and counsel that can help you in a future search situation. How detailed this evaluation will be will depend on how well you know the consultant and how sincere he or she is in wanting to be of assistance.

Another appropriate question to ask is whether there are any other searches on which the consultant is engaged that might be of interest to you. This indicates flexibility and an ability to move on. You will have to accept at some point that, although you were convinced that you were right for the job, the organization did not agree.

Even though you really know you are the perfect candidate for the position, the organization has the right to decide that someone else crossed the finish line slightly ahead of you.

Distinguishing between a Search Firm, a Contingency Firm, and an Agency

A decision to go with an agency or contingency firm is primarily an economic decision. Neither one operates on the same principles as an executive search firm. Executive search firms and contingency firms represent the *client* for whom they will identify and attract executives. Agencies represent individuals for whom they will find employment opportunities. The agency's payment usually is one month's salary.

A search firm's consultant generally has a great deal of information about the organization as well as the position, and will be interested in "selling" an opportunity only if there is a good match between the client and candidate. Contingency firms usually are less informed about client organizations because they spend less time getting acquainted with the client. More importantly, a search firm is paid a retainer fee, but a contingency firm is paid *only* if it identifies the individual who is hired. Hence, payment is contingent upon the firm's finding a candidate quickly—obtaining the most qualified candidate and the best match between the candidate and the client organization may not be primary considerations.

An agency is paid by the candidate, and is not really related to the others except as part of the broad continuum of employment services.

A FINAL WORD

This book is written by well-regarded consultants who want to provide information on how executive search and compensation consulting can benefit you, whether you define yourself as a prospective candidate or client. The information reflects a particular firm's practices.

This chapter has focused on helping you identify the qualities and characteristics that differentiate the best firms from the large group executive search firms. As a client, you should expect outstanding service. What is most important is to develop a relationship with a firm that reflects your values and service expectations.

NOTES

1. "Hospital Needs Assessment—Southwestern States," conducted by B.J. Cunningham, PhD, and the University of Dallas Graduate School of Management, September, 1986 (unpublished).

2. David H. Maister, "Quality Consulting: What the Client Says," 1985. (Unpublished research sponsored by the Association of Executive Search Consultants.)

3

When the Hospital Board Must Recruit a CEO

Michael C. Kieffer, President, Kieffer, Ford & Associates, Ltd., 2015 Spring Road, Suite 510, Oak Brook, IL 60521

J. Daniel Ford, Executive Vice President/Senior Partner, Kieffer, Ford & Associates, Ltd., 2015 Spring Road, Oak Brook, IL 60521

It happens. For one reason or another, hospital boards find themselves needing new Chief Executive Officers (CEOs). CEOs take other jobs or they retire. Some are not doing the kind of job needed to keep pace with the marketplace, and others are sought to launch a new venture. Each organization's situation is unique and each shares major similarities with others.

A TALE OF FOUR HOSPITALS

To illustrate typical situations that trigger the search process, members of four health care search committees agreed to share their stories. The members pointed out interesting challenges they met along the way, showing that there may be more than a candidate to be gained if the search process is utilized fully.

The first hospital was a thriving institution; its CEO had done a terrific job in a competitive marketplace. He had done such a terrific job that he was hired away. How do you fill the shoes with a quality candidate without losing momentum? This hospital board had the advantage of a strong CEO who was willing to advise on some parameters of the search. There was no obvious internal replacement who clearly was a leading candidate, so interim leadership was appointed when the CEO left.

Since the board member designated to head the search committee had clear memories of the time he thought he could handle a search internally, the decision was immediately made to hire an outside firm. The firm was identified primarily through talking with others in the field whose institutional philosophies were similar, and by inquiring about which firms were doing the most successful searches.

In recalling what special talents the chosen firm brought, the committee chair said the major influence was the ability to triage the candidates. This reduced the tendency to revert to previous biases and continually forced committee and board members to be open minded. In the process, a list of more than 200 potential candidates was narrowed to 3 in a way that allowed a change from predetermined beliefs. In the end there was agreement that the best finalist was an unemployed CEO. Few on the committee initially would have predicted that outcome.

The second hospital's CEO, a long-time, benevolent dictator, much respected in the community, had to retire because the institution was not keeping up with the changing times. The CEO did not want to leave and the board did not want to do anything "to hurt" the CEO. In this situation, the dynamic of retirement is as much a part of the search as the identification of a new leader.

The board member facilitating the search was part of a corporate, multihospital system board and chose a firm she had used previously. She stated strongly that working with this particular search firm and profiting from its ability would enable the committee to move past the retirement issue into an organizational assessment of the institution. The corporate system could then begin to balance its needs with the legitimate local board concerns over its relationships in the community and its desire to retain some autonomy. Assessment brought into the open the consequences of putting the reluctant retiree into another position that would affect the status of a new CEO. It freed some local people to say, "Yes, the incumbent CEO has got to go." Also, some internal biases were uncovered. For example, the hospital medical staff members expressed foreboding about the impact of the situation on their practices.

The new CEO came from within the region, was identified early in the search process, and came through the entire search process with a better chance at success because the hospital had identified its needs and its goals.

The third board faced the "no longer the right person for the job" dilemma complicated by the fact that its CEO had been recruited only four years before. He had done some good things, but obviously was not equipped to carry the institution into the future. There were difficulties with the medical staff, and the CEO had little success in building a management team. The hospital was in trouble.

Another complication was that the hospital had joined a corporate system a year earlier and the current severance decision had been made without total acceptance by the local board. Indeed, the local board tended to prefer a caretaker CEO, a role the incumbent had accepted, while the corporate system board wanted a "go getter." Clearly, there was a need to clarify a leadership strategy that both boards could accept before bringing on a new CEO. Fortunately, the departing CEO agreed to a mutual separation and made the path smooth for the system board to bring in an interim CEO who was not a candidate for the job.

The first order of business faced by the system board in choosing a search firm was to determine if the firm understood the style and values of the hospital and the system, since there was a religious mission to consider. The second was to determine if the firm had the expertise to encourage the local board to relinquish some control and hire a CEO with leadership strength. Specifically, one who would understand the difficulties of providing health care to the poor while meeting, head-on, the harsh realities of the marketplace. The firm chosen had a strong track record meeting these kinds of challenges.

It was a long, hard organizational assessment and search process. The search firm helped to stimulate strategic planning for the institution, develop criteria for measuring candidates and show the local board members that the new CEO would need the freedom to replace ineffective managers. The search firm taught the local board members the process of understanding contracts, benefit packages, and negotiation techniques—the prevalent issues in a recruiting marketplace. The consultant was blunt but respectful in his approach to adjusting the board members' perceptions to the realities of the day and the situation: Clearly, the hospital could not afford to make another mistake. The new CEO doesn't resemble the "preconceived" candidate the local Board might have recruited.

The fourth institution wanted to recruit a CEO for a new venture. A number of partner hospitals were coming together in an alliance, and they needed a process and a facilitator, as well as a CEO. The new organization had no tradition, few preconceptions and undefined leadership qualities. It needed a search firm to bring it all into focus. The organization also needed a search firm to deflect the favorite candidates of all the partners until a systematic process was established.

Several of the partners had positive experiences with a particular search firm, which they chose after interviews with several other firms. There was good chemistry with the principal who would conduct the search and who quoted a reasonable fee structure and described an intelligent approach. According to the organization, the search firm brought the search committee from the theoretical to the real by forcing a hard look at criteria, then probing and testing those criteria, and breaking through preconceived notions about where to find the best candidate.

Initially, the committee members thought they should be looking for a seasoned administrator who "knew" hospitals. Through the educational process of the search, the committee hired an entrepreneur whose business had "involved" hospitals.

So, four health care organizations have new CEOs. Each story is unique, yet each shares a critical event that was facilitated by a search firm. Each experienced an honest, no-holds-barred assessment of the institution's past, its present, and its future. More important, however, the assessment wiped away preconceived ideas, broke up insider camps and banished damaging sacred cows in favor of growth and leadership.

THE SEARCH PROCESS

When you are faced with recruiting a CEO, you, too, can gain more than a candidate for your efforts. There is no scientific formula for a successful assessment and search, but there are some things to think about and things to prepare for, so in the event that you need a search committee, it will work as efficiently and effectively as possible.

The Board's Steps

Design an Anticipation List

- How will the hospital be run in the interim period?
- How will the search be done?
- How will the selection decision be made? Who are the key players and which groups need to be accommodated?
- How will the search committee facilitate the search?
- Does the institution have a set of expectations for and desired accomplishments of a CEO?
- Is there a clear definition of the philosophy and values of the institution and affiliations? What is it?
- What is the hospital's reputation?
- Which management team members are capable of an unprejudiced explanation of the workings of the organization?
- Will the search committee name and acknowledge internal problems, recognize the existence of damaging "camps," and evaluate entrenched ideas?
- What is the market value of CEO positions, and who will face the responsibility of compensation discussions?

- Who will gather and selectively share confidential data that may expose weaknesses in the organization, but help to better choose a final candidate?
- Which trustee and board families will prove helpful to the institution's sales job in the final stages of selection?

If you can answer the questions positively or believe you can lead a selection team to answer them positively, then you are ready to have an honest, tough but productive, search experience. If you think you will have major problems with all or any of these questions, now is the time to begin working on them. After all, you never know for certain when you will be faced with recruiting a new CEO.

Consider Organizational Issues

Assume you are facing that very challenge. Begin by thinking positively of the opportunity it presents to revisit the past as well as look at the present and future of the organization. Realize that you will be able to assess the programs and services being offered and look into whether or not the organizational structure is appropriate for the fulfillment of the organization's goals and mission. And, perhaps most exciting, you can begin to assemble a list of capabilities and skills of leadership that will be required to take the organization into the future. This time of reflection offers the opportunity to consider the leadership potential of those within the organization and to determine if the departing CEO has been successful in grooming a possible replacement.

Now is also the chance to consider potential affiliations or business relationships with other organizations. Rest assured that if your hospital is a small or medium size, stand-alone facility in either a highly competitive environment or a rural setting where you can become a feeder institution, your hospital is likely to be approached for affiliation discussions by a larger, stronger, or multi-institutional organization. A word of caution here: the board would be well served to divert active discussions in this, or any other major change in operations, until a new CEO has been selected. Waiting to make major decisions tells a strong candidate that he or she will be influencing those decisions if selected. Without the direction of a skilled CEO, the hospital is at its most vulnerable point for such negotiations. However, knowing that the possibilities for major change exist helps in designing the expectation and experience lists for the recruiting process.

Appoint an Interim CEO

A major step in organizing the search process is deciding how the hospital will be run in the interim, assuming the incumbent CEO is no longer in office. Forward-looking boards will avoid a management committee consisting, even in part, of board members, because that structure paints a picture of board-controlled operations and gives a bad signal to strong candidates. Prevailing wisdom also discourages a bipartite or tripartite management team and encourages choosing one person to do the job even though a management team may be brought together for consultation. If an internal person will take over during the search, be certain not to give out false signals—name him or her an *interim* CEO versus an *acting* CEO, leave the CEO office vacant, and do not raise the pay of the interim person. An appropriate way to reward interim performance is a financial bonus at the end of the period.

An interesting solution to this interim leadership void, perhaps brought about by the current volatility of the marketplace, is using an experienced CEO, who does not have a current affiliation, as a "loaner" to the institution. The danger here is that this person may immediately begin maneuvering for the job. Your best success will be with a person who, for whatever reason, is a noncandidate and, therefore, will not attempt to make political decisions to build a constituency.

Choose a Search Method

Now, assuming that the board acknowledges the need to recruit from outside the organization, it then needs to decide how the search will be done. It can conduct the search on its own, placing ads in appropriate newspapers and journals, and then face mounds of resumes reflecting vagaries from professional resume preparers to job shoppers who reply to every ad across the country. Perhaps the most unfortunate result of this kind of search is the missing candidate—the skilled, experienced professional who does not answer ads for any number of reasons including the possible compromise of confidentiality.

Another approach is to contact state hospital associations, and other associations and ask for referrals. The challenge here is to separate the solid performers from the "good ole boy" networkers. Your hospital does not want to be the recipient of a favor repaid.

Then there are employment agencies. These are a good place to find nonmanagerial and technical talent, but their services often do not extend to the needed consulting talent and time commitment necessary to hire a CEO. Employment agencies work on a contingency basis, which means they get paid if they complete the assignment, and they get nothing if they don't. Therefore, they are less likely to challenge the board's preconceptions and indeed may rush through the process as quickly as possible.

Clearly, the most effective search process for the organization that is truly serious about attracting the best potential executive is the retention of an executive search firm. True, the fees are high (although often not higher than an employment agency) with the industry norm at 33⅓ percent of the hiring salary. However, some firms have put in place an approach they believe to be more professional—a fixed, front-end fee based on an estimate of the time and effort that will be expended depending on the nature and scope of the assignment.

From your Anticipation List you have already addressed what constitutes an efficient interim management team. You have acknowledged the importance of selecting an executive search firm to facilitate the recruiting process. You know you need a search committee—now you are ready to determine its members, because its first job will be to engage the search firm.

Form a Search Committee

The search committee functions as a selection committee representing the interests of the full board. This group will be involved intimately in the assessment process including looking at today's tough problems and tomorrow's needs. These are the people who will be establishing the criteria and the standards against which candidates will be evaluated. If the group has the trust and respect of the board and can work industriously for the good of the organization, the board ratification process will be a perfunctory matter and the transition will be smooth. Obviously, choosing who shall and who shall not sit on the committee and who will represent which key groups is an extremely important task.

The board must choose the members with the following in mind: the most visible and probably the most important decision that the board makes is the selection of a new CEO, and it must never allow even a hint of a perception that it has abdicated this responsibility to any other group. For example, depending on the circumstances, this is a popular time for the medical staff to exercise its muscle and try to wrest this responsibility from the board. Obviously, this can't be allowed. And yet, since the medical staff has such a vital part in supplying the lifeblood of any health care organization, there is clearly a need to balance its important and legitimate need for involvement with the integrity of the role of the board. The answer is to ensure a place on the committee for one or two of the most influential leaders on the medical staff, making certain that they are objective and represent the broad general interests of their colleagues, not those of a polarized camp.

If the hospital is part of a multisystem, the corporate CEO or other logical corporate representative or both should be included. A search committee, which ultimately reports to the full board, works best if it doesn't exceed seven members. However an additional one or two more members may be appropriate depending on the environment, circumstances, and politics of the situation—often times the wishes of both a local board and a corporate board must be accommodated. Also, if the chairperson of the board does not wish to be a formal member of the committee, he or she should certainly be an ex-officio member and participate throughout the entire process.

Having reviewed the Anticipation List, you are ready to act should you have a board member who thinks it useful to invite outsiders, who are not on the medical staff or the board, to sit on the committee. Search committees have been known to want to include chief executive officers of state hospital associations or employee representatives. In one case, a board member suggested inviting the CEO of a competing organization—sort of like General Motors inviting Lee Iacocca to help it select its next president. Even if the conflict of interest is not apparent immediately, these representatives would seriously impair the committee's ability to work effectively and would certainly detract from the quality of candidates generated for the search. Strong candidates might have serious doubts about the ability of the board to understand how organizations operate.

Select an Executive Search Firm

Once a search committee is in place it is ready to select an executive search firm. The first place to look is at the organization's own experience. If you have had a very successful recent experience with a firm on a senior level assignment, you may want to engage that firm again. However, a committee may be served best by inviting three or four firms for interviews.

Some hints for making the right decision:

- Insist on professional references prior to the presentation, and check these references before meeting with the search firm. This is a place where your Anticipation List comes into play. You have thought about what makes your organization unique; now you can describe that uniqueness to the prospective consultant and insist that references from similar organizations be provided. Automatically exclude from consideration any firm that fails to honor this request, because you need these objective check points, not two or three good friends of the firm.

- Insist that the person making the presentation also handle the search—you don't want to get caught in the trap of being sold by someone you will not work with or see again.

- Check the experience of the individual who will be doing the assignment to satisfy yourself that this consultant has experience in similar kinds of situations. Find out how many other assignments the consultant is currently working on and what the typical work load is. At the CEO level, no consultant can adequately and appropriately serve your needs if he or she is handling more than six assignments simultaneously. A word of caution here is that if two people from the consulting firm are making the presentation, assume in every situation that the junior member of the team will be the person doing the assignment—that's the person whose experience you need to check out. And be sure it's the consulting experience you check. Just because a person has multiple years experience in health care does not mean that individual understands how to *consult* with a board. Running a hospital from an operational perspective and working with a board on a consulting basis are two very different skills.

- Schedule all of the interviews for the same day to prevent any one firm from having the very distinct advantage of presenting after a time lag. In fairness to the firms that accept your conditions, you should eliminate from consideration any firm that, at the last moment, says it cannot make the presentation date and asks for a rescheduling.

- Allow adequate time for presentation purposes when you interview search firms so that you have an opportunity to understand the significant differences in style, approach, and process. An hour certainly is adequate and you should never schedule less than 45 minutes.

- After the interviews, make your decision quickly and notify all of the contenders of your decision. No firm expects to win the assignment in every competitive situation, but each incurs the cost of travel and time for preparation and presentation, and deserves to be notified, win or lose, in a timely manner. This kind of professional courtesy can only enhance your reputation.

Ensure Your Effort

So, you have put in a lot of time and thought to select the right search firm. Now is the time to ensure that you get the maximum benefit for your efforts. Remember, the reason you engaged a search firm is because it knows how to recruit candidates more effectively than you do. Make certain that the members of your committee do not share a common, destructive philosophy that the only way to control consultants is to treat them like hired hands and make them jump through hoops. That approach is one way to guarantee that you will not receive the maximum effort, the best the consultant has to give. Instead, you will get exactly what you are paying for—a professional, but most likely perfunctory job. On the other hand, if the committee takes the attitude of viewing the consultant as a professional colleague, sharing a relationship of trust and partnership, it will receive in turn that extra special something that translates to extra attention.

The Search Firm's Responsibilities

Now a new stage of the search begins with a thorough, comprehensive, organizational assessment led by the consultant or consulting team. This onsite exercise lasts several days and includes personal and confidential interviews with members of the search committee (allow at least one hour each); other key leaders of the board; key leaders, both formal and informal, of the medical staff; members of the religious community or corporate structure if applicable; and key members of the senior management team if appropriate. Remember from your Anticipation List that management's role is to help the consultant get an objective view of the inside workings of the institution, not to play a key role in developing the selection criteria.

Organizational Assessment

The assessment, and the fact that you have anticipated its importance, is useful in some major ways. It provides the consultant with the opportunity to know and understand the mission of the organization, its goals, aspirations, and vision. It lets the board, through its representatives on the search committee, translate these values into the skills, experience, and style required of an executive who can lead the organization to reach its potential—to be all that it is capable of being. Also, since organizations each have a distinct personality, the assessment visit provides a consultant with the opportunity to know the organization. He or she will not only see the skills and experience needed to do the job at hand, but will be able to "get inside the soul of the institution," to recognize the style, personality, and value structure needed in a new CEO. Understanding the chemistry of the players from the various constituencies and finding a good match is one of the major accomplishments of a successful search process.

Remember that during this visit the consultant will develop a composite profile describing the characteristics of the ideal CEO and a list of the objectives against which the new executive's performance will be measured. Therefore, each member of the search committee must be ready with the answers to key questions from the Anticipation List. Committee members also should be able to define what needs to be accomplished in the organization in order for the CEO to be considered successful after the first 12 to 18 months on the job.

Immediately after the interviews the consultant should meet with the search committee to provide initial, first-hand feedback and to validate the candidate profile and areas of expected accomplishment. It is at this meeting that the consultant meets a very serious responsibility to the client—reviewing in depth any issues, problems, or concerns which, if unaddressed or unresolved, will have detrimental effects on the search process and prevent the institution from attracting the best possible candidates for the position. These issues range from compensation and structural issues, to such issues as a perception that the board does not understand its proper governance role, severe conflicts of interest at the board level, any major quality issues in the organization, or any unrealistic expectations relative to the future of the organization.

Here is where your committee will profit from hiring a strong, professional search firm. The style of some consultants, or perhaps it is simply lack of experience or courage, is not to raise these hard questions at this time, because the obvious risk in being this candid at the front-end of the assignment is to potentially alienate the client and be disengaged. A consultant with this attitude, who waits until the end of the assignment, when the candidate exposes the problems, is guilty of performing a major disservice. The reason it pays to work so hard in finding the right search firm is that a responsible consultant will have a track record that proves it able and willing to take this risk.

This meeting also affords an opportunity to clarify the number of candidates the committee can expect the consultant to present. A word of advice: potential candidates are not hard to find, but real candidates are developed. Because it is quite difficult to actually develop the candidacy of even one person (making certain the candidate fits in the client's environment while addressing the candidate's needs in considering a career move), the committee should understand that within a reasonable time allotted to a search it should not expect more than five exemplary candidates to be presented. If the committee demands a long list of candidates, the situation is likely to be reminiscent of the old vaudeville act where the juggler is spinning plates on the ends of bamboo canes. By the time he has the sixth plate spinning, he must run back to the first one to try to catch it before it falls. You can only keep so many in the air at the same time!

As a follow-up to the meeting, the consultant should provide a written report covering everything discussed. With that accomplished, the search for candidates can begin. Search firms "source" (the term used to describe the process of contacting potential candidates) in a variety of ways: mailings, listing positions in professional journals, using sophisticated computer systems, and so forth. However, the most professional and valuable sourcing technique is personal contacts made by the consultant through personal networks established over years of consulting experience in the field. Clearly, having an experienced consultant who has a vast network and is well seasoned in recruitment at senior levels is your greater resource.

Consultant Interviewing

Through the sourcing and networking process, the consultant will develop a short list of candidates who seem to have strong potential for meeting the client's expectations and profile. It is time for indepth interviewing between the consultant and potential candidates. These interviews must be accomplished in person.

During the interviews, the consultant will essentially cover three major areas with the candidate. The first two are designed to evaluate candidate "fit" with the position. First the consultant will want to determine the candidate's professional skills, expertise and experience, and make certain that his or her track record ensures that the requisite talent is there to accomplish the job at hand.

Second, the consultant needs to understand the candidate as a person, that is the candidate's values, style, personality, strengths, and weaknesses—looking for the mix that is the best chemistry match to the client. While it is relatively easy for an experienced interviewer to determine if a candidate's professional background and track record meets the client's needs and expectations, it takes much more experience and talent to master the art of determining whether the individual has the right chemistry match for the particular situation.

Third, during the interview, there must be candid sharing of client data and information; the blemishes as well as the positives. To be a good match, each candidate must determine whether he or she feels it's an appropriate move and correct "fit." You do not want to offer the position of CEO of your institution to a person who cannot adequately determine that the situation represents a legitimate and logical career move for him or her and an opportunity for personal and professional growth. Along with career considerations, candidates need to determine that now is the appropriate time to consider such a move and that family considerations can be fulfilled.

Once the consultant has developed a legitimate slate of candidates, a progress meeting is scheduled at which he or she meets with the committee to review the list. This meeting can take different forms depending on the philosophy of the search firm. Some firms present the candidate's credentials in a boilerplate format (all alike) for consistency. Others believe in giving the committee a copy of the candidates' resumes as the candidates have prepared them; thereby allowing a view of how the candidates present themselves. In addition to the candidates' written credentials, the consultant should give the committee a verbal, comprehensive profile of each: what they have accomplished and not accomplished, how they have accomplished it, strengths and weaknesses, style, values, relationships with various constituencies, what preliminary references are saying, and so forth.

Committee Interviewing

Following this presentation, the committee decides which of the candidates it wishes to invite for an interview. Candidates should be sent:

- the latest monthly financial statement
- the last fiscal year final audit report
- an auditor's management letter
- the annual report
- the current budget
- statistical analyses such as Monitrend reports
- the latest JCAH report
- an organizational chart
- a list of board members and business affiliations
- the corporate bylaws
- a list of medical staff indicating specialties
- medical staff bylaws
- descriptive information on the hospital
- a strategic plan
- newsletters
- a position description (if available)
- literature on the community.

The process for interviewing candidates can take several forms depending on the client circumstances. For instance, it may be very appropriate to invite both candidate and spouse to the client location for a full, comprehensive visit including meetings with medical staff members, the management team, and others on the initial visit. This is quite time consuming, particularly when the committee will be dealing with several candidates all getting the same treatment. However, another approach is to invite several candidates, without spouses, to the client location to meet on a preliminary basis with the search committee, giving the committee an opportunity for immediate comparisons between candidates.

After the preliminary meeting, the committee can determine if there is strong mutual interest with one or more of the candidates, prompting an invitation to return, with spouse, for a more formal and structured interview. A variation of this approach, useful in unique situations, is for client representatives to have a preliminary interview with multiple candidates at a neutral site. No one of these or other possible formats is necessarily good or bad, right or wrong. It really depends on the nature of the assignment and the disposition of the group. A good consultant, however, certainly should make a definite recommendation on a process that will be the most effective and beneficial to the client. In any of the formats, it is critically important for the consultant to be onsite and present during all of the interviews in order to observe firsthand the dynamics of the meetings.

If the committee chooses to have multiple evaluation interviews, the following are some guidelines that will help the process:

- Don't try to do more than three interviews on any one day.
- If you're interviewing on more than one day, make sure that the days are consecutive so that the first interviews are still fresh in the committee's mind when it comes to decision time.
- Schedule the interviews in two-hour blocks of time, allowing most of that time for the interview and the remaining 15 to 30 minutes for some immediate reflection.
- Make certain there is a private room in which the next candidate waits to alleviate the embarrassment of candidates crossing paths in the hallway.
- Use the same core group of questions you developed with the consultant for each candidate, adding others as the situation dictates.
- Allow time for the candidate to ask questions of the committee so that both sides feel they have learned by the experience.
- Understand that any interview situation is a two-way exchange.

Certainly the candidate must impress the committee with his or her credentials, skills, and ability to do the job. But it is also important for the committee to convey its pleasure at having the opportunity to meet and discuss the position. Unfortunately, there are some organizations that allow their institutional ego to stand in the way of an effective search process. The board members may think that the organization's stature is so great, candidates must certainly line the streets and hope for an opportunity to work for them at any cost. Strong candidates have many options and any organization needs to sell the position as well as be sold on the candidate.

An additional guideline, another that sometimes causes problems for the committee members, is to be prepared to ask and receive tough questions. When a candidate and a search committee meet, there is no such thing as an unfair question from either side. After all, there is simply too much at stake for the institution and the individual's career to get caught up in dealing only with surface issues. Also, the candidate will want to use this meeting to ask questions about the materials you sent all candidates selected for an interview (materials you gathered as a result of the Anticipation List).

At the conclusion of the last interview, the committee's most critical work begins—the dissection of the interview sessions and the selection of its first and second choices. (It always is wise to have two choices. In case the number one candidate declines the next interview, an invitation to the second choice can be rendered without a need to reconvene.)

Choosing a deliberation method that most members are comfortable with will help to expedite the process. The committee can choose secret ballot, totalling scores on a weighted system, or other method. Or it can choose a participatory, open process whereby each committee member describes his or her first, second, and third choices, with justification for each. This process allows an opportunity to draw out all the issues and lay all the opinions on the table where they can be addressed appropriately.

The deliberation process must take place immediately, and the result communicated in a timely manner. When candidates are in a competitive situation and do not receive word of a decision soon, they assume another candidate has been chosen. They then prepare themselves psychologically by thinking of all the reasons they "didn't really want that job." This declining interest level malaise may affect your number one choice, and it is almost impossible to revive his or her interest level once it has waned.

Handling Return Interviews

To keep the interest alive in the top two candidates, a wise consultant will handle the notification in a candid, honest manner by informing the leading candidate that the committee wishes to invite him or her back for a return visit. The number two candidate will be told that while the committee is impressed with his or her background and credentials, it has opted to invite another candidate back for a more formal visit. The number two candidate will be informed regarding the outcome of the visit with the number one candidate. That way both candidates will know where they stand and those not chosen, who also have been informed of the committee's choices, can go on with their lives.

The consultant has an important task to perform before the return visit. Because the leading candidate is no longer part of a pack, the preliminary and peripheral references checked early on are not sufficient. The consultant must dig deeply into background and relational experiences. At this point, the candidate should give permission for the consultant to talk with members of his or her board and medical staff and others. These references should be contacted in person by the consultant with the results of the conversations transcribed for the committee's review. Educational credentials will have been verified during the preliminary investigation.

You and your committee have worked hard and well to arrive at this point in the search, and you will want to ensure maximum effectiveness from the return visit. The candidate's spouse should be invited, keeping in mind that spouses play an influential role in the candidate's decision. A good consultant will have spoken with the spouse by this point and have an understanding of what is important to him or her and to the family. The committee should be apprised of those needs and plan to be responsive to them in selecting who meets with the spouse and in structuring an appropriate schedule.

This is a formal visit and should begin with a dinner meeting the evening of the candidate's arrival. The dinner can be relaxed and low key, but should be attended by several, if not all, of the people on the search committee and their respective spouses. The introductory dinner serves several purposes. First, it gives the board an opportunity to see how the candidate and spouse relate in a social and public situation. After all, this is the person who will be perceived as representing not only the institution, but in many ways the board itself. Second, the dinner extends a warm welcome, letting the candidate and spouse know that the committee and the board are genuinely interested in them. It should provide a relaxing atmosphere for the remainder of the process.

If the candidate is male, married and has children, the dinner provides an opportunity for his wife to interact with other wives and discuss schools, recreational facilities, career opportunities for her and other concerns. If the candidate is female, married and has children, the process will not work in quite the same manner, and the consultant may suggest a forum outside the dinner to discuss these matters and the husband's concerns. These dinners are designed to be more social than work-oriented, but invariably the topic of the organization comes up in the conversation. Responses should not be staged one way or the other; the normal flow of conversation should take it to an appropriate level.

A word of caution regarding the candidate's spouse and his or her extremely important role in the interview process. There are situations where the spouse has acted so rudely and temperamentally because of a first reaction to the community that, although the candidate was the most skilled, the committee opted for a visit from the second choice candidate and spouse in order to make a comparison. The second candidate usually gets the job when this situation occurs.

Spouses would be well-served to remember that, while their reactions to a community may be less than enthusiastic, it is home for the search committee members and families. Disregard for their feelings will, and should, have negative consequences. There simply is a polite, professional way to handle a negative reaction. It should be done with sensitivity and appropriate timing—usually in private with the consultant, and certainly not at dinner with the search committee.

The next morning should begin with a confidential hour to hour-and-a-half breakfast meeting with the key leaders of the medical staff. This group needs to be alerted in advance to two important considerations. First is the need for confidentiality. Unfortunately there is more than one example of a medical staff member picking up the phone after this kind of meeting and calling a friend who has a friend who has a friend who works in the candidate's hospital. This kind of third-, fourth-, and fifth-hand information can be disastrous, but more importantly, it violates a sense of ethics and integrity that the candidate has every right to expect from all members of the organization. Second is the admonition to the medical staff that this is not an interview situation as such, but rather an opportunity for the medical staff to get to know and understand the background, style, and ideas of the board's leading candidate. Conversely, it provides an opportunity for the candidate to understand the medical staff and its needs and ideas. A smart consultant will be involved in this meeting in order to watch the dynamics unfold.

The Final Steps

The next scheduled meeting time is designated for the candidate to spend some appropriate and quality time with key members of the senior management team that you identified on your Anticipation List. They may include individuals from finance, nursing, marketing, and other departments, and it is critical that these management members are aware that their role is not, under any circumstances, to interview the candidate. Rather, they are a resource to the candidate so that he or she can ask appropriate questions to get an objective sense of the workings of the organization. The search committee should not solicit this group for reactions that may be self-serving and given from a perspective of apprehension. A mediocre management team, for instance, will be intimidated by a very strong candidate.

Following these meetings, the candidate should spend time with the chairperson of the board. This is obviously a critical relationship and it is important for both to determine if they can work together. If your organization is sponsored by a religious body, it may be appropriate for the candidate to spend time with the congregational leadership to ensure that there is a good match from a religious mission perspective. As in the first formal interview, there should be no such thing as an unfair question, because there is simply too much at stake for everyone.

The last formal meeting of the visit will be a wrap-up session with the full search committee. By this point, the candidate will have had an opportunity to see the organization from an augmented perspective and will have much more information in his or her mental computer. This meeting gives both sides an opportunity to ask more insightful questions. The committee shouldn't hesitate to ask the candidate's views of the organization, the senior management team, the medical staff, the board, the religious leadership, the future of the organization, or any other question pertinent to selecting a CEO.

While the married candidate is in this series of meetings, the spouse should have been met for breakfast and escorted on a tour of the community to look at residential areas, schools, recreational facilities, or cultural facilities. This time should be directed toward resolving the spouse's concerns. The tour works best if two or three spouses of committee members, who approximate the age of the candidate's spouse, are involved in the tour.

Getting back to the candidate, if for some reason there has been a breakdown in the process and this visit does not validate the committee's opinion of the candidate, the process must halt. Likewise, the candidate may give signals that this indepth visit does not make him or her comfortable. In either case, the committee faces the question, "What do we do now?"

Assuming that the committee has had proper consultation from the consultant throughout the search, this breakdown should not be the result of poor planning, but simply a possible outcome of this step of the search process. If this is the case, it is time to reassess quickly and move to the second candidate. However, if all is going well, the stage is set to begin preliminary negotiations.

Typically, this should not be done by the full committee, but rather by a subgroup. If the chairperson of the search committee is different from the chairperson of the board, these two individuals, meeting with the candidate, usually suffice. Indeed, it is not at all inappropriate in situations where the chairperson of the board also heads the committee if that person meets alone with the candidate for purposes of compensation discussions. In a multi-institutional structure, it may be appropriate for the corporate CEO, with or without local input, to lead these discussions. Remember, you have prepared for these conversations as part of your Anticipation List, and there should be no surprises.

Part of the job of the search consultant is to recommend to the board, at the front-end of the assignment, the market value of the position. The consultant should have developed a formal compensation analysis depicting the candidate's current compensation, benefit, and perquisite package against what the candidate feels is a fair package and expects. The full committee should have this information already, making this final negotiation session somewhat perfunctory, but nevertheless important, because it solidifies a bonding between the candidate and the organization.

Assuming the consultant has the trust and confidence of both parties, he or she may play a strong, objective role in the negotiation session, keeping either side from making hard, fast, concrete decisions and requests from which there is no return. After all, the candidate and perhaps the client may deal with this kind of situation rarely, while the experienced search consultant deals with it all the time and brings expertise and experience to the session.

Remember that this is a preliminary negotiation meeting. You need to provide the candidate the opportunity to spend quiet time alone with his or her spouse to determine the reaction to the community and their combined reaction to the change. If a candidate feels that more than two or three days is needed to arrive at a final decision, your chances have just gone below 50-50. However, take heart. The process described here is so thorough and comprehensive for all parties that at this stage the candidate should have had preliminary feedback from the spouse and will be in a position to give strong signals as to acceptance or rejection.

THE TALES REVISITED

Now is the time to look back at the four situations, the four stories that began this chapter. Having reviewed the basic steps and processes necessary for a successful search, the preparation and hard work that went into those recruiting challenges should be clear. Each institution found the right candidate to be its CEO, and each institution got an added value as a result of using a strong, experienced search firm for the process. What kinds of added values? The search committee members had no problem supplying examples.

In the situation where the hospital replaced a strong CEO, the biggest added value was the search firm's ability to convince the committee to have an open mind about what kind of candidate and from what environment it would hire—even to looking seriously at the unemployed candidate it eventually chose. This board and committee were strong, the chairperson had headed several searches, so it took great skill on the part of the consultant to get this group to listen. The consultant's ability to present the hard questions and poke at preconceptions, without causing uncomfortable moments, was the key to expanding the horizon of the group.

The committee chairperson who survived the deposing of the benevolent dictator says the added value the search firm brought was organizational assessment. The search firm reported its findings fearlessly (but not recklessly) forcing the system board and the local board to look at the hard questions, like power camps and sacred cows, straight on. For this long-time board chairperson, this experience changed how she interviews search firms—if they can't convince her they know how to bring a board through an assessment, she isn't interested in hiring them.

When the existing CEO is simply no longer the right person for the job, what added value can the search firm contribute? The firm can address leadership strategy—what the institution must know about itself before bringing on a new CEO, what changes the replacement will be willing and able to make, and how the board will react. Not easy issues, but nonetheless they must be addressed.

What was the added value in the search for a CEO to head a new venture? The search firm showed the committee how a thorough review of the backgrounds and perspectives of the institutions that came together in the alliance was the path that would lead the members to an understanding—individually and collectively—of what was needed for the alliance, allowing them to maintain mutual respect for each other. After all, the recruiting process was the first, important activity of the new group.

And so it is, the search for a CEO—perhaps the most important project any board undertakes. Now you are ready.

4

Physician Recruiters: The Good, The Bad, and The Ugly

Susan A. Cejka, President, Cejka & Company,
222 S. Central, Suite 400, St. Louis, MO 63105

INTRODUCTION

You may ask yourself, why a chapter specifically on physician recruiting? Is it really different than executive recruiting? In fact, it is. The difference has more to do with the population than with the search process.

Why is Physician Recruiting Different?

Administrators move primarily for career advancement and secondarily for increased compensation. Unfortunately, these two factors largely are absent in the field of physician search. A practicing obstetrician/ gynecologist (Ob/Gyn) does not advance to become vice president, Ob/ Gyn. Practices look very much the same in San Diego, Peoria, or New Haven. They all require delivery of babies. The job responsibilities remain pretty constant. Night calls don't go away. Compensation does vary geographically, but not very much. This lack of career advancement and consistency of work leads to a double problem.

First, because of no career advancement, physicians do not move with the frequency of administrators. As a result, a much smaller potential pool of talent from which to recruit exists. Second, when physicians do move, they almost always move for personal reasons. These reasons usually are hard to uncover and difficult to deal with. The impact on the recruitment effort is that, in general, there will be far fewer qualified physician candidates available to be interviewed. There also is a higher probability of interviewing a "problem" candidate since personal problems are a major motivation for a move.

Once on an interview physicians are harder to attract, requiring more care and feeding on the interview than the average administrator. Their reasons for accepting your position may never be clear. These differences do not change the actual recruitment process. It does, however, alter the intensity and the attention with which each candidate must be handled, because there truly may not be another.

A final difference worth mentioning is the difficulty in segmenting the population. At last count there were 522,608 physicians in practice, 28,831 of which are Ob/Gyns. Administrative search lends itself well to referral recruiting. Physician search does not. The 28,831 is an unwieldy population. You cannot call all of them and they don't know each other. All of which makes the initial contact cumbersome.

RECRUITING RESIDENTS VERSUS PRACTICING PHYSICIANS

Given the difficulties mentioned earlier, you may have decided to focus all your attention on the recruitment of residents. If fact, that may be your best option, but you should know the merits of each.

Residents are far more malleable than practicing physicians. Since they have never been in a practice, yours will look normal to them. "The way we do things around here" will be easy to teach a resident. Conversely there are problems with residents. Generally speaking they are slow. Because they have never been in a practice before, they do not practice with the efficiency of a seasoned physician. Usually they require a manager; an older, more seasoned physician to offer second opinions and business managerial advice.

Practicing physicians on the other hand, generally are firmly grounded in their craft, start up time is fast, they operate with efficiency from the first day, and can fly solo with no management on your part or buddy system. They also have seen what the world is like, so are less idealistic and less likely to be disappointed if your situation is not nirvana. Practicing physicians also are more willing and able to cope with political problems. The down side to recruiting a practicing physician is that you may be buying someone else's problem. Many physicians move from one practice to another each year for very good reasons. A few do not, but it is only a few.

Advantages and disadvantages to both residents and practicing physicians exist and both are equally desirable groups from which to recruit. Your own situation, as well as the time of year, should dictate which group you go after. Obviously if you need a start date other than August 1st, you should recruit a physician already in practice since residency programs are year-long programs beginning July 1. Given the fact that there are 28,000 practicing Ob/Gyns and only 2,000 residents, you may well have better success looking at people already in practice.

TO USE OR NOT TO USE A RECRUITER

The first obvious question that comes to mind when considering recruiting a physician is: should I use a recruiter? If you find yourself in the luxurious position of recruiting with more than a year lead time, in a field in which recruiting is not terribly difficult, and with good support from your own staff, go it alone. If not, there are two reasons to use a physician recruiter: (1) quality of candidates and (2) time.

A good recruiter should allow you to see better quality candidates than you would see on your own. The recruiter gives your assignment full time and attention, something an administrator rarely is able to do. Generally, recruiters look at a larger pool of talent before making their final selection of candidates. Finally, when a search firm is hired client expectations of the caliber of talent generally rise. What clients may have hired on their own, they will not hire through a search firm.

Almost without exception a search will be completed faster using a recruiter than if you do it on your own. The reasons are simple. It is not so much because the recruiter is more talented at this than you are, although this should be true, but because recruiting is the recruiter's full time job. Recruiting on your assignment is the number one and only priority. It is highly unlikely that it is the number one, two or three priority of any administrator. Therefore, recruiting may, at best, have only your partial and sporadic attention.

Recruiters often are described as "pushy." It is true. Most people are pushy regarding anything that is their number one priority. Since filling your position is important to the recruiter, she or he will be pushy. This, by the way, works to your advantage. If you want the position to be filled quickly someone needs to be in charge of shuttling it through the system and getting the job done. The recruiter accepts that responsibility.

Who Is Responsible for What?

It might be worth a little discussion on the various responsibilities of the recruiter and the client. The recruiter's responsibilities are to seek out talented candidates, screen them for appropriateness, do background and reference checks on those candidates, and present the client to them in as positive and as fair a light as possible. The client's responsibility is to make the final selection of those candidates and make the hiring decision. Ultimately the client has the final impact on whether the candidate accepts the decision or not. Once an interview takes place, the recruiter has relatively little influence over the search. A good recruiter will accept full responsibility for the recruitment and presentation of candidates. In a good client relationship the client accepts full responsibility for the final selection and successful hiring of the chosen candidate.

For What Positions Should You Use a Search Firm?

So, back to the original question: should you do it on your own? You can fill positions on your own and undoubtedly do. Recruiters do not work magic. Any position they can fill, you can fill too. So you should use a recruiter because you probably don't have the time you need to devote to fill the position on your own. Even if you could make the time it probably isn't the best use of your time. Recruiters are like any other type of consultant. They should be hired for a brief but intense project requiring specific expertise and a large quantity of concentrated time.

Obviously a great many positions are filled each year without the use of a firm. However, a few positions will be inordinately difficult. Those positions should go to the search firm. And they should go to the search firm before you have expended large quantities of time or candidates. How to determine which positions will be difficult and which will be easy before you begin your own search is, of course, the problem. Answering the following questions should help you decide.

- Have you recruited this position in the past and found it to be difficult? If so, chances are it will be again.
- Do you have an unusual political or internal situation that will cause an otherwise easy position to become difficult?
- Read the classifieds in the *New England Journal of Medicine*. If there are many positions advertised just like yours, chances are it will be a difficult position for you to fill.
- Has something extraordinary occurred in the field to cause a shortage? (For example, in 1987-88 cardiology switched from a 2- to 3-year program causing an extreme 1-year shortage.)
- Are you under extreme time pressures to have the person on board immediately?

- Are your specifications for filling the position so narrow, or is the position so unusual, that there will be a small pool of talent who might meet your needs?

Most physicians move for a combination of factors. Those factors are a better practice and location and more money than they currently are making. If you have two out of three your position probably will be relatively easy to fill. If you do not have two out of three, chances are your position will prove to be difficult to fill. If the examples below sound familiar use a recruiter.

- Joining a hospital whose only other cardiac surgeon threatens all candidates with his scalpel may not scare off every candidate, but it will certainly weed out the faint hearted.
- Everyone in Pond City, Nebraska likes it, but few outside the area would call it attractive.
- There may be a family practitioner practicing in Minneapolis for $28,000, but we certainly can't find him.

Under any of the above circumstances it would be wise to bring in an outside recruiter immediately.

Why the Good, the Bad, and The Ugly?

This does not refer to the recruitees, but rather the recruiters. Historically recruiters have received mixed reviews in the field of physician search. To help you separate the good, from the bad and the ugly, follow the recommended strategy.

WHICH SEARCH FIRM TO USE

At last count, over 200 firms in the country recruit physicians. This gives the administrator a fair range of choices. In fact, one might say it's an overwhelming task to select one. There are some easy rules of thumb to follow when selecting a recruiter.

First, acknowledge this as a "soft field." In a soft field the most important element in the success of a venture is personal chemistry. There is only one way to determine personal chemistry—through a personal visit. Obviously you do not want to interview 200 firms in person. You could spend more time interviewing recruiters than doing the search on your own. Before inviting firm representatives in for a visit, request and read their literature and check references.

References will tell you a great deal. Certainly results achieved are the most important test of a good search firm. However, you are equally interested in the methods used to get results. The methods used by the firm and its compatibility are ultimately what will make you satisfied or dissatisfied with your selection.

The closest analogy to the importance of fit is in surgery. Of all the traits important in a surgeon, certainly results are first and foremost. But, poor personal skills can ultimately overshadow good technical skills and turn an asset into a liability. Don't let it happen with your recruiter.

Never hire a recruiter without a face-to-face meeting. Realistically, you can interview no more than 3 or 4 search firms in person before making your selection. As a result, much of your selection will be done long distance. It is better to interview only a couple of firms in depth, than to have a cattle call where you get to know no one. Once you get to the finalists, trust your intuition. Personal chemistry is the make it or break it factor in the relationship with a search firm, so choose the one with whom you feel most comfortable. Your goal and tasks, and the consultant's must be similar.

If you don't own a shirt that doesn't have buttons at the collar, it is improbable that a search firm representative wearing enough gold jewelry to weight down a small cow will be your cup of tea.

There are some standard questions to ask when interviewing a search firm which will help in your selection.

- How hard do you think our position will be to fill?
- What other positions like ours have you filled in the recent past?
- Have you had a disaster on a recent search? Describe how you coped with it. (All firms who have been in business longer than a year have had a disaster.)
- What will be the most critical factor to the success of this search?
- How long will you work on the position if it proves difficult?
- What happens if you don't fill the position?
- What happens if the candidate doesn't stay?

You will learn as much from the tone of the answers to these questions as you will from the answers themselves.

BUYER BEWARE

Beware of grand promises and upcoming miracles. If three consultants tell you your position looks difficult and will probably take six months, and one consultant tells you it should be "a piece of cake" and he or she can have a candidate on site in 30 days, look further. It is improbable that the other three firms are wrong.

Beware of money-back and time guarantees. They are easy to sell and hard to produce. If you choose to deal with a firm offering a money-back guarantee, make sure you speak with some references who have been refunded their money. (They may be hard to find.) Also, beware of blanket guarantees that promise your search will be filled in "X" period of time. No recruiter has absolute control over the filling of a position. You control at least 50 percent of the time factor. It is therefore impossible for recruiters to make a blanket promise since they don't control the events.

Look into the fine print of bargain basement deals. If three recruiters quote $20,000 as a fee and one quotes $5,000, make sure you're buying what you think you're buying. Deals that look too good to be true usually are.

Finally, beware of firms who have candidates they could send out to interview immediately. If your position is hard enough to warrant putting it out on search, it is unlikely someone is sitting with the very candidate you want.

CHOOSING BETWEEN A RETAINED AND CONTINGENCY FIRM

Finally, the issue of money. Contingency firms charge nothing until they fill your position. Retained firms may charge an initial retainer and nothing more until they fill the position, or they may charge their entire fee spread over several months. In the latter case you have the possibility of paying the entire fee before hiring a candidate. There are advantages and disadvantages to each type of firm.

One advantage of hiring a contingency firm is obvious. You have no financial risk until a candidate is hired. The disadvantage also is apparent. No one (including contingency firms) works for free; or at least they don't work long for free. If your position is one that will be filled easily, there is a probability it will be filled through contingency. If it is not easy to fill, there is little probability that the contingent recruiter will be financially able to stick with your position long enough to produce the results you need. The old adage that you get what you pay for remains true with recruiters. Mostly we are capitalists.

When you pay retainers you are buying a recruiter's time and attention. If your search will be lengthy and complicated, your retainers give that recruiter enough operating capital to stick with you long enough for a successful resolution. Once the recruiter has accepted your money, he or she also has the obligation to stick with you until a successful resolution. Whereas a contingency firm has the absolute right to back out of any search that looks difficult, the retained recruiter has no such right. Once accepting your money, they owe you performance. Performance does not necessarily mean your position will be filled. It means you'll get your money's worth as measured by time, information, and suitable candidates. The job of hiring remains yours, even with a retained firm.

The disadvantage of using a retained firm is that you are at financial risk. If the recruiter you choose is unethical or incompetent you may be throwing your money down the toilet. At the end of the search you may have a smaller bank account, but no results.

This is an appropriate time to point out that sometimes when a search doesn't get filled it is not the recruiter's fault. Because the recruiter controls only 50 percent of the hiring process, the recruiter controls only 50 percent of the success or failure of the venture. You, the client, control the other 50 percent. It is possible a search will fail and that the recruiter did a good job. For this reason, it is important to work out responsibilities and a game plan before the onset of an assignment.

HOW TO MAXIMIZE YOUR RESULTS FROM A FIRM

To stave off the possibility of money spent on a failed search you need to invest some time, as well as your money, into the search effort. No recruiter can do a good job for you if he or she doesn't have a complete understanding of who you are and what you want.

Up front, the recruiter must have a chunk of your time. Time spent at the beginning of an assignment with the recruiter will pay off approximately ten-fold at the end of the search. The number of candidates to be interviewed will be considerably diminished and the success ratio of hiring them considerably enhanced. This also means that you and the recruiter need some person-to-person time. It can either be done during the recruiter's initial visit during the selection process or, more probably, during a follow-up visit.

Most recruiters will want to spend approximately a day in your organization. They will want several hours with you in order to completely grasp the scope of the assignment. (For future reference, note that there is some benefit to working with the same recruiter over and over. Much of this up-front time will not need to be repeated on every assignment, although every assignment should have a personal visit.)

Many administrators think they speak with their recruiters more frequently than they do with their spouses. It may be true. There are portions of an assignment which require very frequent telephone contact. The early part of an assignment, when the recruiter is defining the position against the market place, requires constant feedback from you to make judgment calls on definition. During the final selection process, when candidates are being interviewed and ultimately one is hired, the recruiter will once again need frequent contact with you by telephone.

Recruiters can be managed, although some administrators would argue to the contrary. If the contact becomes a problem, set up a specific time of day and a specific allotment of time to deal with the recruiter's needs. Not returning the recruiter's phone calls for a week is only postponing your search, since the recruiter is stopped from making any progress until whatever questions he or she has are answered.

Once you have selected a firm, let that firm do its job. It is possible for you to so tie the hands of the recruiter that he or she is incapacitated. Typical things that tie a recruiter's hands are: an inability to disclose to candidates where the practice is, who the practice is with, or what the financial package looks like. Put yourself into the shoes of the candidate. Would you be willing to go on an interview if you didn't know the organization, location, salary range?

You also can tie the recruiter's hands by being inaccessible or by having a cumbersome process for scheduling interviews. Candidates will remain interested in a position for only a brief period of time. If it takes your organization two weeks to decide when to interview someone, or if you can see a candidate only two days per month, the probability of your search being filled in less than a year is remote. It is a good idea to work through all of these issues as well as time frames before the search commences.

The average search takes 3 to 4 months from the day you hire a recruiter to the day you sign an agreement with a physician. This time frame can be altered by your availability. Additionally, you can expect to see 3 to 4 candidates to fill the average search. This too can change depending on the attractiveness of your position and how good a salesperson you are.

Most recruiters will work better if you give a very tight position description and ideal candidate profile. Deviation from the profile is likely; but the recruiter needs a clear target to start.

THE END JUSTIFIES THE MEANS

The heart of the issue in recruiting physicians is the process. The process of recruiting is as important as finding a qualified candidate. From the moment the recruiter decides that a candidate is both interested and qualified for your position everything that follows deals with process. Process relates to the scheduling of the interview, the interview itself, travel and hotel arrangements, dealing with the spouse's needs, salary and contract negotiations, and the final agreement.

Obviously, process is a big issue. In fact, when searches run into trouble, lack of candidates usually is not the problem. Searches run into trouble because the process has fallen apart. Either candidates are not able to be scheduled, and therefore become disinterested, or candidates are not hired because the process is too cumbersome. A general rule of thumb is that you should expect to see between three and four candidates for each hire you make. Some searches will be better and some will be worse. The process of interviewing those candidates will make or break the search.

Costs

A recruiter should be hired only when the benefit justifies the cost. The cost of physician recruiting is somewhat easier to justify than most fields. The lost revenues from an undeveloped practice, a practice that has been vacated and is now dwindling, or a market share that is not being captured are easily computed and far outweigh the cost of the recruitment.

Because all recruiters price their services differently it is difficult to do a true comparison of financial exposure. Total exposure includes: the recruiter's fees plus expenses, which are charged back to the client. The largest area of variance among recruiters is in the area of expenses. Policies range from recruiters who bill back no expenses, to recruiters who bill back the cost of xeroxing and Federal Express, not to mention telephone and travel. It is always wise to get an estimate, in writing, of what your total financial exposure will be. Financial exposure also varies with the number of candidates interviewed by the recruiter and the scope of the search.

In general, your financial exposure to the recruiter will be as follows:

- Fees: $15,000 to $25,000
- Expenses: (includes travel, telephone, advertising, mailings and miscellaneous): $2,000 to $10,000

- Interview expenses of candidates: (will vary with geographic disparity and number of candidates) $2,000 to $10,000
- Total direct costs associated with the recruiter: $19,000 to $45,000

As expensive as recruiters are, their cost is relatively insignificant to the total cost of recruiting. Table 4-1 outlines the time and cost of recruiting without a recruiter. These are actual figures from a real group practice. Table 4-2 further outlines start-up costs and the break-even point for the new associate.

Many reliable publications estimate that the average internist generates over $550,000 dollars per year for a hospital and that the average orthopaedic surgeon generates over $300,000 per year. So, is a one-time expense of $25,000 worth an annual revenue stream of $300,000 to $550,000? The answer usually will be yes. On the other hand, is the cost of $25,000 a good investment if no results are produced. Obviously, no.

Ethics

The line between ethical performance and good performance is fuzzy. The line between unethical performance and incompetence is even fuzzier.

Table 4-1 Costs of Recruiting a Physician

Steps in Process	Time (Hours)	Number of Individuals Involved	Dollar Value
Identification of need	Variable	—	—
Development of criteria (candidate)	3	12	5,292
Placement of advertising	3	1	441
Receiving initial screening of CV's and telephone calls	10	3	4,410
Board review of primary candidates	2	12	3,528
Recruiting committee review	5	5	3,675
Contact with top three candidates to set up visit	6	3	2,646
Visit with three candidates and spouses (average 1½ days each)	36	1 per hour	5,292
Contact references	3	3	1,323
Second visit of top candidate (2½ days)	20	1 per hour	2,940
Negotiations with top candidate	8	2	2,352
Other miscellaneous contacts spouse/lawyer/accountant	4	1	588
Total recruiting costs			$32,487

Table 4-2 Analysis of Starting Costs for a New Physician

Salary	$ 60,000	to	$150,000
Fringe Benefits	15,000	to	40,000
Moving Expenses	3,000	to	5,000
First year expenses	$ 78,000	to	$195,000
Equipment			
Office and 3 exam rooms	$ 6,500	to	$ 8,500
Special equipment	5,000	to	150,000
Total equipment	$ 11,500	to	$158,500
Annual equipment expense	$ 2,300	to	$ 31,700
Total starting costs	$ 80,300	to	$226,700
Production necessary to break even	$160,600	to	$453,400
(assuming a 50 percent overhead)			

You have the right to expect ethical performance from your recruiter. This does not necessarily mean that your search will be filled. You can, however, expect appropriate time and attention from your recruiter, to be treated honestly and courteously, the recruiter to make only promises he or she can reasonably expect to keep, and to be given the best effort of the recruiter. All recruiters should act in compliance with all federal and state laws governing hiring practices (and so should you). Finally, you can expect that your recruiter will refrain from recruiting from your institution for at least one year after the time they last work for you.

What Are Unrealistic Expectations?

There are expectations, which may never materialize. For example, expectations that have not been verbalized to the recruiter have a high probability of ending in disappointment. Expectations which are added after the original specifications have been set forth, also have a high probability of ending in disappointment. There are a number of expectations that are unrealistic and therefore heighten disappointment. It is unrealistic to expect

- 10 candidates to choose from
- the candidates will be able to interview immediately
- the candidates to completely rearrange their schedules to meet yours (across the board, market demand is such that they don't have to)

- a candidate to come to work for you for 20 percent below market because your organization is such a great place to work
- a candidate to be willing to accept a position that is exceptionally undesirable because you need to have the position filled (candidates accept positions because the position meets their needs, not yours)
- a candidate will accept the position and be on board in 30 days.

What About Poor Service?

There may be times when you may have played fair and haven't gotten a fair deal. Is there anything you can do if you think you've been taken advantage of by a recruiter? Fortunately there is. The National Association of Physician Recruiters (NAPR) has been in existence for five years. Not all, but many of the nation's physician recruiting firms belong to this association. Firms who are members of NAPR subscribe to a stringent code of ethics when joining the association. There is an ethics committee, and if you believe that you have been taken advantage of, you should contact the association and file a complaint. The association is interested in hearing problems that clients have with recruiters. You should contact:

Executive Director
National Association of Physician Recruiters
222 S. Westmonte Drive, Suite 110
Altamonte Springs, Florida 32714
(305) 774-7880

SUMMARY

While the field of physician search is one laden with pitfalls, a good result clearly outweighs the risk. To achieve a good result using a physician recruiter, you should decide early whether this is a position that requires the use of a recruiter. Choose the firm carefully. This is probably your most important point of control over the success or failure of the venture. Give the recruiter support and clear direction. The results should be the physician you need.

In general, a search will take approximately 3 to 4 months from the day it is started to the day you reach an agreement with a candidate. In addition, the candidate will need another 3 months in order to close down an existing practice, make the move, and secure licensing. At best, search is not fast. At worst, it can take years. If the end result is a candidate who meets your needs, is a good fit in your organization, and stays 20 years, the effort has been well worth while.

5

Executive Contracts: From the Organization's and Candidate's Perspectives

Peter A. Weil, PhD, Director, Research and Public Policy,
Foundation of the American College of Healthcare Executives,
840 N. Lake Shore Drive, Chicago, IL 60611

Daniel M. Mulholland III, Partner, Horty, Springer & Mattern,
4614 Fifth Avenue, Pittsburgh, PA 15213

INTRODUCTION

The purpose of this chapter is to introduce the rationale underlying the development of contracts between executives and health care organizations. The growing prevalence of contracts in the recent past makes this topic almost mandatory for any executive contemplating a new position. As will be seen, contracts may be a sensible instrument for those executives who are maintaining their positions as well.

In this chapter, we will consider the usual features found in executive employment contracts. Also, the reader will consider features that health care organizations may find especially desirable and features they may want to avoid. Then, we look at the converse situation—the health care executive's perspective—what he or she may want to incorporate or might be avoided. Finally, there are some tips given about the negotiation process itself.

Growth in Prevalence

The concept of executive employment contracts in health care is not new. Since the early 1930s, the American College of Hospital Administrators began to speak out about the merits of formal contracts between hospital executives and boards.[1] But the issue was never really pressed at the national level, and few hospital administrators negotiated written contracts with their boards. A survey at the time reported that only 13 percent of hospital administrators had written contracts.

While business and industry began to institute employment contracts for CEOs on a large scale after World War II, it was not until 1968 that James Ludlam resurrected the issue for hospital executives. He suggested that a friendly letter delineating the prospective executive's understanding of the arrangements is an appropriate vehicle to provide reasonable protection and yet avoid an adversarial relationship that a classical contract might engender.[2]

Despite the growing awareness of the value of executive employment contracts, and even though esteemed professional groups endorsed them, a survey in 1982 of hospital CEOs affiliated with the American College of Healthcare Executives (formerly American College of Hospital Administrators) found that 22 percent of the CEOs surveyed had a formal written contract with their hospitals.[3]

However, only three years later, this figure jumped to 47 percent of executives in freestanding not-for-profit hospitals. The percentage of hospital CEOs with contracts in multihospital systems and in governmental hospitals continued to lag behind the not-for-profit freestanding group. But even these groups showed an average of a 51 percent increase in the proportion of executives having formal contracts in the two-year period between 1983 and 1985.[4]

Factors Contributing to the Growing Prevalence

What factors accounted for the sudden growth in contracts? As with most social phenomena, several causes came together to affect this trend. First, the health care environment underwent tremendous change beginning in 1983 with the introduction of the prospective payment system in the Medicare and Medicaid programs. This new methodology was designed to reward health care organizations that delivered care efficiently. It also led to more aggressive competition between health care organizations as business and industry were simultaneously trying to provide reasonable health care benefits to their employees without suffering the huge annual increases in the cost of premiums, which had become standard.

These immediate changes created greater pressure on the executives to manage their organizations efficiently while providing high quality, technologically sophisticated service. The challenge presented insurmountable obstacles to some. To others, it meant educating their boards to the new competitive situation. To many health care executives, written employment contracts were seen as essential in order to take charge and pursue risky ventures without having to worry about an immediate and abrupt personal financial loss.

The second force contributing to the prevalence of contracts is linked to a more general trend in organizations, to evolve toward greater formalization. Thus, hospitals and other providers have instituted formalized policies and procedures in many areas of their functioning—not just in relation to the CEO's responsibilities and rights, but also in relation to the policies for other employees, for patient care, and for relating with other organizations to name a few.

This phenomenon identified by sociologists studying modern society, has been dubbed the movement from 'gemeinschaft' to 'gezellschaft,' a change from unwritten rules and common understandings to an exactness in expected behavior and a crystallization of procedures in written formalized roles.[5]

Indeed, the executive was studied and defined by one of the great sociologists, Max Weber. In his penetrating study, Weber showed how those in bureaucracies embodied the new social arrangements of modern industrial society.[6] Weber's insights showed how individuals in bureaucracies denoted relationships based on a contract. Thus, contracts for health care executives can be viewed as an expected and necessary concomitant of modern organizational functioning.

The third factor, the long-term trend contributing to the growth of executive employment contracts, revolves around the growing professionalization of health care executives. In the old days, the business manager simply was an employee who served the hospital's board as its loyal functionary. Key decisions were made at the board level; the executive was expected to carry out the board's mandate.

This relationship between boards and executives has been evolving over time. Berle and Means in the 1930s showed that separation of ownership from management in business created a whole new class and with it, new possibilities for the effective functioning of organizations.[7] Hospitals were somewhat late in developing a professionalized cadre of executives. But by the mid-1980s, a majority of health care executives had formal training in business disciplines such as economics of the firm, accounting, finance and marketing, as well as specialized training in health care delivery disciplines including medical sociology, political science, ethics, and epidemiology. Moreover, most have undergone intense scrutiny in apprenticeships of varying duration. Thus, today's health care executives embody a set of principles and practices, which gives them transferable skills and knowledge, provides them with a career in which not one but a series of organizations might be served over time, and makes them accountable to their peers in other organizations as well as to their boards.

On balance, it may be that while the advent of the government's prospective pricing system may have served as a catalyst for the growing prevalence of executive employment contracts, other factors also contributed, namely, the increased formalization in organizations and growing professionalization of health care executives.

BENEFITS AND DRAWBACKS OF CONTRACTS: THE ORGANIZATION'S PERSPECTIVE

On the surface, it may appear as if executive employment contracts principally benefit the executive. However, the organization shares equally, if not in greater measure, in effecting such a formal arrangement. Four features of contracts convey their benefits to the health care organization: (1) improved executive decision making, (2) improved governance, (3) environmental adaptation, and (4) symbolic value.

Benefits of Contracts

Improved Executive Decision Making

First, organizations stand to gain from contracts in that with this limited financial protection, the executive can pursue decisions that most closely effect the organization's mission and strategic goals with less attention being paid to the political implications of the decisions. One interviewed executive stated this argument cogently:

> I've always wanted to be free to make the decisions, which I felt were institutionally sound without any regard for my own need for security and my own interest. I have found that the contract has made my job so much easier, I'm able to take the risks now that I think are necessary in today's environment because every time I consciously examine a risk I remember that contract in my briefcase. It certainly affects every decision—it's that dramatic— at least it is in my case. I can't help but think that it also has to be in the case of others.

In addition, the CEO armed with a contract can exert strong leadership vis á vis the board and medical staff—leadership, which is needed desperately in view of the increased competition among health care organizations.

First, there are very few, if any, hospitals which operate in monopoly markets. Second, hospitals in large metropolitan markets approach an atomistic structure with a large number of hospitals having very small market shares. Third, smaller metropolitan areas tend to be somewhat more concentrated, approximating an oligopolistic structure. However, hospitals in these areas usually compete with regional tertiary care centers in larger metropolitan areas.[8]

Moreover, in decision making, executives have the freedom to implement innovations—new products, services, and methods to enhance health care and streamline the organization, which contributes to its viability. This is particularly necessary today as various community groups look to health care organizations as their principal provider. Since many traditional sources of funding have adopted stringent cost containment policies, those organizations that are prepared to innovate are the ones that will retain the support of the community and attract the financial resources needed to ensure success.

Finally, organizations that offer executives employment contracts can contemplate major changes with greater objectivity and perspective. For example, CEOs with contractually guaranteed termination payments in the event of a merger, consolidation, or affiliation, are in a position to evaluate the merits of such structural changes more objectively than would those without some provision for their financial well-being. While contracts may not eliminate personal considerations entirely, certainly, they do minimize them to a great extent.

Improved Governance

A second benefit to be derived from contracts is improving the performance of the hospital board. This stems from the quality of leadership that executives can exert in their roles when provided with contractual job security. As a result of such leadership, the board's ability to carry out its fiduciary responsibilities of safeguarding corporate assets, assuring quality, and promoting long-term financial health is enhanced.

Other factors that contribute to a board's improved functioning relate to its function to appoint and evaluate the CEO. For example, offering a contract helps the organization attract the best talent to lead the organization. Particularly, in the case of an organization whose survival is threatened, a highly competent CEO will demand the backing of the board most often in the form of a contract. Without such backing, many highly qualified candidates will shun the position.

Another advantage to the board concerns its function to evaluate the CEO. Employment contracts help assure that executives are evaluated on a fair basis—on their stated role and accountability to the organization—not on personal considerations.

Environmental Adaptation

A third benefit of contracts to the hospital is that they enable the hospital to better adapt to the environment. For example, by enabling CEOs to alter their traditional roles and assume risks, the organization will be in a better position to compete for scarce resources. Instructive here is the experience of William J. Williams, a prominent hospital CEO, who has observed that CEOs and boards are moving rapidly from a single hospital focus to a diversified and vertically integrated health care system.[9] The contemporary health care executive often is responsible for managing multiple product lines in a complex multicorporate structure. Such changes obviously dictate an expansion in the role, responsibilities, and risks assumed by the CEO. To assume such risks, reasonable severance compensation is only equitable.

The role of the CEO in dealing with physicians also argues in favor of contracts. In many markets, physicians are in direct competition with hospitals. Many hospitals are competing with physicians directly to maintain or expand the market share by developing ambulatory care centers, emergicenters, health promotion programs, and other services. Physicians also are developing similar activities to maintain and expand their patient base.

A "too aggressive" CEO may become the target of physicians. This is especially true in areas where there is a physician surplus, and it will be aggravated among those physicians who perceive a sense of relative deprivation in the new, tighter health care marketplace. Often, this tension manifests itself through conflicts between hospital management and physicians over the role and functions of the medical staff—with disastrous results for the hospital.

> The [physician] group (roughly 6 to 20 years out [of their residencies]) is the most upset and affected by the changes. These persons are also the least able to cope. They entered their professional careers with some of the same expectations as their older colleagues but have, in effect, had the rug pulled out from under them before they have had a chance to achieve their objectives. It is from this group that most managers are experiencing conflict and unrest. The overall emotional climate of a given hospital's

relationship with its medical staff can largely be judged by the size of this . . . group. Whatever conflict exists is often exacerbated by the fact that the medical staff's formal leaders (chief of staff, clinical chiefs, committee chairs, etc.) are most frequently members of this age group.[10]

Finally, contracts can enable organizations to better adapt to their environment by requiring CEOs to maintain confidentiality should they leave the organization. Clearly, the strategic objectives of a hospital in a competitive environment cannot be divulged to neighboring facilities if it is to compete effectively. Other, more stringent contract provisions intended to achieve organizational viability include "noncompetition" covenants and prohibitions against a departing CEO recruiting other key employees of the organization. (See *Paragraph 3: Annotations to Letter of Agreement*, pp. 82–83.)

Symbolic Value

The fourth and perhaps most valuable, yet least tangible, advantage to the organization of CEO contracts is their symbolic value. A contract communicates the board's expectation that the CEO should make the high risk, innovative decisions that he or she believes will be necessary for the organization to compete and survive. And, as important, the contract communicates to the medical staff and others that the CEO has the strong support of the board.

Drawbacks of Contracts

The drawbacks to an organization in offering the executive an employment contract are:

- The organization may have to pay if the relationship deteriorates.
- A contract does not assure the tenure of the CEO. While the term of the contract may be specified, no individual can be compelled to work against his or her will.
- Certain members of the board or medical staff may perceive that their role in leading the health care organization is being usurped by the CEO.

However, first it should be noted that what the hospital pays as a result of a deteriorated relationship is usually miniscule when considered in light of the organization's entire budget.

Second, financial disincentives can be added to a contract to make premature departure less attractive.

And third, as indicated earlier, contracts also enhance leadership potential and effective board involvement in setting policies designed for the organization's best interests. This should offset any disadvantage in this regard if the contract is approached properly by those involved.

BENEFITS AND DRAWBACKS OF CONTRACTS: THE EXECUTIVE'S PERSPECTIVE

Benefits

A contract for the health care executive has the immediate advantage of providing some financial security in the event of termination. It reduces the incentive not to take risks or pronounce unpopular views. While these long-term benefits are hard to measure sometimes, an immediate benefit is to make the firing of a CEO less precipitous. The CEO also benefits by being in a position to seek other employment while he or she is in a prominent position.

As Earl Simendinger has stated,

> If the parting of company occurs, it shouldn't be a surprise. If the CEO leaves, he/she could help the board find a replacement. If the board initiates, the CEO should be given adequate time to find a new position. And it's much easier for the CEO to find a job when he has a job. He'll find a better job faster.[11]

A second advantage of contracts for the executive is to formalize the relationship between the executive and the organization. Broadly stated accountabilities and specific reporting relationships serve to ensure that the CEO is aware and responsible for the effective functioning of the organization. Moreover, contracts ensure that the role requirements cannot be diluted. Thus, contracts preserve the dignity of the CEO. For example, John Tarrant has written, "On occasion, employers have tried to drive employees to resign—or to accept significantly lower severance pay than called for in the contract by such 'humiliation ploys' as requiring the employee to report to inferiors or imposing demeaning requirements."[12] Thus, the

CEO can be assured via contract that he or she will not be humiliated by, for example, being asked to report to a former subordinate.

A third advantage of the contract is to underscore the CEO's role as organizational strategist and prime determiner of direction. With a contract, the CEO is less vulnerable to attacks from the medical staff or dissident elements in the community if the hospital faces difficult choices in order to provide high quality care with limited resources.

Finally, a contract can provide motivation for the board to establish a systematic performance evaluation of the CEO. Such evaluations are a needed discipline for boards who must commit to definite objectives and priorities. The CEO then has an agenda endorsed by the board that can form the basis for the CEO's annual performance assessment. In fact, contracts and formal evaluations work together to improve executive performance:

> The question is not whether the CEO is to be evaluated. The importance of the role makes this process inevitable. The real question is whether evaluation can be accomplished in a way that enhances performance of executive leadership and management functions. One of the purposes in establishing a well-structured process of evaluation is to minimize the possibility that judgments will revolve around controversial situations which might be highly subjective, inadequately informed, or politically inspired.[13]

Drawbacks

The classic argument that some CEOs have invoked in rejecting contracts revolves around a theme of trust, which supposedly exists implicitly between the CEO and the board. To them, contracts appear as an infringement on that special relationship. Some contend that contracts make the human relationships that bind the executive to the organization cold, and assert that like a marriage, this relationship should not be reduced to a written document.

However, in many instances, a clear articulation of duties and authority, coupled with the existence of a severance clause, can actually serve to enhance the relationship between CEO and board. It does so by making both parties understand their relative positions. What, then, might present real disadvantages from the executive's point of view?

First, as noted by Williams who chaired the ACHE's Committee on Contracts, the process of asking for a contract has affected some administrators adversely, especially those performing marginally.[14] He notes that in a few cases, asking for a contract caused the board to take a hard look at the CEO and sometimes resulted in his or her dismissal. At other times, boards who felt their CEO turned in an average but not outstanding performance, when faced with the demand for a contract, decided to test the marketplace. Therefore, marginal CEOs who ask for a contract may receive a pink slip instead.

Second, a contract once negotiated may give a CEO a false sense of security. However, as Williams asserts, "an employment agreement with severance compensation provisions is not going to make a poor CEO a good CEO."[15] The disadvantage of a false sense of security is mitigated in the annual performance evaluation that some contracts require. If the evaluation is a candid and meaningful one, this false sense of security will be short lived.

Third, a contract may prevent the CEO from leaving to do other things either by exposing the CEO to suit for breach of contract or by preventing him or her from accepting employment in the same community or industry. Of course, these matters are legitimate subjects for negotiation during the contract discussions.

Fourth, contracts, depending on the specific terms negotiated, may hamper the subsequent functioning of the CEO. For example, a contract may prevent the CEO from recruiting key employees after departing from the organization. Or it may prohibit the CEO from subsequently soliciting business from established clients or group purchasers.

Overall, drawbacks of contracts from the executive's perspective can be overcome by negotiation and vigilance on the executive's part. Through a candid self-appraisal of performance before asking for the contract, through candid evaluations by the board, and through careful negotiation of the contract's terms after leaving the organization, many of the potential drawbacks can be avoided.

EXECUTIVE EMPLOYMENT CONTRACTS: DESCRIPTION AND ANALYSIS

Exhibit 5-1 is a model letter of agreement for CEOs. Of course, each contract will have unique adaptations for the specific person and organization concerned, but the general pattern persists in most executive letters of agreement as set forth here.

Exhibit 5-1 Model of Letter of Agreement for Chief Executive Officer

---

(Date)

Dear _____,

_____ Hospital desires to secure your services as Chief Executive Officer of the Hospital. It is understood that your duties shall be substantially the same as those of the chief executive officer of a business corporation, subject to the bylaws of the Hospital and the policies of the Board.

For your services, the Hospital agrees to pay you your current salary and fringe benefits, [as outlined in our letter dated _____ from the Executive Compensation Committee] and such higher salary and additional benefits as are mutually agreed upon at an annual review of your compensation by the Executive Compensation Committee of the Board. Your salary will be paid in equal monthly installments. _____ may elect, by proper notice given to the Hospital prior to the commencement of any calendar year, to defer such portion of said salary for such year to such date as he may designate in such notice of election, such deferred amounts to be credited with periodic interest in accordance with policies established by the Hospital.

The Board may, in its discretion, terminate this Agreement [prior to its expiration date] by giving written notice to you. Upon such termination, all rights, duties and obligations of both parties shall cease, except that the Hospital shall continue to pay you your then monthly salary for a period of _____ months (including the month in which termination occurred) as an agreed upon termination payment. Such pay shall be made in all instances except in the event of intentional illegal conduct by you. During this period, you shall not be required to come to the Hospital or to perform any duties for the Hospital, nor shall the fact that you seek, accept and undertake other employment during this period affect such payments. Also, during this period, the Hospital agrees to keep your life, health and long term disability insurance fully in effect, and provide you with outplacement services.

Should the Board, in its discretion, change your duties or authority so it can reasonably be found that you are no longer performing as the Chief Executive Officer of the hospital, you shall have the right, in your complete discretion, to terminate this agreement by written notice delivered to the Chairman of the Board. Upon such termination you shall be entitled to the termination benefits described in the preceding paragraph. You may also terminate this agreement for any other reason, by giving written notice to the Chairman of the Board, but if you do, all rights, duties and obligations of both parties will cease and you will not be entitled to any termination benefits.

This agreement may be extended for a term beyond its original term by a letter to that effect exchanged between the parties prior to the expiration date of this agreement.

(Name of Hospital)

BY: _____

(Chairman of the Board)

I accept the offer contained in the above letter.

_____

Chief Executive Officer

DATE: _____

Source: Reprinted from *Contracts for Healthcare Executives,* pp. 48–49, with permission of American College of Healthcare Executives, © 1987.

Annotations to the Letter of Agreement

Paragraph 1: Duties

This paragraph sets forth the basic terms of the contract. It should be noted, however, that the specific duties of the CEO are not spelled out in the contract itself. This is done for three reasons: (1) Since the CEO should be involved in virtually every area of hospital operations, he or she must not be limited by a "laundry list" of duties that narrowly circumscribe the scope of responsibility. (2) Such lists can relegate the CEO to the status of a "hired hand" or they can lead to a challenge of the CEO's authority to perform or carry out functions not included on the list by those who are threatened by the CEO's proposed actions. (3) Since the duties of the CEO constantly change as the hospital changes, it is unwise to lock the CEO and the hospital into a set routine from the start. The contract likens the CEO's role to that of a CEO in a business corporation to underscore the broad responsibility entrusted to him or her by the board.

Paragraph 2: Compensation and Benefits

This paragraph sets forth the consideration given the CEO in return for his or her services. It is best that the CEO's actual salary and benefits not be laid out in detail in the letter of agreement. Rather, they should be set forth in a separate letter from the executive compensation committee of the board to the CEO. This letter should be kept strictly confidential. All too often the CEO's salary and benefits will be used by dissident elements on the board or medical staff as a means of attacking the CEO. Although those benefits may be appropriate for the CEO of a company with a budget greater than ten million dollars, they will not be perceived as such by rank and file hospital employees or the news media. A separate document will minimize the risk that this sensitive information will fall into the wrong hands. Newly recruited CEOs should delete "your current" and insert the phrase in brackets in the first sentence of the paragraph.

After each annual salary review, the CEO's salary presumably will increase. New salary levels should be contained in a letter to the CEO from the board chairperson, which will become incorporated into the initial contract. The contract also permits the CEO to direct that a portion of his or her salary go into tax shelters as deferred income to the extent permitted by law.

Executive compensation, besides being in the form of the base salary, also can be in the form of annual bonuses which often are made explicit in the form of stock (in proprietary or investor-owned hospitals), cash, or other bonuses. Long-term incentive rewards also are a part of executive compensation, and may take the form of stock options, stock, appreciation rights, and in industry, performance share awards. Compensation may be further amplified in terms of such items as deferred compensation agreements, incentive compensation tied to performance objectives, and relocation expenses for the new employee. Tax exempt hospitals, however, should consult with legal counsel when structuring executive incentive programs, so as not to violate Internal Revenue Service restrictions on private inurement.

Flexibility is needed, too, when it comes to the benefits afforded the executive. Ideally, the benefits should match his or her needs. Also, some benefits may be considered taxable income especially when not offered to other employees. Thus, it behooves CEOs to consult with their accountants regarding the personal income tax implications of fringe benefits.

Typical benefits offered to the executive today are life, health, and disability insurance, provisions for retirement and early retirement, and profit-sharing plans. Particularly in the case of CEOs who have been with the hospital for a long time, retirement and early retirement provisions often are defined in great detail. Besides those benefits already mentioned, there also can be club memberships; spouse travel; credit cards for business expenses; and an automobile with insurance, fuel, and maintenance.

Other benefits on the increase because of the increased pressure of today's competitive health care environment concern vacation leave—now an average of four weeks—but more and more CEOs obtain five or six weeks of vacation. A related benefit to prevent the executive from becoming stale are sabbatical leaves based on years of tenure.

Still other ways to compensate executives are nonwage forms of payment:

- tuition grants for executives' children
- whole life insurance paid up
- health insurance co-pays and deductibles not currently covered
- Supplemental Executive Retirement Plans (SERPs)

Executives also can be provided with specific services to assist them now or in the future. Examples are

- Professional assistance in tax and financial planning.
- Legal counsel for personal legal problems up to a limit of perhaps $5,000.
- Executive outplacement services to assist him or her in assessing strengths and weaknesses and to enhance interviewing skills if the current employment arrangement ends.

Paragraph 3: Termination and Severance Pay

This paragraph commonly is referred to as the termination clause. It is by far the most important part of the contract. In the event that a majority of the board decides the services of the CEO no longer are required, for whatever reason, the contract is terminated. However, the CEO is entitled to a stated amount of salary (along with group life and health insurance benefits) even though he or she no longer is working for the hospital. Outplacement services also are provided. Other benefits may continue as negotiated.

The exact number of months of termination pay to which the CEO is entitled is, of course, the subject of negotiation. The figure should reflect accurately the risk and challenges of the position, as well as the relative difficulty the CEO will face in finding a comparable position. Maximum protection is afforded to the executive in a rolling or "parachute" contract, which provides compensation and benefits for a specified period of time. The American College of Healthcare Executives has advocated that severance compensation should not be for less than 12 months nor more than 24 months. The clause referring to the expiration date obviously is used only if the contract is for a stated term.

The purpose of this clause is to protect the CEO from threats of termination aimed at making him or her act with unnecessary caution. It is in the interest of the board, the hospital, and the patients. The CEO must be able to exercise authority to the fullest extent possible. The CEO also must be able to make hard decisions without fear that his or her job may be in jeopardy simply because someone on the board or the medical staff dislikes the decisions for reasons unrelated to the best interests of the hospital.

Termination pay should be made except in the event of intentional illegal conduct on the part of the CEO. The board must have the clear authority by contract to terminate the CEO if it desires. But if it exercises that right of termination, the agreed upon termination payments should be made regardless of the reason for termination. The danger of arbitrary termination for political or personal reasons, which was the basis for recommending termination clauses in the first place, is still real in the hospital field—perhaps more than ever in today's volatile environment. Therefore, it is in the best interest of the corporation, from the standpoint of assuring decisive leadership, that the termination clause be operative in all but the most egregious situations. This is not unfairly weighted in favor of the CEO as some have suggested, rather it is in the interest of good institutional management and thus should be the goal of any conscientious governing body.

Apart from the various events that may lead to termination, termination arrangements can include at least three other clauses: (1) noncompetition covenants, (2) confidentiality provisions, and (3) arbitration. The hospital may insist that the CEO not work for a competing facility for a period of time following resignation or termination. However, the noncompetition clause must not impose undue hardship on the employee, such as forcing him or her to stay at the hospital or else leave the area. Generally, a restriction against the CEO taking a similar position in the hospital's service area for up to two years should be upheld.

Confidentiality provisions in the contract can prevent the CEO from divulging or taking confidential information pertaining to the hospital's operation after being terminated. This merely restates the common law duty with respect to the same. Other provisions can prohibit the CEO from recruiting key employees when he or she leaves.

A clause concerning arbitration, also known as an "alternative forum for dispute resolution," often is inserted to allow informal arbitration of disputed issues between the CEO and the hospital. To resolve disputes, arbitrators can be provided by the American Arbitration Association, a not-for-profit organization. This method of resolving disputes may be less costly than court mandated enforcement of the contract. On the other hand, arbitrators often have the tendency to "split the difference" when deciding a case, which can work to the disadvantage of a party who has a clearcut right to relief.

Other termination agreements may require the executive who voluntarily terminates to remain on the job for some period of time in order to ensure continuity of management. However, as stated previously, a person cannot be forced to remain in a job, so the only practical way of enforcing such a requirement would be to cause the CEO to forfeit his or her termination pay or incur some other financial penalty.

Paragraph 4: Change of Duties

This paragraph is similar to paragraph 3, except that it comes into play if the board substantially changes the duties of the CEO, either by appointing another officer with similar duties or restricting the authority of the existing CEO. This would be one way to avoid the applicability of the termination provisions of paragraph 3.

One of the intentions of the employment contract is to preserve the dignity associated with senior executive positions. Agreements have provisions to deal with a situation when employers try to drive employees to resign by humiliating ploys such as requiring the employee to take on demeaning duties. Typically, if the executive's duties or compensation are diminished during the period of employment, this can be construed, at the discretion of the executive, as invoking the parachute. For example, if the title is reduced or pay is halved, in effect, the executive has been terminated. As in the case of paragraph 3, the CEO in this case will be entitled to full salary plus group life and health insurance for the number of months specified in paragraph 3.

Paragraph 5: Term

This paragraph makes it simple for the hospital and the CEO to continue the agreement beyond its initial term by signing a simple letter of agreement as an extension. The letter need only state that the initial contract has been extended for another specified period and the CEO's new salary. All of the initial provisions and benefits continue in force during the extension.

The critical element in the term is the length of time for which the health care organization commits itself to the CEO in the contract. As long as the contract is in existence, the organization is bound by it as is the CEO.

Since the term is not specified in this particular letter of agreement, it should be specified in the letter to the CEO from the executive compensation committee referred to in paragraph 2. Alternatively, contracts that omit a specific term are presumed to be terminable at will, that is, continuing for an indefinite period of time until terminated.

In business and industry, executive employment contracts range from three to five years. If a CEO is appointed for a stated term, it should be for at least five years in view of the inertia CEOs need to overcome in health care organizations; anything less than that is too short a time to accomplish the objectives set out by the board with respect to the CEO's performance. The rationale for this view was noted by Simendinger who explains, "It requires one or two years to clean house and three to five years to establish programs."[16]

The renewal process should consider the issue of a set term versus a rolling term contract (sometimes referred to as a parachute). In a set term, the contract expires at a specific date, and if not renewed, the executive is terminated. In a rolling term contract, the contract's protection in terms of such things as compensation and benefits will run for a specific period of time into the future (usually one or two years) with no formal termination date. A variant is to combine a set term contract and add a rolling term to it.

The execution of the contract should be authorized by the board. It becomes effective when it is signed by the Chairperson of the board and accepted by the CEO, or on some later date agreed upon by the parties.

Features Organizations and Executives May Find Advantageous

In negotiating contracts with executives, health care organizations may find it particularly advantageous to require a certain number of months notice be given if the CEO wishes to terminate the contract. This will allow adequate time for recruiting a replacement. A similar clause might be included in key executive contracts for the same reason.

Executives may wish in specifying benefits to include a "drop and add" or "cafeteria" fringe benefit clause. For example, if a CEO elects not to use one of the benefits provided in the contract, but would rather substitute for it another benefit of equal monetary value, this should be permitted. In one instance, for example, disability permitted to the CEO and not allowed or provided to any other hospital employee was rejected on principle by the CEO. However, the CEO would have liked to substitute another benefit for this.

Also, in regard to term, executives may wish to stipulate no set term. Apart from giving reasonable notice by each party, this allows the executive the prerogative to change positions without being subject to breach of contract.

Other Types of Executive Employment Contracts

The following types of executive contracts or agreements have been identified:

- A long-form, "classical" contract contains an extensive set of provisions pertaining to the authority and responsibilities of the CEO, as well as compensation, fringe benefits, and renewal and termination arrangements. John Horty has commented that this type of contract is better suited for the newly appointed executive.[17]

- A short-form contract is limited to certain specifics regarding the appointment or continued employment of an executive. The letter of agreement detailed previously illustrated the short form contract. As discussed, basic elements of the governing board–CEO relationship may be defined in collateral documents, such as bylaws, personnel policies, and other policy statements. This essentially is a termination agreement which is a part of the more extensive "long-form" contract. Occasionally, such letters are negotiated between key executives other than CEOs, for example chief operating officers and the hospital. Of course, such a letter allows either the CEO or the executive to terminate the employment relationship and does not involve the board.

NEGOTIATING THE EXECUTIVE EMPLOYMENT AGREEMENT: THE PROCESS

Raising the Subject

Changes in the health care industry have affected the burden and risk executives assume in their roles. However, in spite of this changing climate, asking for a contract still remains a sensitive issue. At least one recruitment spokesperson has suggested that a lawyer, consultant, or recruiter raise the subject to avoid giving the impression that the employee does not trust the new employer. Alternatively, the employee can simply state that a contract is useful to clarify points and to deal with any contradictions or important omissions in the employment arrangement. As it is increasingly becoming the standard for the industry, those who are currently employed need to raise this subject with their boards. Board members themselves often work under employment contracts, and thus, should realize the importance and worth of contracts.

Occasionally, when relations between the board and executive are especially good, contracts have been initiated by the boards. In other instances, boards will initiate a contract based on the advice of an administrator. The health care executive has to be aware of the nuances of his or her situation and relationship before undertaking the process of asking for a contract. The particular circumstances will determine the executive's strategy for obtaining a contract. For example, some boards will be more receptive than others, and an administrator doing a superior job might find it easier than one whose performance is mediocre.

Who Should Negotiate the Contract?

In canvassing various executives and consultants about who might be involved in negotiating a contract, lawyers, executive recruiters, and consultants were the most commonly cited third parties. Most agreed that CEOs should have expert legal counsel who can review the wording of the contract, suggest points that should be introduced, or suggest issues that must be clarified. The attorney, in essence, serves as a useful balance to the hospital's legal counsel who reviews the contract from the hospital's perspective.

The individuals canvassed cautioned that while legal advice is appropriate, a CEO should negotiate the contract directly without his or her attorney being present so as to preserve the trust and goodwill of the board. The attorney's advice should be relied on before concluding the agreement.

Executive recruiters and consultants can facilitate an agreement between a CEO and board. Acting as "shuttle diplomats," these third parties can assist in the negotiating process. And, while the search firm's primary obligation is to the employer, in most cases, their long-term interest lies in achieving a balance of interests—an equitable contract from the perspective of both hospital and CEO.

Authorization Procedure

While the contract negotiations with the CEO are best conducted by the executive committee or an *ad hoc* committee of the board, a majority of the full board must vote to authorize the contract. If the CEO is an *ex officio* member of the board, he or she should be absent from that portion of the board meeting when the employment terms are discussed. Once the board has authorized the contract, it should be signed by the chairperson of the board for the hospital corporation and the CEO. The contract becomes effective when signed or on such other date as agreed to by the parties. The contract should then be filed along with other essential corporate documents, such as the hospital's bylaws and articles of incorporation, and a duplicate should be given to the CEO. Needless to say, the terms of the contract and all subsequent amendments to it should be confidential.

Renewal

The contract can be amended or renewed by another letter signed by the chairperson and the CEO, stating whatever new terms (such as salary increase or additional benefits) have been agreed upon.

Negotiations for renewing the contract should take place allowing sufficient time before the contract is terminated and after the executive learns that the board intends to renew it. One executive recommends that the process begin at least a year before the end of the contract ". . . so no one's surprised—otherwise, all of a sudden the contract is up and the CEO gets his pink slip or the board gets the letter of resignation, and the CEO is sitting around doing nothing for a year except looking for a job."[18] This allows sufficient time for both parties to deal with any eventualities.

CONCLUSION

Recent studies by the nonprofit Project on Adult Lives shows a new breed of careerists, usually between age 25 and 40 who have attained influential positions. They are characteristically less loyal to the company they work for. Instead they are concerned with their own career progression and their personal development. They are the product of a generation, which grew up under the influence of an educational perspective that believed subjects and work should be relevant. The director of the project says

> What I'm finding now is that a lot of urban careerists talk about a kind of hunger for leadership in their companies. . .that would articulate a vision that transcends the short-term selfish interest. They want to integrate their desire for success with a larger meaning of society.[19]

Today's younger executives are pursuing a course of enlightened self-interest with respect to the firms they manage. Since they are more vulnerable themselves, they are more prone to negotiate an agreement with their organizations in which both parties know that the relationship will last only as long as it is productive for both. This readiness, according to Bob Swain, chairman of Swain & Swain Inc., a New York out-placement firm, is resulting in people who are "experiencing what they really want to do—a meaningful job without worrying about the politics and hierarchy of the organization."[20]

These are healthy developments for the American society. Played out to the fullest, the pattern of executive decisions based on personal visions can only lead to greater efficiency and innovation in health care delivery.

NOTES

1. American College of Hospital Administrators, Report of the Model Contracts Committee, *Contracts of Hospital Administrators with Suggestions as to Form* (Dallas, Texas: September 26, 1938).

2. James E. Ludlam. "Contracts for Hospital Administrators," *Administrative Briefs*, American College of Hospital Administrators, vol. 2, no. 2 (July, 1968).

3. American College of Hospital Administrators, *The Evolving Role of the Hospital Chief Executive Officer* (Chicago: American College of Hospital Administrators, 1984), p. 96.

4. American College of Hospital Administrators, unpublished data: Membership Advancement Study, Chicago, 1985.

5. "Ferdinand Toennies" in *International Encyclopedia of the Social Sciences*, vol. 16, ed. D. Sills (MacMillan Publishing Co., Inc. and Free Press, 1968), pp. 98–100.

6. Max Weber, "Bureaucracy," in *Max Weber: Essays in Sociology*, Gerth and Mills, eds. (New York: Oxford University Press, 1958).

7. Adolf A. Berle, Jr. and Gardiner C. Means, *The Modern Corporation and Private Property*, (New York: MacMillan Publishing Co., Inc. 1932), see especially pp. 124–25.

8. Richard Arnould and Lawrence M. De Brock, "Competition and Market Failure in the Hospital Industry: A Review of the Evidence," *Medical Care*, vol. 43, no. 2 (Fall 1986), pp 253–292.

9. American College of Healthcare Executives, "Contracts for Healthcare Executives" (Chicago: The Foundation of the American College of Healthcare Executives, 1987), p. ix.

10. Stephen Shortell, "The Medical Staff of the Future: Replanting the Garden," *Frontiers of Health Services Management*, vol. 1, no. 3 (February, 1985), p. 12.

11. American College of Healthcare Executives, "Contracts for Healthcare Executives," p. 25.

12. John Tarrant, *Perks and Parachutes: Negotiating Your Executive Employment Contract*, (New York: Simon and Schuster, 1985).

13. American College of Hospital Administrators, *Evaluating the Performance of a Hospital CEO.* (Chicago: ACHA, 1984), pp. 18–19.

14. American College of Healthcare Executives, "Contracts for Healthcare Executives," p. 19.

15. Ibid., p. ix.

16. Ibid., p. 25.

17. Ibid., p. 23.

18. Ibid., p. 23.

19. Don Oldenburg, "Loyalty and the Work Place," *Washington Post*, January 5, 1988, B5.

20. Ibid.

6

Effective Incentive Programs That Attract and Retain Executive Talent

Mark M. Cox, Senior Vice President, Witt Associates Inc., 724 Enterprise Drive, Oak Brook, IL 60521

Joan Bourke, Senior Associate, Executive Compensation, Witt Associates Inc., 724 Enterprise Drive, Oak Brook, IL 60521

INCENTIVE COMPENSATION

Five years ago, a book about executive recruiting probably would not even include a discussion about incentive compensation—and the information about compensation in general would be brief. Today, the compensation package developed for the key executive staff is a significant issue in the recruiting negotiations.

Recent survey reports indicate 25 to 35 percent of today's chief executive officers (CEOs) in health care organizations are participating in an incentive compensation program. However, search consultants claim that the percentage of new CEO hires negotiating for incentives as part of the job offer probably is closer to 75 percent. If an incentive plan exists, the CEO, executive vice president, and chief financial officer are almost sure to seek inclusion, and other functional executives at the "number 2" level also will negotiate for this benefit. If no plan exists at the time of hire, the new CEO will want board approval to develop such a program, at least for his or her own position.

Because of this growing trend toward incentive plans, with 25 percent having a plan and 75 percent seeking one, it is important to review the executive compensation package in general. Incentives are just one component of a pay plan, and need to have a solid base or foundation if the plan is to be successful. The components to be considered are *BASIC*:

B—board involvement and basic compensation
A—appraisal and evaluation methods
S—setting goals and target objectives
I—incentive planning (fund, distributions, etc.)
C—communications and constant reviews

Board Involvement and Basic Compensation

This is really far too broad a category, but does represent the very cornerstone of a compensation program. The charge to a board of trustees will include the responsibility to *attract, retain, motivate,* and *reward* the key executive staff. Just as the board will appoint committees to deal with other aspects of the overall charge (such as medical staff committee, finance committee, plant and facilities committee, personnel committee, and executive committee), so should it appoint an executive compensation committee to deal with this issue.

The executive compensation committee of the board will be responsible for the annual evaluation and appraisal of the CEO and the definition and maintenance of policies on executive compensation issues such as target pay level, compensation mix, and the incentive compensation plan. The policy statements will reflect the board's philosophy on compensation, and that philosophy should be defined in a statement of purpose for the committee. All of the policy statements developed by the executive compensation committee should be reviewed on a regular basis (usually about every three years) and revised as necessary to keep the compensation program in tandem with the overall strategic plan of the organization. The American Compensation Association (ACA) developed a position paper on Principles of Executives Pay Programs that stated:

> ACA recommends that the evaluation of any given executive compensation program be based on the following factors:
>
> - The required performance level
> - The achieved performance level
> - Existing pay levels for similar positions
> - The risk the executive is required to take vis-à-vis the risk required of other executives in equivalent positions.[1]

Base compensation needs to be equitable and competitive before any consideration is given to an incentive plan. A process for assessment should include review of survey data from multiple sources and be adjusted for relevance. The purpose of an incentive plan (or a discretionary bonus plan) is to provide additional rewards for extraordinary or superior performance. If the base pay plan is not adequate the bonus award will be viewed as something already "owed" to the executive. It will not motivate, retain or reward executives, and may, in fact, have a negative impact.

Appraisal and Evaluation Methods

Any compensation plan that seeks to provide pay for performance must have a system for measuring that performance. An executive appraisal system should have two directions—reviewing past performance and targeting future objectives. Also, the system should include input from both the executive and superior as well as a written documentation of the process.

Although institutions in the United States report an established performance appraisal system for the lower level employees, the lack of evaluation procedures for key executives is appalling. The individuals who are in a position of risk and authority receive minimal direction, review, and support. By comparison, those employees in closely supervised positions with limited autonomy may receive a detailed, written evaluation on an annual basis. In fairness to the executive, agreement on performance standards and priorities is essential for personal growth and development as well as the success of the organization.

Setting Goals and Objectives

The process of setting goals and objectives should be looped, with ongoing communication and coordination. In practice, the process should be initiated by the executive compensation committee in the beginning stages of the CEO's appraisal. The executive compensation committee, reflecting the board of trustees, should indicate to the CEO the three or four major targets for the organization. These frequently are in fairly general terms, and pinpoint the specific areas in which the CEO will target his or her own performance.

For example, the executive compensation committee may identify four major organizational goals:

1. financial stability, with revenue growth consistent with the past two years;
2. development of programs and services, both inpatient and outpatient;
3. management contract or outright purchase of the 115-bed institution in the adjoining county; and
4. continued and improved quality of care, and recognition of same within the community.

From this statement, the committee will direct the CEO to prepare his or her own list of goals and objectives that will support these organizational targets. The CEO's listing should identify organizational goals and goals for his or her own position, each with a defined standard of performance. (It is recognized that the standards of performance or measurement will not be precise in the early years of this process but will, with practice, become refined.)

The CEO's listing will be submitted to the committee for review, revisions, and rankings. These frequently are accomplished within the committee, exclusive of the CEO's participation. A session is then scheduled to finalize the goals and reach a mutual commitment.

Once the CEO's goals have been set in priority order, the CEO will charge the key executive staff members to prepare their own goals (organizational and individual) that will serve the already approved CEO goals. Again, the list should be submitted, reviewed, and revised, followed by mutual commitment to the listings. The CEO, of course, will coordinate the charges to each individual to maximize team effectiveness.

This process is based on the concept that the individual, functional executive is best able to identify the direction of his or her own position. The "wish list" comes from the executive; the final approval and coordination come from the CEO and executive compensation committee.

Incentive Planning

If the executive compensation committee of the board recognizes an incentive compensation arrangement as one component of the executive compensation package, such a program merits planning and development and subsequent review. A checklist of basic questions to be addressed includes:

1. What is the purpose of the plan?
2. How will the fund be established? (Where is the money coming from?)
3. Who will be eligible to participate in the plan?
4. What is the maximum award available to any individual?
5. What is the criteria for distribution? What will trigger availability of the fund in general, and what will determine an individual's eligibility for a distribution?
6. What is the timetable for goal determination, year-end evaluation, and award distribution?
7. What is the timetable for review and revision?

Several of these features are discussed in more detail in the balance of this chapter. At this point, suffice it to say that the development of an incentive compensation merits substantial planning efforts to maximize the productivity of the individuals and the effectiveness of the program.

Communications and Constant Reviews

An incentive compensation program, in fact the entire executive compensation plan, is an active, "alive" concept. The programs are supportive of the institution's planning process, and will change in scope and direction from time to time. The executive compensation committee, the administrators of the incentive program, must constantly address the questions: For what behavior or accomplishments are we seeking to provide the incentive? What are appropriate measurements or standards of performance?

For years the authors have considered *"Communicate!"* and *"No Surprises!"* the two slogans for any executive compensation program. Truly, they go hand in hand.

INITIATING INCENTIVE COMPENSATION

This book is focused on recruitment and job seeking and this chapter will deal primarily with the organization that does not have an incentive plan but is ready and willing to pursue a plan.

If an incentive plan already exists, and an executive candidate is seeking to change it, the selection committee generally can accommodate that request by expressing a willingness to review changes within 12 to 18 months, or by supplementing the existing plan with a discretionary bonus of X percent in the first year and revision discussion in the second year. If a plan exists the selection committee can work concurrently with a time schedule and a plan for revision.

First, consider the situation where a selecton committee is interviewing three final candidates for the CEO position. Each already has indicated he or she is benefitting from an incentive plan and is seeking a similar arrangement. The selecting organization is willing to pay a competitive base pay, but does not have a defined incentive plan.

If an incentive plan does not exist, the selection committee cannot offer an incentive award to the new hire. An incentive plan implies that some planning has gone into the concept, and in this scenario that just isn't true. An alternative arrangement would be to offer a discretionary award of

X percent at the conclusion of the first performance year if for example, targets 1-2-3 are met, and a commitment by the board to initiate the development of a plan for introduction at a specified date and initial payouts at a specified date.

Who Initiates the Incentive Plan Development?

The development of an incentive plan may be initiated by individual executives, by the CEO, or by the board of trustees. Each interest group may have its own reasons; some valid and some less so.

For the individual executive, an incentive award is an opportunity for additional rewards to compensate for superior performance or achievements in a stressful environment or both. Today's health care executives are seeking a total compensation package that is competitive with similar jobs in the nonhealth care environment. Frequently, this means a "risk and reward" component to the pay package. There certainly are some who feel an incentive is a way to keep up with one's neighbors, but once a plan is designed and explained, and it is clear that payment is linked to performance, this attitude fades.

In many instances, the CEO will recommend the development of an incentive compensation plan to use as an effective compensation tool with his or her own executive staff. (In such instances, the CEO may exclude his own position from consideration, but that approach is questionable at best.) Just as the board is charged with attracting, retaining, motivating, and rewarding the executive group, the CEO is charged with the implementation of that concept. Incentives will enhance the compensation package when attracting new executives to the institution. Furthermore, it is an effective retention tool to keep key executives in an unusually competitive market place. Motivation comes from job content and role definition as well as compensation, but financial motivation to coordinate performance and focus on organizational goals is not to be discounted. The CEO also will recognize that incentives provide a reward mechanism to compensate the exceptional performer.

When incentives are first introduced at the board level, the reasons usually reflect the represented businesses. Comments such as "it worked at my place;" "let's separate the wheat from the chaff, let the cream come to the top;" and "who will stand up to be counted?" are not uncommon. Board members must understand the Internal Revenue Service regulations. While the plan may reward fiscal responsibility, a total focus on the bottom line may jeopardize the institution's not-for-profit status. Also, board and the executive compensation committee members must understand that the development of an incentive compensation program will not end their responsibility or involvement in compensation issues. In his book, *Building a Better Hospital Board*, John Witt makes the comment:

> In the last few years board members have increasingly looked to incentives as partial alternatives to compensation adjustments. They feel (somewhat inappropriately, in my opinion) that an incentive system will make adjustments easier. This is only partially true, as the judgment factors are seldom removed from any incentive plan.[2]

Regardless of where the discussions start, the development of an incentive award component of an executive compensation plan must focus on several issues. There is no ideal, prepackaged plan. The whole concept of incentives is based on a personalized, measurable, institution-specific framework. The unique mix of the institution and the key executives will drive the plan, and it will require ongoing review and revision to keep it functional. There are administrative issues as well as participant issues, and each category deserves time and attention.

ADMINISTRATIVE ISSUES OF INCENTIVES

Establishing the Fund

An incentive fund may be developed through a variety of formulae or budget plans. The most common approaches are a defined fund, a dependent fund, or a combined fund.

In a *defined fund*, an established dollar amount will be budgeted, just as other compensation expenses are budgeted. The amount can be a few percentage points less than the maximum potential of the summed awards. For example, if an incentive plan allows participating executives to receive up to 20 percent of their base salary, the defined fund can probably be established at about 15 percent or 15 percent of the summed bases. This arrangement recognizes that most executives will not reach the maximum potential of their award if the goals and standards of performance are defined as stretch targets for superior performance.

A *dependent fund* will be established as a dollar amount, depending on some particular outcome at year end (and unknown at the beginning of the performance year). For example, a dependent fund may be equal to 1 percent of outpatient revenues, not to exceed $50,000; or, x dollars for every half percentage point that the institution exceeds the national targets on

the American Hospital Association's MoniTrend report for revenues, occupancy, and expenses per patient day. It is important that a dependent fund
be capped, or there is risk that the incentive awards will be disproportionate to base salaries or unachievable in subsequent years or both. It is also
important (especially in the initial two years) that the dependent fund be
reasonably assured of some contribution. To develop and introduce a plan
that can have no payouts, will not serve to attract, retain, motivate, and
reward executives.

A *combined fund* combines some aspects of a defined fund and allows an
additional dependent contribution. Once a plan is tested and in place, this
may be the best method, assuring availability of a certain base fund, and
allowing an additional cap tied specifically to productivity and performance.

Distributing the Fund

Fund distribution is frequently a two-step process. Basic accomplishments or "trigger goals" may be defined by the executive compensation
committee as the key to the fund. If certain organizational targets are not
met, no individual can receive an award. (In short, if the dollars are not
available, awards cannot be given.) These trigger goals are usually limited
to two or three, and generally are related to financial viability and overall
quality care.

The second approach to distributing the fund will be the formula or
system for determining the individual awards. It is suggested that each
individual award be composed of three parts: (1) organizational performance, (2) individual performance, and (3) a discretionary component. As
the plan matures, and the executive's participation is refined, the balance
of these three components may vary. For example, in the first year, an
individual's award potential may be in equal thirds. As the standards of
performance are refined, and all participants and evaluators mature in the
plan, the discretionary component generally will decrease and the other
two components will increase (perhaps to 40 percent, 40 percent, and
20 percent). In many organizations, the award composition also may vary
by job. Line positions may emphasize individual goals and staff positions
may have a stronger emphasis on organizational or group goals.

Characteristics of a Plan

Whether an incentive plan is designed by the staff and board committee
or by outside counsel, there are certain basic plan characteristics.

- The plan is an addition to or a *component* of an executive compensation system. It is not a substitute for a competitive base salary structure.
- The plan offers awards for *specific achievements* beyond normal expectations. It is not a method of increasing gross compensation or circumventing an established salary increase policy.
- The award is *variable*, depending upon performance. There is no guarantee of payment.
- The award is *meaningful* in terms of effort expended.
- The formula and rationale are *understood easily* by the plan participants.
- The award is based upon specific, mutually agreed upon, *predetermined objectives*.
- It is possible (even preferred) that the plan has its own *time schedule*, distinct from any annual salary adjustment.
- The plan may consider both *short-* and *long-range* achievements; both *financial and nonfinancial goals*.
- The plan is *reviewed regularly and adjusted* as necessary. Changes and revisions in goal emphasis will maximize productivity.

What about Outside Consultants?

Many organizations question whether the development of an incentive compensation plan is something that should be done internally or charged to an outside consulting firm.

There are real advantages in using outside counsel for plan design. Time commitment and experience are two major considerations. There also is a distinct advantage in having an outside, impartial individual assessing the climate of the organization, assessing the existing compensation program, and identifying the plan and communication needs. If the CEO and his or her key executive staff stand to benefit financially from the award distributions, their proposed plan may appear to be self-serving. It also is valuable for the executive compensation committee to have a consultant on call for questions, comments, and ongoing committee assistance.

PARTICIPANT ISSUES REGARDING INCENTIVES

Who Should Participate?

It is suggested that the initial participant group in an incentive compensation program be kept small and manageable. A guideline figure is to calculate one-half of 1 percent to 1 percent of the total employee group. So, in an organization with 700 full-time employees (FTEs), the participants probably will be four to seven key executives. With 1,800 FTEs, the group may expand to 9 to 12.

In the initial interviews with potential plan participants, the executives frequently may express a desire to include their own management staff in the plan. No doubt some sort of reward program will develop at the lower levels in years to come. Initially, however, it is prudent to keep the participant group small until the plan has been tested. If the plan is well designed, and it truly rewards those in risk positions, it will not expand easily to lower levels. If rewards are designed for "Indians" rather than "chiefs," the nature of goal setting and measurement must be adjusted. An initial incentive plan should be targeted to the risk takers; those executives upon whom the success of the organization truly rests. One client organization described participation parameters by indicating the plan was for those situations where the incumbent was as important as the job—"who is doing it" is as critical as "what is being done."

Most employees can recognize the reward component, but the risk component in an incentive plan is just as critical. When determining the size of the participant group it is suggested that the core group be considered as the natives. The plan should, over time, make the natives converts to the system and eventually missionaries for the plan. Once the individual participants are in the missionary category, the organization is ready to consider a related plan for the next level of executives and the cycle then repeats. The individual executive (or board committee) finalizing on goals and standards of performance must be committed to the incentive concept if the plan is to be successful.

What Will Be Rewarded?

The process of goal determination and identification of standards of performance will mature with the plan. In the initial stages of an incentive plan, it frequently is helpful to separate the base pay issues from the incentive issues. Many organizations have a defined policy that states an above average, competitive base pay will be provided for above-average performance of the basic job responsibilities. In addition, incentive pay will be available for the performance of targeted goals and objectives that are beyond the basic job responsibilities. One could think of incentive goals as one-time charges, or some project-type achievement that is only required every three or four years. Base pay for basic work: additional rewards for extra or project-type efforts. As the plan matures, incentive emphasis may be related to superior performance of basic responsibilities, but this is harder to measure and not suggested in the first year or two of the plan.

How Much Is an Appropriate Award?

Current executive compensation surveys are suggesting that incentive awards for the CEO may have a potential of 25 percent to 35 percent, with payouts being closer to 18 percent to 22 percent. At other executive levels, these amounts generally have a 20 percent to 25 percent potential, with payouts ranging from about 12 percent to 18 percent.

Since an incentive plan is, by definition, dollars at risk, it is suggested that the award potential be limited in the first year or two of the plan. It is not unusual to see a plan design that provides up to 25 percent for the CEO and perhaps 20 percent for the key executive staff. It is not fair to risk a significant dollar amount until the process of goal setting and evaluation has been tested and the standards of performance or measurement for each job have been defined.

While industrial incentive plans may provide awards in excess of 50 percent or even 100 percent of base pay, such plans are unlikely in the health care setting. External forces in health care (such as third party payors, government regulations, and community needs) limit the control of any individual executive. If the department that puts casts on broken arms is not profitable, the institution cannot eliminate it in the same manner that an unsellable widget can be discontinued. Although some incentive plans currently allow payouts at 35 percent or 40 percent of base pay, it is unlikely that potential payouts will go much beyond that level. A well-defined and administered plan that allows 30 percent of base pay will quite likely be the high range for some time to come.

HOW SUCCESSFUL ARE INCENTIVES?

The reported results of incentive compensation programs are very good. To date, the authors are aware of no organization that developed an incentive compensation plan and then discontinued the program.

However, this is not to suggest that incentive awards are the answer to compensation problems. Realistically, situations where incentives may have failed probably are not talked about. With current literature announcing the growing trends and increased interest in this concept, few organizations are going to step forward and announce failure if their plan doesn't work. It also should be recognized that the incentive plans in health care

are still relatively new. What the impact will be 5 to 10 years from now is not known. What is known, is that the best results seem to come from the simple, uncomplicated plans that are well administered and maintained. A publication of the American Management Association commented on this issue:

> The key to making any incentive scheme work is for management to have the will to manage the system actively and be willing to differentiate on the basis of performance. Managers will be more likely to enforce a pay-for-performance approach to the administration of rewards if they know that their own pay is determined according to the same philosophy. Within the organization, the will to manage is like a snowball that, if practiced by top management, gains momentum as it rolls down the ranks of management.[3]

There is little documentation of incentive successes in health care beyond the increase in activity. Industrial programs have been tested, though, and one such study was reported in the *Journal of Compensation and Benefits* in late 1986.

> The organizations that were most successful financially used employee compensation plans to communicate the chief executive's performance priorities and to distribute rewards consistent with accomplishment of priorities. The organizations whose performance was poorer had no such communication link.[4]

Aside from the financial and productivity results within the organization, an incentive program will support the planning process within the organization, underscoring directions, programs, and services.

SUMMARY

Incentive compensation, as a significant component of the executive pay package, will continue to play a role in job offer negotiations for key health care executives. If an incentive plan exists, the top executives will seek inclusion. If no plan exists, it is suggested that the search committee provide an alternative through a discretionary, one-time payout and concurrently commit to the investigation and development of an incentive plan. If a plan does not exist, it obviously cannot be offered. However, the concept is valid and merits consideration and review and, quite likely, development.

NOTES

1. American Compensation Association, "Position Paper on Principles of Executive Pay Programs" (Scottsdale, AZ, American Compensation Association).

2. John A. Witt, *Building a Better Hospital Board* (Ann Arbor, MI, Health Administration Press, 1987).

3. Charles G. Tharp, "Linking Annual Incentive Awards to Individual Performance," *Compensation and Benefits Review*, November-December 1985, pp 38–44.

4. Jay R. Schuster and Patricia K. Zingheim, "Tying Compensation to Top Performance Can Boost Profits," *Journal of Compensation and Benefits*, September-October 1986, pp 69–73.

7

Causes of Executive Failure in Health Care[*]

*Terence F. Moore, President, Mid-Michigan Health Care Systems, Inc.,
4005 Orchard Drive, Midland, MI 48640*

*Earl A. Simendinger, PhD, Professor and Chairman, Department of Health
Education and Health Sciences, Central Michigan University,
Mt. Pleasant, MI 48859*

Executive failure usually brings to mind someone being fired, but some would argue that the two are not synonymous. Clearly, executives may sometimes be fired because of circumstances beyond their control. Conversely, executive officers may retain their jobs until retirement yet be considered failures because they misused their powers while in office and/ or did not maximize the potential of either the organization or the staff.

Many health care organizations have had CEOs who served for many years and retired amidst much fanfare and ballyhoo, but when they were replaced, it seemed as if a clot had been removed from the organization. It soon became apparent that the former CEOs were detrimental rather than beneficial to the organizations' health.

Because this definition is so universally accepted by executive recruiters and others, the authors will use the term "failure" to denote an executive who has been fired or derailed from progressing further in an organization.

HIGH LEVEL OF TURNOVER

There was a time when health care executives enjoyed relative job security compared to their counterparts in private industry. They did not suffer from the ravages of great economic recession or product life cycles or foreign competition. That time ended when third party payors began to emphasize controlling the amount of rate increases granted to health care

---

[*]Adapted from "Executive Failure" by Terence F. Moore and Earl A. Simendinger in *Healthcare Forum*, Vol. 30, pp. 61–65, with permission of Association of Western Hospitals, © May/June 1987.

facilities and, more recently, when the DRG reimbursement program was implemented.

As health care institutions have lost their "financial altitude" their executives have begun to lose their jobs with great frequency. In a survey conducted in 1984, the researchers determined that the turnover rate of hospital chief executive officers (CEOs) in California was 24 percent that year.[1] A similar survey in Michigan in 1985 indicated that approximately 25 percent of all hospital CEO positions changed occupants between October 1985 and October 1986.[2] Some of these executives retired, some went on to other positions, but many were simply released to seek employment elsewhere. At least one recruiter has indicated that on the west coast the turnover rate has approached 35 percent. It was noted that the San Francisco area was a particularly brutal marketplace and the turnover rate per year there was almost 50 percent.[3]

A study covering the six counties surrounding Los Angeles by the Hospital Council of Southern California, Los Angeles, showed the turnover rate in that area to be about 30 percent. But the problem is more severe at investor-owned facilities and particularly in those facilities with fewer than 100 beds. It was indicated that the turnover rate in 1986 in that area was 40 percent at the smaller facilities; and in 1985, 45 percent.[4]

These vacancies did not result necessarily from firing, but there is an indication that many of them did. Dick Dolan, an author and president of Career Decisions, Inc., estimates that of his firm's health care clients, 60 percent are fired, 20 percent leave the field voluntarily, and 20 percent leave to retire, because of their health or for other reasons.[5]

AFTER THE TERMINATION

The real tragedy of these firings is not so much the immediate damage done to an executive's career, but the long-term loss, what happens to a CEO's career after he or she is fired. Of nine CEOs who were fired from their positions in the East Central Michigan region during the past few years, three have not found employment, one has found employment in the health care field, one has relocated to the Middle East and another to El Salvador, one works on an Indian reservation, one is a salesman, and one is in jail.

Every executive recruiter knows that it is much easier to find a position if you already have a job. Looking for a job when you do not have a job is similar to leaping on a galloping horse from the ground. It is much easier to jump from one horse to another. Unfortunately, an estimated 85 percent of all new health care executives entering the field today will be fired or forced to leave their position at least once during their careers if the current trends are maintained.

Another tragedy of these terminations and high turnover rates is that it has a "churning effect" throughout the entire organization. The CEO who is only at an organization for a short period of time makes numerous changes. If a new CEO is hired, he or she again changes things. This type of convulsion can have a disruptive and deleterious effect on morale and operational efficiency. Employees at all levels are continually told to change direction.

GENERAL REASONS FOR EXECUTIVE FAILURE

What makes or breaks a top executive? An exhaustive study of executives who had been derailed provides some interesting insights. Reporting the results of this study, behavioral scientist Michael M. Lombardo and Morgan W. McCall observed that all of these derailed executives were near the top of a Fortune 500 company and all had gotten there because they appeared to have the same traits as their successful counterparts.[6] As the derailed executives rose to higher levels in their organization, however, certain events tended to expose one or more of their faults. Situations leading to their derailment included at least one of the following:

- They had lost a boss who had covered for them or compensated for their weaknesses.
- They were in a job for which they were not prepared. (A new boss with a different style often was a factor in exposing their lack of preparation.)
- They left behind a trail of little problems or bruised people; they handled these problems poorly or moved so quickly that they failed to handle them at all.
- They moved up during a corporate reorganization and were not closely scrutinized until after the reorganization had fully settled.
- They entered the executive suite where getting along with others under highly stressful conditions is critically important. What these situations exposed was "people factors" or so called "personality flaws" in the failed executives.

These same authors compared twenty-one derailed executives with twenty arrivers, those who had made it all the way to the top. Detailed observations through interviews with insiders of several Fortune 500 companies turned up ten fatal flaws in the derailed executives:

1. Insensitivity to others; an abrasive, intimidating, bullying style.
2. Display of cold, aloof, arrogant behavior.
3. Betrayal of trust—the "one upping" of others or a failure to follow through on promises.
4. Overambition—thinking of the next job and playing politics.
5. Specific performance problems with the business.
6. Overmanagement—an inability to delegate or build a team.
7. Inability to staff effectively.
8. Inability to think strategically.
9. Inability to adapt to a boss with a different style.
10. Overdependency on an advocate or mentor.

Most executives were derailed because of only one or two of these ten flaws. Insensitivity to others was cited more frequently than any other flaw. The ability or inability to understand other people's points of view represented the most difference between those who "arrived" and those who were derailed. Only 25 percent of the derailed managers were described as having a special ability to deal with people; among the arrivers the figure was 75 percent.[7]

Another author, Richard Conarroe, describes ten reasons why the best executives do not always get to the top.[8]

1. They do not always make themselves known. (Sometimes it enhances one's reputation and pays off to do projects inside an organization, in professional societies, and in the community.)
2. They do not look the part. (You can dress for success or you can dress for failure.)
3. They do not act the part. Executives must be consistent and have absolute integrity.
4. They do not speak the part. (Learn to speak in concise, positive terms and not focus on petty issues or personalities.)
5. They do not know how to sell themselves. (The section in this book about marketing yourself covers many aspects of "selling yourself.")
6. They do not know how to sell their ideas. Many executives probably have failed to advance their careers because they simply cannot get the decision makers in their organizations to support their ideas and projects.

7. They do not take chances or they take too many chances. (It is essential that executives take some calculated risks and not fear failure.)
8. They do not learn the rules of survival soon enough. Actually, they do not learn some basic administrative tactics. These tactics are similar to well-established military principles.[9]
9. They do not know how to conserve their own energy. Often they focus on doing things right rather than doing the right things. (What activities produce the most benefit for your organization? What activities produce the most benefit for you?)
10. They do not understand the value of specializing. (You must not get into the habit of only doing those things which you enjoy.)

WHY DO HEALTH CARE EXECUTIVES LOSE THEIR JOBS?

Enough about the failure of business executives in general; specifically, why do health care executives lose their jobs? Several years ago three top executive recruiters in the United States answered this question. All responded that this subject had been foremost on their minds and they shared their comments in typewritten letters. Mark Silber, Ph.D., an author and a well-known lecturer, consultant, and executive recruiter from San Diego has given considerable thought to the causes of executive failure. He believes that the primary cause is often a mismatch between the executive's style and the organization's culture. This mismatch is revealed in ineffective board relationships and is exemplified by noncommunicative, emotional, or manipulative behavior—even the exploitation of "perks" and benefits by the executive.

The second major reason, according to Silber, falls within the category of the managerial skills/relation factor. Indecisiveness or the "paralysis of analysis" is often a characteristic of failing executives who gradually lose touch with their objectives, opportunities, and the perceptions others have of their actions. Their leadership becomes lopsided: they focus on one aspect of managing at the expense of another. For example, they may focus on the visionary aspects of the organization at the expense of bottom line results. These same executives also fail to network adequately with peers, board members, members of the medical staff, and others.

The third major reason Silber gives for failure is "personal factors." Executives with this problem may project a poor image, be insensitive to power and its use, and exhibit many of the fatal flaws cited in studies by McCall and Lombardo. In an unpublished paper, Silber focuses on assistant administrators and their slow and subtle decline into personal and political ineffectiveness. He believes that failing assistants often have the attitude that they are annointed rather than appointed. These self-styled experts believe their position must be accepted totally and feel frustrated and personally rejected when it is not. They do not know when to listen or when to leave.

Mike O'Brien, president of Harper Associates in Detroit, stated that there is a significant reason why health care executives fail, one that has not received enough attention. Assistant administrators learn early in their careers that they are rewarded for good news—not bad news. When they become CEOs they continue to focus on bringing good news to board members and when really bad news is communicated, the board terminates the CEO. The best time to introduce bad news to the board is when there is some really good news and vice versa.

Bob Hampton, a former vice president with Witt Associates, indicated that the selection of weak, nonthreatening people in key management jobs is the primary cause of executive failure. He also echoed the findings of McCall and Lombardo, believing that "poor people skills" are a major cause.

More recently, another top executive recruiter, John Lloyd, a managing partner of Witt Associates and author, outlined five key problem areas which lead to executive failure.[10] He stated that, based on extensive interviews conducted by Witt Associates with health care executives over the years, the most frequently given reasons for firing CEOs are: poor medical staff relations, lack of responsiveness to the board, poor financial performance of the organization, low visibility in the community and in the hospital, and lack of adequate management staff. He also noted that these are not problems that occur overnight. They can be anticipated and these issues should be an integral part of an evaluation process between the CEO and the board. The CEO should not assume that just because there are no negative comments by the board members that they are satisfied with his or her performance.

THE IMPORTANCE OF BOARD RELATIONSHIPS

One of the recurring reasons for CEOs being terminated in hospitals pertains to their relationship with board members. In analyzing this further, it becomes clear that CEOs often do not work effectively with all members of the board and fail to groom potential board members. Richard Gifford, managing director of Russell Reynolds Associates, stated that often CEOs are not blameless for their own failure.[11] He believes that many hospital executives do themselves in because too many of them have very narrow relationships with board members, focusing only on the chairperson and not on the board at large. If that is the case, they are secure only as long as the board chairperson holds the seat. As often as not the CEO has not forged a relationship with the next board chairperson.

According to Gifford, the situation is exacerbated when the chairperson elect does not take the job and someone else who has no previous relationship with the CEO is made chairperson and wants things done a new way. For the new chairperson, it may be a vital time in his or her life and the new chairperson often has no patience for someone who is not responsive, who has a different energy level, or with whom there is an awkward chemistry.

In a conversation with Art Lepinot, president of Art Lepinot Associates, he stated that a CEO's best effort toward survival is to work with the board carefully in the selection of new board members and make the best possible effort to work with each personality on the board to achieve good results. Even though some executives realize that it is important to assure that only capable, constructive people who are willing to work hard at carrying out their responsibilities are selected for board membership, these executives do not provide the mechanism for it to happen. Qualifications of potential board members in many hospitals are often not evaluated as much as those of lower level employees. Such an evaluation of board members is particularly critical, not only because of the powerful position they occupy, but because once they are elected, board members are almost never asked to resign unless there is a definite period of time they are allowed to serve.

All too often, new board members are selected by several board members or a single powerful board member who has seen them function only outside a health care setting. The autocrat who runs his or her own company with an "iron fist," making all the major decisions and many of the minor ones, finds that dealing with a group of highly educated medical specialists who essentially work "with" and not "for" him or her is different than dealing with a group of subordinate middle managers. Most often the board continues intact, but the administrator becomes a casualty.

An evaluation process should be established so that potential board members can be "tested" in front of their future peers, administrators, and the medical staff. Potential board members should function for a period of time in the institution's standing committee structure before being nominated for board membership. Hospitals may establish either an association or advisory board and should have a progression philosophy that requires individuals to serve on some of the institution's standing committees before they become board members (see Figures 7-1 and 7-2).

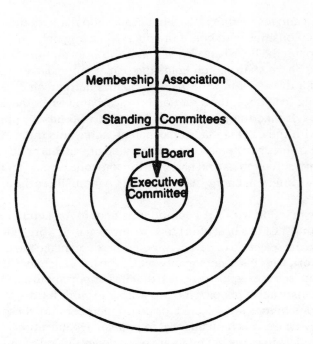

Figure 7-1 Progression to Board Membership from a Membership Association. *Source:* Reprinted from *Organizational Burnout in Health Care Facilities: Strategies for Prevention and Change* by E.A. Simendinger and T.F. Moore, p. 133, Aspen Publishers, Inc., © 1985.

In Figures 7-1 and 7-2, the arrows denote the potential sequence of membership. In other words, individuals must be in an association or advisory board to be selected for a standing committee and they must serve on a standing committee to be considered for full board membership. Once on the board, they must serve for a period of time before they can serve on the executive committee. If an organization does not have an advisory board or an association, then these members can simply be drawn from the community. However, they still must be required to serve on a standing committee for a period of time before being considered for board membership.

This type of progression not only allows the board to "test" potential members, but also has three other advantages: (1) it enables future board members to become more familiar with the institution's operation, organizations, and personalities; (2) members of the association or advisory board can help the board with the work load (a 20-member board needs extra strength if there are a large number of standing committees); and (3) with more "outsiders" on these committees there is greater input from

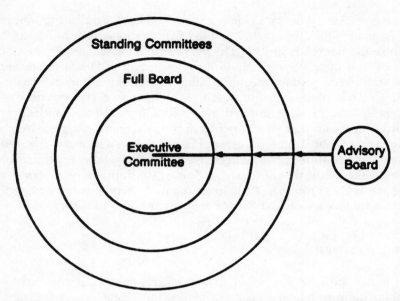

Figure 7-2 Progression to Board Membership from an Advisory Board. *Source:* Reprinted from *Organizational Burnout in Health Care Facilities: Strategies for Prevention and Change* by E.A. Simendinger and T.F. Moore, p. 134, Aspen Publishers, Inc., © 1985.

the community and, equally important, greater input back into the community.

Drucker stated that the primary function of the board is to communicate with the major elements in the community, but instead they waste their time talking about the linen contract. "They are usually hard-working and decent people, but nobody has told them what their job is."[12] Telling them their job is a task of the CEO. Although the CEO has not done this in most instances, Drucker believes that those who have have not been fired.

Administrators should be the trustee's most credible source of information. Given the choice, more information is better than less, although a judgment is necessary. Perhaps the best test comes from asking: "If I were a trustee, what would I need to know?" Unfortunately, the first time CEOs meet some of their board members is when they are introduced to them at a board meeting. By this time, it is too late to make a change and the CEOs find themselves in a situation that is similar to playing Russian roulette.

FOCUS ON THE DECISION-MAKING PROCESS

Chief executive officers often recognize that much of the breakdown in relationships between board members and the CEO results from the decision-making process. Decisions may be made too quickly or they may not be made quickly enough. It is the CEO's responsibility to develop the agenda and not the board's.[13] The board should be reacting to the CEO's agenda, not the reverse. Sheldon King, president of Stanford University Hospitals, writing about executive failure, stresses the importance of the CEO's relationship with the board. Too many hospital executives, he observes, have found themselves relieved of their responsibilities by the board over issues that should not have gone that far. An aggressive planning process that identifies potential issues well in advance is important. Equally important is a committee structure, which allows for the involvement of the medical staff, board and other appropriate members in the decision-making process. Time investments by executives to ensure that these activities are carried out will help assure their own survival.

USE OF POWER

It is not the need for power that motivates health care executives or enables them to become peak performers or at least avoid failure. The actual need for power has been rated very low by health care executives. In a 1981 study, of 104 CEOs of health care facilities, only 3 percent said the need for power had a significant effect on their success. Forty-six percent said that the need for power had a moderate effect, and 61 percent said it had no significant effect at all on their success.[14] One of the respondents noted, "Most executives, in my opinion, have more power than is necessary for achieving their goals and complaints about lack of authority usually mean that the person making the complaint has not learned how to respect his subordinates."[15] Also, executives often do not understand the concept of empowerment.

One of the major shortcomings of failing health care executives is the failure to exercise power appropriately. They either fail to use the power available to them or, in some instances, misuse their power. Most commonly, they fail to empower others in their organization.

The subject of empowerment has received a considerable amount of attention in the literature during the past several years, but some executives are slow to grasp the significance of empowering their employees through involvement, including them in the decision-making process, providing them with a consistent flow of information about the organization's operations, developing a relatively flat organizational structure, and eliminating the bureaucratic hurdles for the front-line workers.

The opposite of empowering behavior is depowering behavior, which often is the reason both the executive and the organization or group for which they are responsible, fail. Depowering executives exhibit several traits. The first of these is the focus on coercive power rather than reward power. Users of coercive power tend to be overly critical of others. These same executives often are autocratic and tend to be too involved in their subordinates' decision-making process. They are like people who pull young plants up by the roots to see how they are growing. They also remind keen observers of drivers who "oversteer" their vehicles and cause unnecessary, counterproductive anxiety to their passengers.

The depowering executive places great emphasis on policies and procedures and often is interested more in process than in outcome. The result is that there is a great deal of emphasis on conformance rather than performance and that is what the organization receives—conformance.

In one case, a CEO of a large hospital exhibited many of the traits of a depowering executive. He had seventeen top executives report directly to him and often berated his subordinates in front of others. One of his tactics was to attack department heads at meetings and make them cry. Each year, he took a two-week vacation in the fall and another two-week vacation in the spring. His new administrative assistant suggested to one of the senior vice presidents that he, the administrative assistant, should take his vacation at the same time as the CEO to whom he reported. The senior vice president said, "Are you crazy? No one takes their vacation when the old man takes his vacation; that way you get two vacations—one when he takes his and then your own." Indeed, when the CEO left for vacation, the executive parking lot was vacant before 9:30 in the morning and after 4:00 in the afternoon. Fortunately for the organization, the CEO had a temper tantrum in front of the board and was terminated. The damage that he had done to that organization and its employees during his 15-year reign, however, will never be fully known.

Silber believes that, in their desire for conformity, the health care executives need emotional support for their authority.[16] If they permit disagreement among themselves and the associate administrator, dietitian, director of nursing or whomever, they see it as a threat to their own power. The result is that they order everyone around in an autocratic manner.

As times goes by, subordinates decrease their initiative and their risk taking. The executive becomes the "emperor without clothes." Because the failing executive cannot decide what decisions he or she wants others to make, he or she makes most of the decisions. Silber suggests that all executives should occasionally ask: "Have I surrounded myself with a team of non-sinkers or do I have a swimming team of champions?"[17]

Top health care executives have an intuitive feel for power and its use or have somehow acquired an understanding of power and empowerment through reading and experience. All health care executives would do well to develop such an understanding.

NOTES

1. Unpublished data compiled by T.F. Moore and E.A. Simendinger using 1984-1985 *American Hospital Guide* issues.

2. Unpublished data compiled by T.F. Moore and E.A. Simendinger using 1985-1986 *American Hospital Guide* issues.

3. Frank Sabatino, "The Revolving Door: CEO Turnover" *Hospitals*, 6 (October 5, 1987): 80–84.

4. Ibid., p. 80.

5. Ibid., p. 80.

6. Michael M. Lombardo, and Morgan W. McCall, *Psychology Today* 12 (February 1983): 10–13.

7. Ibid., p. 12.

8. Richard Conarroe, "Climbing the Corporate Success Ladder: A Self Marketing Program for Executives," *Management Review* 20 (February 1981): 25–43.

9. David Rogers, *Waging Business Warfare* (New York: Scribners), 1987.

10. John Lloyd, "Where Did I Go Wrong," *Healthcare Executive* 2 (May/June 1987): 18–21.

11. Richard Gifford, "More Than One-Third of CEO's Feel Threatened," *Hospitals* 6 (October 5, 1987): 81.

12. Peter Drucker and Karl Bays Discuss the Toughest Job—Running a Hospital—*Hospital Management Quarterly* (Summer 1982): 4.

13. Terence F. Moore and Earl A. Simendinger, *The Effective Healthcare Executive: Guide to a Winning Management Style* (Aspen Publishers, Inc.: Rockville, MD, 1986): 136.

14. Walter J. Wentz, and Terence F. Moore, "Administrative Success: Key Ingredients," *Hospital and Health Services Administration* 26 (Special II, 1981): 85–93.

15. Ibid., p. 90.

16. Mark Silber, "Are You an Effective Hospital Administrator?" *Osteopathic Hospitals* 20 (August, 1976): 11–13.

17. Ibid., p. 12.

8

Diagnosing Corporate/ Candidate Compatibility*

Michael D. Caver, Partner and Manager, Health Care Practice, Heidrick and Struggles, Inc., 125 S. Wacker Drive, Chicago, IL 60606

By now it is clear to most thoughtful observers—if not always to legislators, regulators, and critics—that health care delivery has been changed irrevocably by the events and decisions of the past five years. Yet for all the attention paid to new technologies, shifting economics, market forces, and other such important factors, no aspect of health care has been affected more profoundly by these changes than human resources.

Trustees, executives, and senior managers alike have felt the impact of these multiple revolutions on their roles and on their expectations. As a result, both board members and managers are active and key participants in helping others sort out how these changes affect them and their roles.

Against this backdrop, the subject of corporate/candidate compatibility takes on even greater importance for board members, executives and their candidates. Selection decisions made in today's environment can have enormous implications for the future.

CONSIDERING ISSUES OF COMPATIBILITY

Individuals in health care have either asked or heard firsthand some or all of these questions:

- Why all the fuss?
- Isn't the selection process in health care an everyday event as it is in every other sector of the economy?

*© 1989 Heidrick and Struggles, Inc., and Michael D. Caver.

- How complicated can it be to make the correct hiring decision when all that is involved fundamentally is selecting the best candidate or accepting or rejecting a job offer?
- Don't both parties, as adults, know themselves—their needs, their assets, and their liabilities? Can this process be any more complicated than sharing expectations, identifying differences, and negotiating these differences, or admitting a mismatch?
- Isn't the worst that can happen learning that some basic incompatibilities were overlooked? If both parties acknowledge that fact and the differences can't be accommodated, what harm can come of parting company, each wiser for the experience?
- Is it truly possible to advance professionally without running into some basic incompatibilities with an employer at some point in one's career? And what employer hasn't faced these types of differences with at least one employee?

Answers to these questions lie at the very root of the mutual selection process—the most basic issue of employer/employee compatibility. Yet because such differences often surface well after employment, they may seem far removed from the original selection process. To ensure a successful match, then, employee/employer compatibility *must* be kept in the forefront of the health care selection process.

Why? *Because there is no sector of the American economy which is as complex as health care delivery.* As sweeping as this statement is, there is no other area in which individuals work to enhance life and alleviate physical and emotional pain within the highest dictates of quality service on a 24-hour-a-day, year-round basis at reasonably affordable costs. There also is *no* other industry in which the needs of the patients, their families and friends must be balanced intricately against those of legislators, regulators, communities, special interest groups, financial backers, employees, and unions. This means that demands on senior middle managers and executives in health care are enormous.

Assessing employer/employee compatibility also is difficult in today's health care environment because in periods characterized by high rates of change, needs and expectations as well as assets and liabilities usually are "moving targets." For instance, what is expected of today's chief executive officer (CEO) is vastly different from what was required of the typical health care administrator even ten years ago. Yet as difficult as it is to get a true "fix" on shifting needs, expectations, assets, and liabilities, they must be considered carefully to ensure fundamental compatibility between employer and employee.

Finally, it is difficult to judge employer/employee compatibility because neither board members, executives, nor candidates can be certain, in advance, how the other will respond in times of crisis. Most sophisticated senior managers understand that it is the unusual board which has indepth knowledge of all the factors shaping health care, which vigorously and thoroughly prepares for meetings, or holds itself as accountable for the success of the institution as it does its CEO. If such a board is atypical, how will the more typical ones react in times of crisis?

Similarly, the decision authority—whether the board or executive—can never predict how an apparently qualified candidate will deal with adversity, controversy, extreme pressure for long periods of time, or acute crisis. Yet, most observers anticipate that, without fundamental changes in trends already set in motion, health care virtually is programmed to undergo more years of severe stress before it is fully reshaped.

For instance, physicians feel threatened economically and are frustrated by the many influences interposed between physician and patient. Payors, whose livelihood depends on the economic success of their enterprises, feel threatened by the rising costs of health care. They have already signaled their determination to seize more control unless a sweeping change is introduced quickly. The government faces demands for universal access to quality care yet cannot even cope with today's demands on already beleaguered budgets. And patients and families feel increasingly powerless when faced with these realities. Those who are fortunate enough to have insurance coverage can only look forward to higher benefit contributions, cuts in benefits, and more restrictions on the use thereof.

The senior health care executive and his or her board are almost inevitably faced with a stressful immediate future. The complexities of health care and the rapid and continuing changes it is undergoing make it impossible to determine, in advance, the exact crises to which employers and candidates will have to react.

Faced with these difficulties—can compatibility be assessed at the pre-employment phase? The answer: it may be difficult, but not impossible. Since the stakes are so enormous, any added degree of precision that can be brought to the process can prove to be important to employer and candidate alike.

It is not true, as some have suggested, that basic incompatibilities are inevitable between employer and employee. Too many examples exist of long-tenured health care executives to reject the reality. Also, it is not accurate to state that if incompatibilities are not resolved, "life goes on." Experience shows that most flawed relationships are *never* salvaged and often end in the departure of the executive. Both the organization and the executive are often scarred by an unsatisfactory experience. Each faces a challenge in recovering from the upset, which often makes a suitable "remarriage" even tougher.

In these unprecedented times of change, the health care industry needs continuity of leadership—leaders who are compatible with their institutions. The demand for highly talented, mature, and proven executives already outstrips availability. At the same time, boards have become insistent on selecting only those individuals who are proven executives. As a result, the search for management is increasingly competitive and has become national, often international, in scope.

Candidates, learning from their experiences and those of their peers, have become vastly more sophisticated and discriminating. The stark truth is that in today's talent marketplace no board member can assume that if a new CEO fails, the search committee will be able to attract another panel of candidates who are equally strong and enthusiastic.

Coincidentally, as a reaction to today's unforgiving environment, boards have never been more selective in choosing their CEOs from among the candidates presented. A candidate whose judgment they question, perhaps because of a failed relationship, may be viewed as too much of a risk. Far from judging a candidate, a prudent board usually feels ill-equipped to separate fact from opinion in such cases. Often the executive search consultant is simply asked to identify others whose candidacies do not present such imponderables.

However, a board is not alone in suffering the repercussions of failure. A miscalculation by the candidate can interrupt and perhaps seriously affect an otherwise successful track record of progressive management growth. In fact, it is hard to exaggerate the potentially negative impacts felt by an executive and his or her family as a result of an unsuccessful career move.

Therefore, there are ample incentives for each candidate and organization to invest in an appropriate, lasting "marriage." Neither can afford to give or dedicate less than the best, most thoughtful, and honest effort to the selection process. In addition, each must ensure that the initial compatibility is capitalized on and not taken for granted when the employee assumes his or her new responsibilities. But before the search committee members or the candidate reaches this point, both have to conduct some soul-searching evaluations.

IF YOU KNOW WHAT YOU ARE SEEKING, THERE IS A MUCH BETTER CHANCE OF FINDING IT!

After 22 years in the field of human resources, the author speaks from experience when he says that much more energy normally is expended by candidates writing resumes and addressing the other logistics of a job search than is spent wrestling with the most fundamental issue—what the candidate is seeking. In fact, many qualified professionals seem to gravitate toward the mechanics of employer or career change or both rather than focus on such important questions as

- Will I truly be better off in a new situation, or will I just exchange one set of negatives for a new less well-known one?
- What are my fundamental strengths?
- What do I most enjoy doing?
- How will my family needs and desires be best served?

Candidates are not alone in concentrating on the logistics of search. Many employers emphasize the selection process as well. They face the temptations to immediately place an advertisement or put out "feelers" to solicit suggestions and nominations of candidates. Among both candidates and employers, the instinct to get on with the search process is logical and understandable. Both candidates and employers, especially the most successful and experienced, believe that time is being wasted if they do not move quickly and decisively to the logistics. Yet precisely because the stakes for forming sound and lasting professional relationships have never been higher, the payout has never been higher for thoughtfulness and thoroughness.

From the Client's Standpoint

Normally, the hiring authority acts conscientiously and responsibly, carefully screening candidates to minimize the organization's risk and ensure that the very best are attracted. Yet screening can be valid only if the hiring authority carefully assesses the requirements of the job in a businesslike, sensitive manner before beginning the interviewing process.

The challenges facing employers are, if anything, more formidable than those encountered by candidates. For all the authority and power they wield, CEOs and board members are faced with a daunting array of requirements. They must

- assess objectively and dispassionately their organization's advantages versus disadvantages and temper the dreams of the organization with its realities;

- take a total and objective view of today's requirements and anticipate those of the intermediate and long-term future;
- anticipate how a candidate would perform both as part of and then separate from the overall team;
- project how the successful candidate and family will adjust to the new environment; and
- enlist support from key team members to ensure the success of the new executive, once employed.

While the hiring authority usually is sincere and has good intentions, there often are limitations on what it can deliver. For example, if several board members are not in tune with the new realities of health care, there is no guarantee that others will take responsibility to teach them or that these naive individuals will make room on the board for those who do understand the health care environment. Nor is it easy to predict whether the board will see its duty as ensuring the new CEO's success or, as so many seem to believe, only one of evaluating performance at year's end.

From the Candidate's Standpoint

A candidate's best chance for success starts with getting in touch with his or her needs and desires at the outset of the search process. This ensures a much better chance of accurately measuring the personal impacts of the positives and negatives of any new role under consideration.

There will never be a more critical time for an executive or senior middle manager to conduct an honest and thorough self-appraisal than before the interviewing process begins. Doing so confirms many self-assumptions and, when taken together, can unveil capabilities, performance records, management style, personality characteristics, and the environment, which best allows for professional growth. Candidates armed with such information have a powerful tool at their command—self-knowledge—which no one else can utilize.

In fact, a professional may not be ready to begin interviewing until he or she can answer at least five basic questions objectively:

1. What are my fundamental attributes?
2. What are my functional strengths?
3. What tasks do I most enjoy doing?
4. In what environments do I perform best?
5. What are my family's vested interests in my career?

Evaluating Yourself against the Basics

Every employer worthy of consideration will want to attract, select, and retain only managers and executives who bring integrity, intelligence, creativity, vision, drive, emotional maturity, and stability to their positions. Each employer also wants to hire individuals who possess interpersonal skills, management ability, and leadership talents, and regularly produce timely results.

Your success to date suggests that you score high on most, if not all, of these basic management criteria. Yet few individuals are equally strong in all categories.

In a very real sense, your future success rests with your ability to identify opportunities which utilize your greatest strengths, do not call on your relative "short suits," and allow you to complement your weaknesses with the abilities of others on your new management team.

Your Functional Strengths

Like most managers and executives, you use certain functional skills to succeed on the job. Your list probably is substantial and includes such talents as the ability to communicate effectively, diplomacy, analytical skills, and marketing instincts. The point is that an honest, thorough inventory of your functional skills prepares you to take advantage of the ideal opportunity—one which calls for, acknowledges, and rewards your functional skills, while making minimal demands on those you do not possess. An appraisal of this sort also will enable you to better assess the talents of individuals you will manage, if you accept the new role. In many cases, these individuals have a day-to-day responsibility for specific tasks. You must understand the details and subtleties of these tasks in order to direct and evaluate your subordinates.

What You Enjoy Most and Where and When You Have Done Your Best

Most people do what they enjoy the most and are the best at doing. These things do not seem to be as much "work" as tasks they do not like. Unfortunately, it also is true that at some point in their careers most people find themselves in roles or environments with limited potential for enjoyment. In fact, a person may work for years in a position or setting that gives little or no pleasure.

If you have not evaluated the "fun quotient" in your career recently, today is a good time to start. More than likely you already have the education, training, and motivation to perform well in any number of situations. Before you grit your teeth and accept a position you might not enjoy, ask yourself: What is keeping me from a job in an environment that includes enjoyment as one of its rewards? This approach is not selfish. Your potential employer likely has an identical interest: studies have shown that the most dedicated, hardest working, and most productive executives are those who really love what they do.

Your Family's Vested Interests

Most ambitious and driven managers have, at some time, sacrificed family time and time for their own outside interests in deference to their jobs. Fortunately, many families not only tolerate job-related excesses, but also are quite supportive—at least in the short term, while the executives are just getting started in their new positions.

Yet you set aside family and personal interests on an ongoing basis at your own risk. What may be acceptable and defensible on an occasional basis can prove to be disruptive, perhaps even destructive, to family relationships in the long term.

The interrelationships of people's careers, their personal interests, their families—indeed all aspects of their lives—have led Richard Bolles and others to articulate the concept of career and life planning. Their work has been helpful to countless executives. Bolles' *What Color Is Your Parachute?* already is a classic. It is updated annually and is available in paperback. Full of commonsense and practical suggestions, this is an easy and "must-read" book for any executive who is facing major career decisions.[1]

None of the advice Bolles provides is more basic than the notion that to have a lasting effect, career decisions must take into account the full spectrum of life's issues, including the needs of families. Yet as straightforward as this concept may be, it is difficult to internalize and practice, especially if you have never done so.

If this thought process is new to you, you may want to consider attending one of the many seminars given around the country on the subject of career and life planning. The very diversity of the groups who attend and their quest to learn may help you "get outside yourself" long enough to understand the important aspects of your total life situation. If you are married, make your spouse an important part of your decision-making team. Most people find it easier to relate to and support a decision they have had a hand in shaping, and spouses are no different.

Your Target

Willie Sutton, the notorious 1930s gangster, gained a place on the long and illustrious list of American philosophers with his reply to the question, "Why do you rob banks?" He is reported to have said, "Because that is where the money is!" Without stretching the point too far, the same holds true when seeking a compatible relationship with a new employer or employee. If you target your search on those opportunities that best fit your specifications, you increase your chances of accepting an offer which will spell success for both you and the organization.

Conversely, making a decision based merely on the positions that have been offered to you may not be a "true" choice. If you have not invested up-front time in the search process, you can never be sure whether you are looking at your best opportunity for success. For instance, if you want to grow in a range of ambulatory and other alternative delivery systems, but accept a position in a single, free-standing hospital that lacks resources and a vision of the evolution of health care delivery, then no matter how good the offer, you have sacrificed your objective. This is true regardless of how attractive the opportunity still is in relation to the other options that have been presented to you.

On the other hand, an executive anxious to further develop board skills can uncover those institutions with boards composed of market-sensitive members whose behavior is enlightened and largely supportive. With this knowledge in mind, the candidate can accept an appropriate offer with confidence.

OBTAINING INFORMATION ABOUT YOUR TARGET

Objective Data

Both the candidate and the hiring authority have a host of objective data from which to draw to help them analyze their choices. The candidate can review OS-1s from the most recent and previous bond issues, annual reports, current financial statements, organizational charts, medical staff bylaws, and current contracts with alternative delivery systems. Similarly, the thorough hiring authority can evaluate substantial objective candidate data which are often not solicited or studied in depth: annual reports and organizational charts from the candidate's institutions, candidate reports and recommendations, and copies of previous written performance reviews.

Subjective/Evaluative Data

Though more subjective in nature, another type of information is available to the conscientious candidate. It can be gathered from knowledgeable sources such as those with particular expertise related to the industry, the particular institution, the area, current or former employees of the organization, and suppliers and previous patients and clients of the institution.

From Your Prospective Employer

Once you have accepted the notion that a sound career decision is in your prospective employer's interest, as well as your own, you may request confidently all but the most proprietary and confidential information about the institution. For example, in addition to talking at length with the individual to whom you would report, you may want to pick an appropriate time to talk with others who will influence your ability to contribute and succeed. Among them are

- medical staff leaders
- key physicians and physician executives
- outside counsel
- the audit partner in the accounting firm retained by the institution
- recently engaged consultants, especially in the area of strategic planning
- investment bankers

Your Family's Data Gathering

Your prospective employer likely will feel a vested interest in the successful integration of your family into the new community. Indeed, at the CEO and chief operating levels, your overall success often depends in some measure on how closely you identify with the community and its needs. Therefore, you can expect your prospective employer to be supportive of your need for a wide range of information about the community.

Some data can be provided in written form. Other information can be collected firsthand through personal investigation. Though most hiring authorities defer the visit of the spouse until the candidate has been designated a semifinalist, your family's interests probably are best served if you gently indicate (firmly if need be) that you are not prepared to make a decision on any offer until your family is satisfied with its prospects in the new community. Often, this can best be accomplished by including any school-age children as an integral part of a visit lasting several days.

A family's commitment to public education warrants research into the public education system available in the new community before making a decision on even the most appealing job offer. All of the apparent advantages of a new role will not balance against an underfunded or out-of-date school system.

During the Interview Process

Interviews can be somewhat artificial unless both parties expend considerable energy on them. If you and your prospective employer share the conviction that mutual compatibility is important, then consider some of the following variations on the standard approach:

- *Preliminary fact-finding visit.* Before the formal interviews begin, the hiring authority may arrange a combination tour and series of orientation discussions with key people to educate the candidate about the institution and its environment. Subsequent interviews and discussions are much more meaningful because the parties are talking from a common basis of understanding about real issues.

- *Targeted interviews.* Few interviewers can be equally knowledgeable about or interested in all relevant matters. However, properly selected interviewers possess expertise or perspectives that are important to the candidate. Consider requesting that each interviewer focus with you on a given area and that you be told in advance the subjects assigned to each one.

- *Lengthened interviews.* At its most effective, an interview is a process by which two people with significant stakes in the outcome get to know one another. The standard hour to hour and a half can sometimes be inadequate for this purpose. Consider requesting a minimum of two hours with each key decision maker at varied sites—in the institution, over a meal, or in the outside offices of a board member or physician.

- *Committee meeting.* When a search or interview committee is involved, request a meeting with the entire group at the end of the visit. This will enable you to discuss matters critical to all parties and minimize the chance that one or more interviewers might miss a key fact or opinion or offer a view contrary to the understanding of the group.

- *Second and subsequent visits.* If properly managed, the planning process will include, as an integral part, a request about the items on your agenda, in advance of second and subsequent visits.

A WORD OF CAUTION

The term "halo effect" describes the strengths or positives we quickly and easily identify. All too often, however, a more thorough examination reveals that we have been blinded to the pitfalls or negatives of a person or position in much the same way as the bright halo of the sun's rays blinds us to its total picture. The only known antidote to the halo effect is thorough, patient, and thoughtful consideration of **all** relevant aspects of both your strengths and relative shortfalls and the opportunities and disadvantages of the position.

Anticipate the Offer

The proverbial "cool of the evening" is the best time to anticipate the offer you expect. Before emotions run high, before you become personally invested in the prospective new situation, before the personalities of others have attracted you, and before the "halo effect" of one or several special aspects of the job appeal to you—that is the time to thoughtfully and thoroughly determine the criteria you will use to reach your decision.

Draft an offer checklist. If married, involve your spouse in creating it. Once you have analyzed your needs, your strengths and desires, and your family requirements, such a list should take shape quickly. If, for example, significant board involvement is critical to your career growth at this stage, then be sure to list it as a factor.

Your checklist likely will reveal some criteria, which will be imperative for you and your family—true "deal breakers." If so, then at the appropriate time inform the search consultant with whom you are working about these elements. Neither you nor your employer need be frustrated by last minute surprises.

Finally, before any offer is extended, act in good faith to keep all parties apprised of your thinking. For example, if you have several possibilities that appeal to you, let each executive search consultant and potential employer involved know that you intend to investigate all opportunities thoroughly before making a decision. It is unbusinesslike and perhaps even unethical to inform an unsuspecting consultant or employer at the last minute that you need more time to make a decision.

Testing Your Assumptions: Final Due Diligence

Before deciding on an otherwise appealing situation, force yourself through a final "due diligence" process. In other words, put aside all your enthusiasm, and that of your potential employer, and challenge your assumptions by testing them against additional relevant facts and data.

If you have not already done so, this might be the right time to talk with several senior former employees, state and local hospital association executives, local lawmakers or regulators familiar with the institution, and community leaders and other "power brokers." Moreover, with extreme discretion and the cooperation of your prospective employer, you can often get in touch with key competition. Listen to what they have to say about their strengths, successes, and dreams for the future. Without in any way misleading or seeking proprietary information, you can compare situations and ask yourself which is most realistic.

Trading Expectations in the Offer Process

If you accept the offer, the implicit commitment is that you will be bound by the criteria used by management and the board to evaluate performance and behavior and, if need be, the discipline enforced for poor or inadequate performance. Often the most effective time for you to have input on these criteria is when the offer is extended. Six months later may be awkward, at the least, for you to discover that the hiring authority and you had different expectations.

Whether orally or, ideally, in writing, you can work for mutual agreement and understanding of the exact duties and objectives you are expected to discharge and the specific measurements that will be used to determine superior, adequate, or poor performance. Decision rights—the authority you will have versus that which is reserved up the line—also should be detailed. Finally, you should establish a clear feeling for style and behavior issues that are compatible with the institution's culture. If these have not been discussed, talk about them now.

Getting Off to a Good and Lasting Start

Much of your prior investment depends on proper and timely execution—you must get off to a good start, literally and figuratively. Reflect dispassionately before you take up your responsibilities on what you plan to do in the first few weeks and months on the job. Undoubtedly you will review some of your former successes and perhaps even a few blunders. You have friends and colleagues whom you admire who can provide valuable input. What has worked for them and what, on reflection, would they do differently if they had it to do over again?

Obviously, getting off to a good and productive start depends on a combination of principles and specific situational considerations. If you vow to manage so as to encourage and celebrate the successes of your staff, you will be much more effective if they focus on the top priorities of the institution.

CONCLUSION

For you, the points discussed in this chapter may be obvious. If they were to all, there would be far fewer interviews scheduled between candidates and search committees with fundamentally incompatible expectations. The truth is that too many executives leave their employers after one or two years. If they gave compatibility the emphasis it deserves, this would not be the case for many.

Correctly diagnosing corporate/candidate compatibility will likely remain one of the most elusive goals in organized human endeavors for a long time to come. The various factors at work make everyone a potential victim of a proverbial mismatch. In some ways, the pressures caused by complexity, rapid change, and the inability to anticipate crisis are so much a part of modern health care that making a correct diagnosis of potential employer/employee compatibility is challenging. However, "When all is said and done, much more is said than done." The truth is that there is much more complaining about the difficulty of attaining compatibility than there is effort expended on earnest, disciplined, and creative ways to achieve it.

No one can want more for you than yourself. Similarly, no one can want more for an organization than its senior executives and board members. If you, as a candidate, and your potential employer are committed to minimizing the guesswork involved in the hiring process and increasing the odds of a successful employment marriage, then you can use these suggestions and your own creativity to bring this kind of situation about.

At this point in your career you have invested at least 16 years in your education, 10 or more years in your profession, and countless hours in upgrading your professional skills. You have sacrificed personal convenience, evenings and weekends, and, at times, your family's preferences. Yet, you still have a third or more of your career to which you look forward. The success and rewards you derive in the future will be influenced heavily by your current decisions.

Given your investments to date and the importance of the decisions you will soon make, surely a week, month, or more is not too great an additional investment in your future. Remember, if your choice is not sound now, you can be assured that you will somehow have to make the time to repeat your search process in a year or two.

NOTE

1. Richard Bolles, *What Color Is Your Parachute?* (Berkeley, CA: Ten Speed Press, 1972).

Part II

The Executive's Perspective

9

Success Strategies: Victor or Victim?

Mark B. Silber, PhD, Mark Silber Associates, Inc., Healthcare Consultants, 16776 Bernardo Center Drive, Professional Suite 110-B, San Diego, CA 92128

Executive success is a mile-high feeling. Your vertical career climb to the top of the health care mountain epitomizes executive success. Performance at the peak, a different vista, expected vision, and new vulnerabilities. Congratulations on your career ascent. You have passed through "the valley of resumes," the extended telephone calls with the health care executive recruiters, and the series of group and individual interviews with their repetitive questions. The medical and nursing staff, key persons of the trustee board, and members of the search committee finally, yes finally, selected you from among the many competing candidates. You won. Congratulations on being the selected victor! You are rightfully proud. Your family is proud of you.

Whatever headaches and heartaches were involved in your position relocation and readjustments have been cured. Your new executive office with its personalized changes of your choice has been completed. "Welcome on board" handshakes have been extended to you as you made rounds from the pharmacy in the basement to the top patient floors. Then there are your line and staff personnel, which you have inherited who, at this point in time, are your present span of executive control. Although your staff members are smiling with you, they are desperately searching out clues to your executive value system.

THE "HONEYMOON"

This is the honeymoon time! Interpersonal romancing and dancing, the initial courtship interplay, is in full sway. When you speak everyone is quiet. When you ask questions others appear sharing and caring. After you have been introduced and have spoken at the multitude of department manager/

supervisory meetings, you wonder whether or not any of them have the courage to speak. Smiles and silence!

This is the job honeymoon. The physicians in the doctors' lounge, in the corridors and even in the parking lot not only extend greetings, but also begin to lobby for their vested interests and concerns. The names of people are crammed into your memory bank along with those first-sight impressions. Are they friends or foes? Are they hindering or helpful people? Where are they really coming from and where and what are their true values? Who is for real and who is romancing you?

While the honeymoon is bright, the future path is dim. Various board members will begin to approach you, usually over a luncheon table, to "help you see the light" and also to lobby for their pet projects and prejudices. Their "correct paths" to adhere to will be pointed out subtly and not so subtly to help guide you through the woods and thickets of your new political environment. Political potholes and the places for pratfalls will be presented through their biases. Board members want you on their team; that is, they want to make up your mind for you. Who can get to you first? Who can get you to think in terms of their categories? Silberism 1: "Prejudice is the hardening of the categories."

Then there are those initial honeymoon times of looking into the management mirror. The leadership looking glass reflects many things during those first kick-off months. The positive reflection is that of a person "who made it," a person who stands tall in dream fulfillment, an executive who now walks tall among his or her peers nationwide in the health care profession of senior management. The positive reflection is of a winner who exhibits graciousness, diplomacy, an assertive voice of values and vision. Frank Sinatra's theme, "Here's To The Winners" is the song you sing. If you jog or exercise the theme music you hum is "Chariots of Fire" or "Rocky." The management mirror reflects you a victor.

The leadership looking glass also reflects deep down doubts. Can you really be your real self here? Are you already caught up in playing games just to get off to a good start in the multitude of races you will have to run in the coming months? Are you a "psychological imposter;" did you really deserve this promotion? How strong should you be or not be in your leadership position and style? How well did you handle the first set of conflicts and disagreements; did you face or flee from them? Since you are the new kid on the block, are you moving too slowly, too quickly, or not at all on the key result areas? The list of self-doubts and the list of questions can go on and on for the newly appointed hospital executive. But guess what? You are not alone, you are human.

YOUR BEGINNING

Welcome to the hospital–world summit of the Ps: political pressures, policy creating, people problems, performance futurisms, and pathfinding. The honeymoon can be short-lived. You are now in the executive saddle and riding the horse of hurry, hassle, and hindrances on a path with an unclear finish line. Peppy zest and enthusiasm will sustain you for a while, but don't be surprised that your pep turns into being pooped. Being at the helm turns into becoming overwhelmed. The pace of change introduction seems passive; people's smiles turn into frowns and initial cooperation reverses to political turfs and territory protectionism. As an advertisement on television states, "What will you do . . . what will you do?" Frustration turned inward can become depression.

Are you a victor or victim? Will it be self-projection or self-protection in your attempt at constructive transformational leadership? Hours at work seem to stretch beyond your expectations and the expectation of your family. The push and pull of strained demands on you may cause strains on a multitude of different components of your leading and living.

Time for time out and rethinking. Make an appointment with yourself to reaffirm that you have a long occupational history of having proved your adequacy. Leadership starts with, is sustained by, and succeeds with self-esteem, the inner power that lets you know that you are adequate. Remember, revitalization starts with you.

The first suggestion to assure your success is: appreciate the fact that you cannot control everything. The transition from managing to leading means letting go. The transition from your former orientation to manage to your leader responsibilities represents moving from control to competence and having the trust of others by fixing accountabilities. Accountability dictates who has what key result areas and who has the ball to make what touchdowns. Leader transitions are reflected in your letting go of pushing for achievement to pulling by vision and values. *Stop Achieving Yourself.* Transition to leading through direction and destiny/destination! *Stop Trying To Prove Your Adequacy* by being an expert with expert answers. Start asking expert questions of others. Pros accept themselves without needing to prove themselves as all-knowledgeable and always in control of everything.

The second suggestion is to write your priorities on the back of a matchbook, not on a three-page laundry list. The author calls it "matchbook managing." Select your priority battlefields for prioritized changes. Victory will ensue through ego control and through pinpointed choice. Choice is within you, not in reactive circumstances of trying to be everything to everybody. Choose your chaos, there is enough chaos external to yourself to choose between and among without reactively running from crisis to crisis. Select your challenges. Remember, organizations are not changed overnight and by quick fixes. Time can be your friend. Not everything must be done immediately.

The third suggestion for your successful strategy is to take the time to think. The open door policy does not mean that your door has to be open all the time. Every day set aside on your executive calendar at least one hour without personal or telephone interruptions. Personal control takes the place of political reactiveness—thinking time is not wasted time, it is an investment. Either you are in control of time or time will control you. Be willing to see anyone about anything, but *not at any time*. Time will not be given to you; that is why you must take time.

The fourth suggestion is to surround yourself, both inside the hospital and in your community relations, with positive and inspirational persons. Winners love winners and winning ideas. Constructive ideas and positive feelings are generated in and through positive interactions. "Doom and gloom" negative personalities will get to you and wear and tear you down to their level of perception. A kitchen cabinet and network of exciting people to be around are worth your time for mutual stimulation and mutual relief from the world of whiners and complainers. Excitement comes from exciting people. Comfort comes from being with collaborative and creative people. The recommendation is to gravitate to gifted personalities who have ideas, rather than people who limit their conversations to talking only about people and problems.

The fifth recommendation is to sharpen your senior skills in negotiating. In your tenure on "executive row" you will not be alone in facing conflictual encounters. Conflict is life and life is conflict. Life at the top of the hospital is conflict management and conflict resolution. Silberism 2: "Patient care, progress, profitability and personal relations are forged-out on the anvil of conflict." How skilled are you in negotiating conflict? Contention, argumentation, and emotional wrestling over vested interests is leadership. The American College of Healthcare Executives (ACHE) has an effective course on negotiating and conflict resolution as well as a course on introducing change and dealing with conflict. Compromises in the resolving of conflict may be an effective strategy; there are other conflict modes.

Healthy = *heal thy*. Your body is your money machine; when your body goes, your executive career goes. Stress, distress and dis-ease will be your bed partners. A conducive life-style and self-management are critical for you and your family. So far you have invested in your career ascent. Now is the time to also invest in overall holistic life management. The core and critical value on which you must keep focused is your well-being.

You want and wish to be happy. Happiness is your choice. But the hobgoblin of the harried and harassed executive is perfectionism. Silberism 3: "Perfection is only found in eulogies." Only one perfect person walked on this earth. Let go of searching for perfect solutions, let go of the goal of being a perfect hospital executive, a perfect spouse, and a perfect parent. "Go" are the first two letters in the word "goal."

It would be more healthy and helpful to choose action—the antidote for anxiety—rather than perfection. The more you insist on the perfect plan, the perfect staff study, self-perfection and the perfection of others, the prediction is career and self-demise. Trust others not to be perfect. Proactive action and action implementation will produce errors and mistakes at times. Give yourself permission not to be perfect; forgive yourself for being human in a nonperfect health care world, a world of judgment calls. The syndrome of success is not founded on perfectionism. It is founded on short step-by-step progress toward commitments.

POWER VERSUS EMPOWERMENT

Power and prestige sometimes inflict a mission to self-destruct on senior health care officers. Some begin to believe their own public relations. A health care systems president had a sign on his desk, "To partially win is to totally lose." Compare this relationship-destroying belief with another sign on another hospital president's desk: "No Games Played Here." Will you "hit bottom when you hit the top?" Power is there to facilitate the achievements of others, rather than power for your ego. Failure often is self-inflicted. The transformational *Leader* has discovered one of the secrets of success—to transcend power games and empower others. Like love, give power away so that it will come back to you. By retaining power you will find that people will ingratiate themselves to you and will manipulate you through your own need for power show and blow. Will you be a victim of your own personality need for power? If so, empowering others is the cure.

THE RIGHT STUFF FOR HOSPITAL LEADERSHIP

Are you getting a little tired of hearing theory upon theory of supervision? Will you be at your string's end if you have to sit through another workshop on the theoretical frameworks given by college professors who lecture on leadership laws? After nineteen years of applied, hands-on consulting to hospitals, after listening to and learning from those men and women who have bottom-line accountabilities through their leader effectiveness, this author questions whether there are leadership laws and executive absolutes.

Leadership theory is helpful as a border to a picture, but it is not the picture. There are a multitude of brilliant people who dream and conceptualize beautiful paintings in their heads, but there is a scarcity of persons who are painters. Today, as never before, health care corporations need "painters," the doers of leadership. Performance and productivity result from men and women who are the painters in the hospital world, whose achievements require real results obtainable through their leadership sensitivity, skill, strength, and style.

Leadership Lessons

The Holy Bible brims with lessons of leadership. Political history books are replete with repeating lessons of "leader losers"—people who have misused their positions. Current newspapers and popular magazines report on leadership effectiveness and ineptness throughout the world scene. There is scarcely a night on television which does not deal with demonstrations of leaders and their effects on others. Readers and viewers of leadership in action are amused and bemused by men and women in leadership situations. Leadership, its success or failure, is a daily companion in print, in movies, and on television. What can be learned from these lessons of leading? Women are not born leaders; men are not born managers. Leaders and managers are cultivated and nurtured, shaped and strengthened, by practical classroom grooming and experimental experiences in the safety of a positive, not punishing environment. This is not to discount the real value of reality testing through success and setbacks on the firing line of the job. The proof of learning really is successful performance in the hospital world. The secret is learning from leadership successes. And, to critique yourself after your successes to learn from your successes. Mismanaging mistakes also should be critiqued to help you learn from your errors.

Lamplighter Leadership

A leader is one who lights a lamp so that others can know the way. People want and need to know the path leading to successful performance. Today, in hospitals, the cry is for more productivity. People are accused of no longer being motivated. Silberism 4 is quite to the contrary: "People want to be productive, and people want to please other people. If they only knew what it took to please other people in their performances!"

Hospital executives are paid to be pathway lamplighters. If they want results, they must invest the time with their staff, eliminating the productivity hazards on the pathway to the expected results. Organization psychologists call this process "providing structure." Staff persons seek structure from their supervisors. Structure is defining or lighting the pathway to the results that specifically are needed. A secret of leadership is expectations, so that the Pygmalion effect (My Fair Lady effect) can occur. Liza Doolittle clearly knew what Professor Higgins' expectations were and what would please him in her performance. People have a way of fulfilling expectations of others if they have the structure of knowing what the expectations are.

Leaders light others' lights. Silberism 5: "Leaders light employees' lights so that their performances can be seen by others." Are you keeping your employees' lights under baskets so that no one else in your hospital can see them as individuals or see their effects? A secret of being an empowering leader is letting others' excellence shine brightly by focusing the lamplight on them, not on you. Are you employee-driven or self-driven? A secret is to encourage others to burn brightly so that they will not burn out or cop out on being productive with you. Lamplighters look good in the reflected glow of lights they light.

Lodestar Leadership

Lodestars are stars that lead as a guiding star. Leader stars also are out front, providing direction and purpose. Lodestar leading is guiding and gaining project identification through discussions of purpose and of values. A difference between leading and coordinating is found in the degree to which one provides clear vision to projects. Are you up-front and out-in-front with your staff persons on the whys of task necessities and the whys of assignments, which are needed? Silberism 6: "Involving interaction with people produces involved identification."

The lodestar leader shows concern, caring, and compassion for personnel. She or he provides a heart and a trustworthy relationship. People-perspicacity carries a bonus of enhancing inspiration through building human dignity.

Leader Qualities and Behaviors

Successful executives in health care corporations have clear-cut characteristics:

- Commanders and "demanders" use their authority to control others. Leaders facilitate the work and performances of others.
- For executive effectiveness you must understand your boss' goals and objectives; pressures; strengths, weaknesses and blind spots; and style, values, and visions.
- The leader's maturity is demonstrated in abnormal situations. How does he or she behave in an emergency, in the "clinches," under stress, pressure, and chaos?
- The leader who is out of touch with himself or herself cannot touch others.
- Leadership style is acquired, like graciousness and class.
- Leaders must change. Failure to change is the failure that leads to career demise. You are a change agent.
- The leader's expectations create the Pygmalion phenomenon—a self-fulfilling prophecy, the result of attitudes and definitions asserted by the leader for staff persons' adaptation.
- Risk taking is a must for effective leadership. Make a decision.
- A leader is the orchestra conductor, not first violin player.
- The higher you rise on the leader ladder, the more you must change from a competitor to a cooperator; be a collaborator, not a competitor.
- Leaders are willing to argue, but they are not argumentative.
- It is a great source of strength to know yourself and your strengths and weaknesses.
- Every person carries the seeds for his or her own failure or success. Whether or not the seeds grow depends upon the corporate culture.
- Leadership is the art of caring and utilizing other people well.
- A leader's ability to lead with excellence is dependent upon self-image.
- Intelligence may have little to do with success. Action is the main cause for success.
- Leadership is awe-full—full of awe.
- A good manager manages with love, not for love.
- There is no one best way of managing people.
- Leaders get paid for making decisions, not solving problems themselves.
- Trust does not grow back once it is destroyed.
- Leadership belongs to the ones who make the choices.
- The leader needs a combination of skills, credibility, competence, and the ability to empower others.

- Leadership is the ability to influence others.
- Success comes to leaders who identify and focus on doing a few things well, as contrasted with trying to do many things well.
- Leaders may listen to gossip, but they never repeat gossip.
- Leaders have a high need for integration, not achievement; the process is collaborative, not individual.
- A secret of leadership is to "catch people doing things right."
- A leader is like the shepherd, not the herdsman. The leader draws out from people their potential.
- Leaders see the differences in other people as just differences; not one person better or less than another person.

In the leadership process, people are the vital ingredient. The more concern your hospital leadership is demonstrated in a caring and considerate leadership style, the more likely you are to be perceived and received as trustworthy. Consideration is the degree of concern or caring others see in you when you ask them to do something for you.

When your staff persons experience you as "truly listening" and empathetic in communications, they will gravitate to collegial responsiveness. People will become consultative, not compliant or conforming. To be effective, the hospital executive must relate to others' vested interests, with a readiness to manage confrontation with concern for his or her opposer.

Leadership is not being the biggest; it's striving to be the best. It is never being comfortable with the status quo; it's seeking new challenges and needed changes. It's setting a standard of performance that inspires and challenges associates. Being a leader is a lot tougher than being a follower.

It's not the critic who counts. It's not the man who points out where the grown man stumbles, or how the doer of deeds could have done them better. The credit belongs to the man who actually is in the arena, who strives violently, who errs and comes up short again and again, who knows the great enthusiasms, the great devotions, and spends himself in a worthy cause, who if he wins knows the triumph of high achievement, but who if he fails, fails while daring greatly, so his place will never be with those cold and timid souls who know neither victory nor defeat."

Theodore Roosevelt—
the Twenty-sixth President
of the United States

PEAK PERFORMANCE

Climbing to ever higher levels of peak performance is like shaving . . . if you don't do it every day, you will become an also ran. Champion athletes are world class pros in the arena because they discipline themselves to practice daily, to prepare themselves by daily rehearsal so they are up for the field competition. Olympic hospital stars are not born, they become star producers because of their daily mental exercises, which extend their excellence.

Various health care corporations have invited this author to present seminars and keynote addresses on Peak Performance: Turning Personal Power into Performance Power. The theme is that outward successful achievement starts with successful innerspace, a successful you. You are your attitudes. What are your "be-attitudes," your attitudes being you? Do you have the attitudes of a sustainer or do you have the attitudes of a success-seeker? There is a psychological truism that our attitudes either land us on our feet or land us on our seat. Attitudes separate winning from whining, and separate champions from minor league people "who just play" at the game of life and their occupational calling. Innerspace of attitudes produce or reduce external performance; your behavior is the result of your mindset.

"Setting-of-the-mind" for the production of peak performance goes beyond the ritual of looking in the mirror every morning and asking your reflection in the mirror, "who has the most positive mental attitude this morning?" Specifically and with practicality, peak performance is launched by "meta-talk" (meta is the Greek word for beyond) beyond puffing one's personhood in front of a mirror. The performance psychology of meta-talk offers exciting growth potential.

Look inside the attitudes of champions, the meta-talk of the innerspace of winners. A prime attitude is the commitment to constructive discontent, a restless commitment to what can be done better. In a sense, winners have mental "ants in the pants" in asking themselves what they, not others, can do to be more effective. Peter Drucker points out that effectiveness is focusing on the needed effects, the needed results or outcomes, which will make a real difference in the real world (the right results rather than just plodding along trying to do everything right).

Champions dare to dream. Their dreams keep them awake while others hide in sleep, and produce a restlessness, which produces a zest to quest. Their healthy discontent focuses on what can be, not whining and whimpering about what is, what could or should have been. Their attitude is "I can make a difference!" Do you dare to dream about what can be?

Comingled with this focusing on the right effects, which will make a difference, is a sense of urgency. Some people are day dreamers. Others are dream-doers. Peak performers have an action attitude that if a person is to climb a mountain, if one is to move the world, the movement starts by moving one's self.

The psychology of those who are leaders seemingly relates the value of time to their personal value. The worth of time is hinged and hooked on personal worth of making a difference. Leaders are not interested in passing time, spending their time, or doing time in a job; time has real value and worth to them. Winners respect time. Time and achievement have a healthy sense of urgency. Time is life and life is time; their innerspace of focused dreams does not stop with day dreaming and wishing, but dreams are acted on through their creative restlessness and a sense of urgency to run the race.

Looking into the mindset of peak performers, psychologists have found an exciting factor, which facilitates self-starting accomplishment. They call it locus of control. At times this differentiating human factor is called the control of fate or the control of destiny. Another name for this human factor is center of choice.

The center of choice or locus of control might be explained as the difference between persons. Some see life as one big Reno roll—roll the dice and whatever will be will be (that is, external fate will determine what will happen). On the other hand, others like the champion bowler see the impact or results of their bowling under their control. That is, the number of bowling pins knocked down by the champion bowler is seen as mostly under his or her control, concentration, and choices, but not fate. Champion bowlers meta-talk (innerspace visualization of their control).

What happens to peak performers is controlled by their influence, their choices, and their changes. Peak performers see power within themselves, rather than the potency of winds blown at them externally. They choose to see themselves in control, as victors, not as victims of circumstances. As a result of seeing the locus of control within themselves, rather than in external events, peak performers seldom make excuses, wring their hands, and wear hairshirts placing blame on others or circumstances.

Look a little deeper within the center of choice and locus of control concept. What are some of the miles driven by superior hospital officers on their road to higher levels of achievement (M.I.L.E.S.):

- **M**entally focusing or centering in on what will make a difference; mentally visualizing the results, imagining positive outcomes or "positive coming attractions."

- Imagine or mentally rehearse actions, which will lead to the focused result, image the actions and think through the assets, which will be needed.
- Live in the present, live with the realities of people, political, performance, and progress barriers, which will have to be confronted and surmounted. Do not live in a fantasy world nor live in the past of what might have been, a world of "if onlys."
- Enthusiastic expectancy. Winners expect to succeed. In *My Fair Lady*, Professor Higgins expected to succeed in transforming Liza Doolittle (power of expectations).
- Self-discipline to stay with the plan; self-control so as not to jump from idea to idea. Concentration and persistence of concentration on the opportunity. Stop worrying yourself out of performance, but rather start planning your success. Work your plan.

Are you a leader who gains mileage by being proactive in your life at work or are you a reactive responder to fate and a blamer of what does not happen on external circumstances? Do you see the locus or location of control within you or external to you? Peak performers see themselves as their own choice makers; they make choices and accept the consequences of their decisions. Have you taken charge of your life or is life in charge of you? The choice of choices is yours to make or will you let the trustees and medical staff make the choices for you?

"Giveupitis" is a positive attitude and behavior of Olympians in sports and leadership. This is a strange word, giveupitis, but Olympians do give up. They have the personal persistence to give up distractions and time robbers, which steal their concentrated consistency of being consistent. Giveupitis is another way of saying the will to sacrifice. The willingness to give up some or many of the things you would like to enjoy for immediate pleasure in order to gain greater reward. "Later on" is a hallmark of peak performers. They have learned the lesson to say "no." "No" is one of the shortest words in the English language, but one of the most difficult words to say. Winners say "no" to distractions. Wimps have a terrible time saying "no." Chumps end up saying "yes" to everyone else's wishes, wants, and whims. That is, losers say "no" to themselves and "yes" to everyone else. A healthy "no" is not being self-centered, but rather keeping priorities as priorities.

Superior executives accept that it is A-OK to be wrong at times, that errors and mistakes are the human condition. Imperfection is not a failure to hospital presidents—failure is not trying. Results come from calculated risk taking, from venturing a few steps into areas of anxiety. The search for perfection often results in taking the status quo and super-safe course or no action. Perfectionism is fearfulness. Performance courage is not the absence of fear, but rather courage is the conquest of fear, the conquest of procrastination in making health system decisions.

Have you ever thought about people who have nothing in life? While there are a multitude of causes for having and giving nothing, possibly one of these many reasons is that they think they do not deserve anything for whatever psychological reasons. It seems that those individuals who accomplish and lead have something called belief power. They believe or trust in their worthwhileness and the goodness of their goals and efforts. It is truly worth noting the biblical notion that a person's thoughts determine who the person is and who the person will become. Could it be true that people who have nothing are still achieving? That is, achieving what they think they deserve, which is nothing.

What do you think of yourself? What do you think you deserve . . . the peak or the pits in your leadership? Do you have self-esteem? Self-esteem is the calcium of your personality bones, the calcium of your spine to evaluate and take executive risks. No judgment a leader can pass is more significant than the judgment that he or she passes on to himself or herself. No single factor is more responsible for the shaping of one's life than self-judgment and self-esteem. Self-esteem is the degree to which one is comfortable with who one is and comfortable with who one is not, being at peace with one's self. While restless for performance, hospital officers have self-esteem and do have a power of belief.

Leadership does call for paying your dues, and a different mindset of attitudes and self-perceptions. If your future is to be better than your present, your future must be paid for today. If you are unwilling to be a person with giveupitis and pay the price for tomorrow's success, at least be happy with the lack of success in your life. Peak outputs and success demand setting your sights on higher levels beyond your psychological safety zone and safety net. If you set your limits on being average, that is what you will be. Peak performance starts in your head, is sustained by your attitudes, and is achieved by your behaviors.

In the competitive health care industry today, magnified by the pressures of PPOs, DRGs and interhealth system rivalries as never before, peak performing senior officers are needed. Health care decision making must be more rapid, risk-oriented and tough minded in these turbulent, transformational times. Challenges and choices are being faced daily in the 5,000 or more hospitals. Some hospital presidents "will hack it" and others will be asked by their boards of trustees to find a success experience with another health delivery system. Peak performing presidents are this industry's critical need. As you look into the leadership looking glass, do you see a hospital peak performer?

THE CAKEMIX OF SUCCESS

Success is not the goal nor the end of the trail, but the consistent achievement along the pathway, which has the accumulative effect of sequential success. Success is the way of traveling life's path based on an internal set of attitudes toward self, work, and overall living, rather than a final destination.

Success is only a word in the dictionary, but yet it is individually defined. Each person has to define the perimeters and parameters to give success meaning. For some success is the accumulation of monetary wealth, for others it is a state of self-pleasure, and what happiness means for them. For some it is the accumulation of status and ever increasing higher levels of the symbols of status. Others might describe success as their relationships to their God as well as holistic living, marriage, children, and health.

The Ingredients

Success does not necessarily follow working hard and putting in long hours. Success seems to relate to working both hard and smart. Working smart means the concentration of your time and the concentration of your effort for a reward. Leaders learn that a multitude of others are followers seeking strength, structure, direction and guidance from others. Hence, the followers are willing to work for leaders and visionary people.

Satisfaction is a personal factor or personal dimension. Success is external and created in the external world. This is a secret of success—to identify opportunities and unsatisfied needs external in the marketplace, which have not been met. Successful leaders do not have to impress themselves, but rather the consumer, customer, or client external to themselves. If a person can identify the unrequited and unmet "needs, greeds, bleeds, and fears" external to themselves, those are the areas where there is a probability of success. If a person takes care of meeting other people's needs, success will take care of itself. This calls for identifying by listening to these needs which, in turn, are developed into success opportunities.

The subsequent ingredients are then concentration, concentration, concentration and bulldogged persistence, persistence, persistence of focusing time and resources on those areas of opportunities. Do not try to be everything to everybody; do not spread yourself thin. Specialize in limited areas of other's needs and your own areas of competence, skills, and abilities. Do not try to do multiple things simultaneously, but rather do many things sequentially. Set a few goals and set up benchmarks or mile markers to calibrate or monitor how you are progressing against those few goals. Be honest with your own setbacks regarding how you are progressing; do not delude yourself. A successful leader is a realist and a dream doer—not just a dreamer, or a person of self-deception.

Do not throw good money and good time after a bad decision. If progress and achievement do not measure up, cut your losses after you evaluate honestly why it is not working. Do not ride a dead horse. Extensive greed also is an enemy; be willing to take moderate and above-average gains, rather than "trying to eat the total elephant."

Successful senior officers probably make more of their share of mistakes because they make more decisions. There is no gain without pain and there is no reward without ventured risks and vulnerability to downside slippage, changes in the marketplace or a poor judgment call. Successful health care people are moderate risk takers but not high Las Vegas risk rollers; conversely, they are not low or no-risk takers. Successful people are constantly estimating in their venture

- the probability of success
- the significant worthwhileness of the reward compared to the risk
- the probability of failure
- the severity of consequences of failure compared to the risk

Leadership starts with an identified clear vision. It is not based on reactiveness, impulsiveness or unclear thinking. Effective leaders do not operate with a ready–fire–aim philosophy. They clearly identify customer needs or expectations, plan the necessary steps and resources needed, and constantly consider the downside danger regarding the contingencies of failure. How quickly and easily can you get out of a poor decision? Successful people stay in touch with the arenas of action, rather than sitting back and expecting what they do will satisfy the marketplace. They "mind the store" with ongoing discipline so that they can spot problems early and take corrective action if the darts are slipping away from the bull's eye.

Almost without exception, winners define success in terms of a service, a higher purpose, or a mission. This dedication to a calling, this commitment to a customer-driven purpose is genuine. It is not self-serving but serves others. There is a zest or zealousness attached to this defined destiny. Supporting the zest for the quest is doing the hard thinking because it marries with that a sense of calling and purpose. Hard work comes more easily when you do the things you believe in. Time passes quickly when you are having fun at what you are doing.

Ethics and morality, which may or may not come from institutionalized formal religion, are a core of success. Successful health care leaders want to, and as best as they are able, do the right thing at the right time in the right way, because it is the right thing to do. They do not cut corners on the ethical and moral thing to do. Your executive behaviors will reflect your ethical beliefs and values. The pace of time is equal for everyone. But, how people see the value of time and how people discipline themselves in the habit of using time produces differential success. Time is money; time is life. Part of the investment of time is the recharging of your physical and mental batteries. The recharging and revitalization of self (physically, spiritually, emotionally, and intellectually) is vital to the vitality of successful leaders; they invest in themselves for such diversification and recharging. Friends, spouses, and other emotional support systems are vital for your success. Few successful people are successful by themselves or because of themselves only. They invest themselves for mutuality and conviviality in other individuals.

The gains of accomplishment are supported by frugality and the conservative conservation of what success has produced. Real leaders are not meteorites that flash and quickly burn out in the sky. Health care leaders retain their critical mass. Acquired gains and amassed honors are sustained in a frugal, savings-conscious manner. As success is not an instantaneous experience, the leader does not dissipate nor instantaneously utilize what has been acquired. A rainy day may still come and the successful person knows the precariousness of success and its fragility. This is called the "terror of triumph." Success can be lost quickly.

Health care executives are persons of imaginative recognition who see possibilities, how a novel way can be applied to fulfill needs that have not been met. They are individuals who are willing to turn ideas into a pragmatic way of applying resources, to come out with a working system, and to flexibly redefine problems. They don't accept the problems just as they are given to them. They can redefine the problem and come up with new possibilities.

Health care executives are not afraid to be their own judge. These persons have a low fear of expressing unconventional ideas and proposals. They conform to what is accepted in social behavior, but at the same time they are unconventional, independent thinkers. They generate uncommon ideas and proposals. These individuals are free from personality needs to think as others would have them think. In their courageous thinking these executives are productive in thinking on their own. They are not victims of groupism. They will challenge preconceived thinking, resist stereotype judgments, and question traditional judgments. These are "pro's pros" who have little fear of being wrong in the eyes of others and of being critical of their own thinking.

Successful persons possess a healthy knowledge of themselves, a knowledge of their own strengths and of their weaknesses. These are individuals who are struggling to become better at fulfilling their own areas of endowment and strength, concentrating on making their own endowment even better. These courageous people will make decisions and be decisive. They will make decisions in spite of ambiguity, even though there is information uncertainty, recognizing the time when a decision must be made. Complete certainty may mean failure altogether.

Another ingredient of success is the capability of divergent thinking under pressure. Individuals who can think in an expanding manner under stress, rather than a contracting manner by focusing on the details or dangers, have the psychological ability to absorb danger and to continue to think openly. Such individuals do not immediately fixate on traditionally bound methods, the old ways of thinking, the customary way of responding, and the usual patterns of problem solving.

The successful leader can think and tolerate stress, disorder, complexity, and time delay. This is the individual who is emotionally geared to tolerate inner tension while examining the question at hand. She or he has the patience to see deeper possibilities that are inherent in the problem. The winner focuses on possibilities and tolerates uncertainty and risk-taking behavior. The winner does not focus on apparent facts and embrace the first solution which suggests itself or the first solution that is suggested.

Supporting success on the psychological level is "bounce-back resiliency." Living means exposure to pain, disillusionment, and failure. The successful person has the psychological resiliency to bounce back from all this. She or he does not pretend that all is well, does not live in a world of rose-colored glasses. But, here is an individual who accepts set backs. The key here is the word accepts, accepts that set backs must be borne by human beings. Leaders recognize mistakes. They realize that mistakes must be corrected and they do something about them. Leaders do not waste time agonizing over the past. They view errors as lessons, not as personal crushes.

ARE YOU EFFECTIVE?

The Prime Thrust of Effectiveness

Effectiveness resides in the ability to direct the hospital resources by pinpointing the efforts of your people toward opportunities for significant results. This is the key for the hospital administrator who increases his or her political leverage and makes that hospital an effective health delivery system in the community.

An effective hospital system is attained first by employees focusing time and attention on opportunities rather than on problems. Second, by staff members putting effort into areas that have maximum impact on the effectiveness of the hospital. The health care leader does not misallocate time and effort in the fundamental confusion between efficiency and effectiveness.

The efficient hospital administrator focuses on doing things *right* but the effective administrator focuses on doing the *right* things. The difference on doing things *right* and doing the *right* things is what you do to get a meaningful return on the investment, what you do that is right rather than compulsively hanging on to sclerotic procedures and practices, and the this-is-the-way-we-have-always-done-it-around-this-hospital attitude. Put effort where there is real contribution—do not be satisfied with activity and people being busy.

An effective leader is concerned with output and with process (results, not activity), with individuals being good rather than looking good. Are they just going through activity, movement, and hospital procedure only?

Earmarks of a Failing Hospital Leader

The failing hospital administrator is a reactor, rather than an actor, who lets occurrences, events, crises, and constant problems dissipate her or his time. This person always is reacting to political requests and events rather than planning or stopping to take the time to think things through. (Do not imitate this person, turn crises into routinized events that other people can handle.) The failing individual also does not plan objectives and does not take the time to set standards of performance ahead of time so people can know what is good work and what is failing work. Hence, they do not have a clear idea of the expectations.

Human relations means asking yourself "What can I predict in my relations with others? Where will I be punished? Where am I going to be hurt? When is the chairperson of the board going to be on top of me for not performing?" If people know where they stand, if people know what is expected of them in their performance, then you have the core of human relations.

Here is an example of clear expectations at work.

An executive of a major hospital said to this hospital's health care consultant, "Come into my office. I would like to discuss a problem with you. I want to fire my controller. It's been quite a while since I fired anyone and I'm pretty rusty. He is doing everything I don't want him to do and doing only the things he wants to do. He came from a major hospital and I gave him a $6,000 increase in salary. They said he was very fine at keeping everything straight. I think he's a loser and want to get rid of him. Can you advise me on how to fire him?"

The author asked, "What do you want him to *stop* doing? What do you want him to *start* doing?" For an hour and a half he paced the floor listing what he wanted and did not want from his controller. The author wrote everything down. Later, that same day, Charlie Controller came walking down the hall. He asked, "Could you come into my office for a minute? I've had it—I want to get out of this hospital. I can't please 'the old man'." The author replied, "I just came from the president's office and he told me what your job was. He told me what was wrong with your performance. I wrote it all down for you."

Sometime later when the author was back in the hospital the president called him in saying, "I don't know what kind of magic you have, but Charlie is a performer! You know that I was going to fire him, but I just gave him a raise. He's a great controller, does everything I want him to do and has stopped doing all the things I don't want him to do."

The message here is if you want your people to be effective, you have to tell them where you're going, tell them what race you want them to run, and tell them what you don't want them to do. That is human relations effectiveness and administrative performance in action.

The failing hospital administrator also wants conformity and needs emotional support for his or her authority. If disagreement is permitted between the administrator and the dietitian, controller, purchasing manager, or chief of nursing services, the administrator sees this as a threat to his or her power. Rather than involving people, he or she orders them autocratically. It is important for this failing administrator to control rather than to get return on human assets. Quite often a weak manager who behaves this way is not after performance, but after conformance. He or she gets wonderful delegation, all upward, and decides everything.

It is easier for the failing administrator to function in a Theory X manner and with great busyness. This individual is everywhere in the hospital. As time goes on, the staff members will decrease their initiative and their risk taking. They will not tell the boss anything, since the boss makes all the decisions. They don't give new ideas, but wait for signals and signs before they take action.

Earmarks of the Effective Hospital Leader

The effective leader spends a percentage of time away from the executive desk to identify where there is significant opportunity to make that hospital more effective. Identify the areas you want to commit your staff's efforts, attention, and output. Live with anxiety of not doing anything. This takes some courage—to plan and identify where your hospital has to be serviced now. Do not tinker with yesterday's problems. The main thought is, "Where is the hospital delivery system going now?"

Concentrate on the following: What is one hour of your time worth? What is the worth of that one hour in terms of overhead, space, benefit package, and salary? The effective leader knows what that time is worth and knows what the staff time is worth. Employees need to know what their time is worth.

Silberism 7: have "the conviction to cut." An executive should have the courage to amputate those activities, noncontributing projects, and processes, that are dissipating time and wasting resources. There is nothing that will kill your career, or kill your effectiveness, more than appendages that sap time. Have the courage to amputate, to have people stop doing something they are attached to, which may have minimal to no impact on the hospital systems' or patient care effectiveness.

Consider the definition of management: the ability to get results through other people. It means let people get their job done. Results through others means you do your job, the tasks of administration, and you allow others the freedom and logistic support to get their job done. What rocks and boulders can you roll off the road so that somebody else can go through and perform? Where are you going to use your power, and political clout, where are you going to use your informal authority to get the rocks and blocks in the hospital system off the road so that other people can produce? These are things the effective hospital leader must consider each day. If people are on a payroll to make things happen, they are the problem solvers. Your job is to get the impedimentia off the road and out of the way, so that people can go ahead and make something happen. Specifically ask yourself *Today*, what needs are to be accomplished in this hospital? What will I facilitate by rolling stones out of the way?

Here is an axiom: When a person walks through the door with a problem, that person must go out the door with the problem and alternative solutions on his or her back. The role of the hospital leader is to be a professional sounding board for the solutions that the staff person has brought in with the problem he or she needs to solve. You are there to help this person think through the solutions that the person has created to solve the problem. The administrator takes the human growth position, "Don't bring me problems—bring me solutions with your problem."

Development of Hospital Human Assets

When the hospital leader asks people to make decisions, they begin to grow. One of the richest things entrusted to a leader is the ability to help other people to develop, to come along in their skills and self-esteem. The hospital leader is a steward of talents. One encourages the psychological well-being of people and gets a return on investment for the hospital system. But one of the greatest rewards that you will have is to develop a team of champion swimmers rather than a team of nonsinkers.

Ask yourself: Do I have a staff that will argue with me, push me, ask questions? Do I allow my staff the three be's? The first be is to give people a chance, to be. That is, to be a somebody rather than be a nobody. The second be is, to belong. They are part of the system rather than just workers or pairs of hands. The third be is, to become. To become what they are capable of becoming, to stretch their necks without breaking their necks. The people have their psychological well-being fulfilled and they know they can enrich their lives through work.

The effective leader is concerned with bringing people along in their own effectiveness. That is one of the things that one has in the way of a legacy of personal and enduring significance. The effective leader becomes a significant other to the people, not just a boss. People are the only hospital asset that can appreciate as well as depreciate in value.

WHERE ARE YOU GOING WRONG?

The demise and death rattle of a health care career usually is a slow and subtle decline into political and personal ineffectiveness. Many newly appointed hospital executives miss and mistake early warning signs of self-destruction, yet wonder about what is or is not happening in their relationships.

Behind closed executive doors, one can hear the wailing and whining of the failing administrator. Comments such as, "They just want conformance not professional performance around this hospital." Or, "Medical staff here is just a collection of robots in this health systems corporation who are afraid to try anything innovative." Or, "I'm getting out of this health care corporation, they don't appreciate me." The blaming, ineffective hostility, and hurt feelings are directed externally on "those" who just don't understand.

Health care corporations need leaders who have multiple skills to present administrative innovation in sensitive ways. The crying need in these transitional and trying times in health care corporations is for tough-minded, yet flexible, pros who handle relationships and proposals for change by avoiding the potholes and pitfalls on the road to organizational intervention. The crying need is for transformational executives in these transformational times.

Explore and examine some of the mistakes and constructive antidotes in keeping the administrative relationship effective and healthy. Particularly at the time of making proposals for change, rethink the ways in which you present yourself and your administrative ideas for organizational intervention. In the following paragraphs are just a few thoughts for you as you propose changes.

It has been said that administrators are their own worst enemy. Their impatience with their inability to have an impact on the health care structure and its processes can be a foe. What apparently occurs in a person's work life is the disparity experienced between what he or she feels is of vital and critical importance to the hospital for change and what "they" will let the person do. But how much of this frustration is self-imposed or self-induced?

One of the signs of an amateur is the casting and presentation of himself or herself as a self-styled expert. This person's self-perception as the end-all, be-all, and change-all person with the hospital world revolving around his or her proposals for change is misguided. He or she is simply the prime change agent. Note the basic psychological truism: many achievements are the results of a stepwise progression of introducing change as opposed to insisting upon a major revolution. The failing person sees his or her introduction of change as primarily above and ahead of what the hospital will accept and where it is in terms of understanding the necessity for that change. This person takes the position that the total process must be accepted and feels frustrated and rejected when the board of trustees will only accept the process with major modifications.

You must examine your own psychological needs. How do you rate your need for organization power in relation to your need to provide service? Where do you stack your need for personal power and the need for acceptance and belonging in your health care organization? Have you confused your own need for dominance and visibility with the professional need for being a change agent? When you were hired, did you see yourself annointed or appointed? If power is your strongest need as compared to the zest to give ideas and support the organization's development, this ordering of values and priorities often may spell the difference between professional effectiveness and career failure. These red flag personality needs so often show through to the board, for example, the need for personal dominance. When a board emotionally experiences an administrator who has a need to dominate that relationship, the members tend to feel threatened and alienated from both the individual and what that professional is suggesting.

The need for power and dominance is a self-induced handicap that interferes with one's effectiveness as one tries to superimpose oneself in relationships. A youthful leader who places power ahead of change-agent service is headed for a win-lose conflict and the result, by and large, is that he or she loses.

The effective leader honestly examines and confronts his or her own need for power. What is your ability to genuinely listen with your "third ear?" Are you genuinely interested in providing consultative guidance or are you there to dominate that relationship? Do you visualize that you sit in a side-by-side relationship with others, or do you see yourself in a selling relationship wherein you talk a person into gaining a personal conquest?

Another death rattle of the failing administrator is his or her need to peddle gimmicks to department managers. The peddling of techniques, for technique sake only, often leads to demise. Unfortunately, hospital consultants see the newly hired executive who is bringing techniques to department management's attention, rather than a rationale for the change. Too many are package oriented and focus on selling the new package. Are you so procedure-bound that you constantly are selling others on the latest program rather than focusing on generic needs and what the hospital itself needs for its vitality?

How comfortable and effective are you in swallowing your ego? The effective leader focuses on what is needed and forsakes his or her own ego. The amateur's operating style focuses around self-opportunism and self-centeredness, rather than customer-centeredness. When department heads feel they are made into objects for experimentation with "that new technique or methodology," they resent it and feel they are being manipulated and exploited. They usually turn the administrator off and tune out the proposal request no matter what its intrinsic value might be.

Look at another self-destructing earmark of the failing young executive, the projection of the "breastplate of armor." Too often, when an administrator makes a presentation, he or she goes in with the expectation that he or she is going to be rejected. The person therefore girds the breastplate of armor over his or her chest for the attack. One's own concern of being rejected often produces an anticipatory fear which is telegraphed and communicated to others. Because of this anticipation of rejection, the amateur comes on either too long, too hard, or too strong and often as an in-gratiating apple polisher seeking the doles, which might be passed off as personal acceptance. The newly hired executive who constantly fears failure could well become a self-destroying person and destroy important innovations in health care corporations.

In these cases of breastplate armor attack and defensiveness, the self-fulfilling prophecy often comes true. Both the purveyor and the idea for change are rejected. This is quite similar to one's premarital courting days wherein if you are a suitor and expect to be rejected by your potential lover, this may become a reality because of the nonverbal as well as verbal messages you send in the dating relationship.

We ask the youthful executive to take a look at his or her attitudes before walking into a presentation. Do you have a do or die attack attitude? Do you see yourself as an effective human being? For your own effectiveness you need to decide before you enter that presentation whether you are there to consult or whether you have your selling shoes on. (If the latter is the case, you are going to telegraph that you are "on the conquest trail.")

You must ask yourself what vocabulary and whose value system you tend to communicate through, your value system or the board's? The amateur in administration who does not do his or her value homework and search the board's background and experiences, including hangups and tender spots, is in for a presentation rejection.   How sensitive are you to your audience's tender spots, specialized needs, and operating values? Have you walked into the nursing administration office without having done your home-work? Have you entered a relationship with a genuine and authentic need to counsel, guide, and listen to what is really operating?

Effectiveness is to put your administrative concept into the frame of reference of others; their value systems, their vocabulary, as well as operat-ing needs. Think in terms of cost as well as payoff. The question is whether others perceive you as an individual who is genuinely concerned about their needs and their career effectiveness. Do you walk in their shoes? Can you work on the other person's emotional and financial side of the desk? Can you work effectively in terms of their values; operating needs; and informal, political, and hospital world realities?

What typically happens to you, emotionally, when the medical staff or a specific person gives you a hard way to go? The amateur bores in deeper, sells even harder, stops listening, gets into a debating contest, and tries desperately to prove points. He or she becomes psychologically myopic, preoccupied with the barriers being experienced emotionally. One tends to hear only what one wants to hear and tends to perceive only what one wishes to perceive.

When the real leader meets resistance, he or she stops. People experience presentation rejection through different signals from the audience. Every person is different and has his or her own way of turning somebody off. Some of the things you might be alert to are loss of eye contact; pinpointed hostility against subpoints within the presentation (away from the main issue at question); and attention to somebody else or something else within the immediate environment.

If you begin to lose the attention of others during the presentation, or if others begin to give you a hard time, this is the time to listen and to ask more questions. It is the time to stay open, not the time to intensify. It is the time to practice the two "d's" of resistance handling—diagnosis and dialogue. Only through diagnosis of what is happening at that point in time and a genuine interest in an open dialogue can you hope for an ongoing relationship.

The failing administrator is that individual who lacks the sensitivity to know when, where, and how to introduce change; when to tactfully and tactically question; when to listen; and when to leave and withdraw from the interaction. These are positive acts within the repertoire of the administrator even though they may be tough to accept internally. However, these vital ingredients pave the way for ultimate, active, and positive results, if these behaviors and attitudes are executed with authenticity.

When another person calls attention to an omission you made within your proposal, for the most part he or she is trying to fill in the gaps to make it more palatable and acceptable. When your board suggests that you are "missing the point," often the members are really trying to help you succeed by recalibrating your organizational compass. If you look at resistance in the light of constructive suggestions, rather than seeing their ideas as personal rejection, you are on your way to being more effective. Few youthful administrators can understand immediately the complete scope of an organization and all of its informal political and subtle potentials.

You must listen for more of these political nerve-end organization signals, signs, and cues so that you can be effective. Only by knowing and listening to these realities within a hospital's informal political world can you be in a service position to have others accept your proposals. Only then can you be effective as a change agent. Are you willing to have your organization sensitivity compass recalibrated in a helpful way by others?

Your New Direction

Stop searching for excellence, start being excellent. Advertisements and bylines in logos of automobile companies, airlines, medical supply houses, and hospital corporations underscore this theme of excellence. At commencement ceremonies, graduates from Masters of Health Administration programs hear the importance of excellence in confronting the challenges facing health care management. Excellence, and the consistency of its pursuit, is the tone of today's renewal and revitalization of health care systems.

Excellence is not a destination of the hospital road; excellence is the way of traveling that road, a health care road filled with potholes, detours, and unknown curves. Excellence is a credo translated hourly each day of executive practice into demonstrative caring and considerate behaviors. Excellence is your commitment to yourself, your esteem and pride in and through the multitude of ways you project yourself. The value of excellence precedes economic value; economic return follows excellence. Excellence is not costly: it is priceless. It is ongoing executive behavior in relationships and for results.

HOSPITAL CULTURE: VALUES AND BEHAVIORS

A health care culture or climate is the invisible interpreter of the interactions among and between persons and hospital departments. It highlights how people feel working in the environment. Hospital climates are value-driven, guiding day-to-day actions or lack of actions in deciding behaviors. Culture is an internal image, the feels and perceptions that prescribe standards of what is and what is not acceptable. It is the collective consciousness of assumptions about your hospital and how it really works or doesn't work.

What are you and your staff really thinking, seeing and believing in your cultural network of values? A hospital culture impacts and affects decision making, performance linkage and bonding for results, productivity, relationships, and commitments. Before renewing common purposes and implementing changes, a health care leader must first know what exists by touching the perceptions of the persons within the corporate climate.

Achieving needed changes requires accurate identification of the positive as well as the negative blind spots, which operate within the hospital. Meaningful data are needed; diagnosis must precede the planning of cultural change. Your hospital's future is its culture today.

Thirteen Critical Concepts

1. *Identification.* Identify what the staff is proud of, and what makes the hospital special. What are the positive, energizing set of beliefs or

emotional forces within your hospital. List the positive attitudes and perceptions that knit the staff together.

2. *Correction.* What does not need fixing? What is working well here and should not be changed? Internally, what is being done right and effectively? Where is cohesiveness and cooperation in meeting the external challenges evident?

3. *Structure.* How clear and effective are assignments, tasks, and the organizational charts? To what extent does the hospital's structure facilitate or hinder the achievement goals? How does its structure facilitate or hinder coordination in getting jobs done?

4. *Systems.* Where do the arteries of information flow or get clogged? Are you getting adequate and sufficient information downward or between departments? Identify where you need more reliable, faster, and current communications about what things.

5. *Symbolism.* A culture rewards and reinforces acceptable behaviors; management pays attention and gives evidence to what it considers important by rewarding different results. What symbolic behaviors tell you what is acceptable and what is not acceptable? What symbolic behaviors are rewarded or punished here? To what does management pay great and ongoing attention, or pay little or inconsistent attention to?

6. *Shared Values.* Cohesive and consistent beliefs provide pride and direction through visions. List positive values and visions of this hospital. List negative values, which hide in the "little corners" among the employees.

7. *Strategy.* Key result areas and identified ways to achieve successful and sustainable effects are critical in competitive times. Identify where you are getting mixed signals (confusion) regarding strategy. What strategy targets of this hospital do you want to know or have clarified?

8. *Barriers.* "We versus they" barriers can paralyze action. Where is the administration enslaved and encumbered by bureaucratic habits, out-of-date systems, unnecessary rituals, and comfort. List silly and dumb ways of working together that put you in a straitjacket. Also, identify old projects or systems that you cling to and should be shut down. Identify ways you can de-layer, de-value, and de-manualize. What rules, which interfere with relations, can you change?

9. *Trust.* Describe the level of team interaction and trust in your hospital. List adjectives you hear, which reflect trust and the openness between people. Identify situations or areas where there is organizational gridlock, lack of decision making because of artificial walls, broken trust, and poor communication.

10. *Conflict.* Describe how contention, conflict, and dissatisfaction are dealt with in your hospital. What are the hidden agendas for handling differences and dissent? How are challenges to opinion handled? What are the ways for talking about the tough and delicate issues? Discuss the cultural norms for confronting conflict and contention.

11. *Future.* What do you mean by greatness? What will it take to get there? Thinking three years ahead: what present core values do you want to retain? Thinking three years ahead, what present values do you wish to discard? Three years from now, what present management behaviors will still fit? Three years from now, what different leader behaviors will be needed? "What if . . ." could happen if you don't change certain cultural behaviors. What will it take to keep this hospital in good shape three years hence?

12. *Measurement.* What gets measured and assessed gets done. If you're looking for ways to change how an organization behaves, change the systems and focus of measurement. What priorities are not measured? List those things you celebrate and reward. What things do you overlook and do not celebrate. Identify things that should be measured, paid attention to, and celebrated. Identify measurement systems which have outlived their usefulness.

13. *Policies.* Identify 3 to 5 policies and practices, which interfere with stated purposes.
    Identify 3 to 5 policies and procedures which interfere with people.
    Identify 3 to 5 policies which contradict people productivity.

How healthy is your hospital's environment? How does it affect the people and their performance and relationship commitments? Today's tough and transformational times of health care delivery demand a corporate culture, which is strong; consumer driven (through cohesive values and shared beliefs); and has a climate in and through which all personnel are linked and emotionally and ethically bonded. Depending upon the vitality of your culture, your managers will play it safe and be less innovative or act in a risk-oriented innovative way in their decisions and managerial behaviors.

The contemporary leader has a change mandate. Every leader makes a basic choice to be the moved or to be the mover. Department managers run hospitals, the successful CEO creates them. Department managers make the trains run, but today's hospitals more desperately need Olympian leaders to select the right track and get the engine going. Do you see your role as a creative leader, not manager, who shapes shared values for performance strength?

Your leadership base for setting the climate for those needed changes comes from having up-to-date knowledge of your culture and knowing how to tap into this network to accomplish your change mandates from the board. The key tasks are to understand the hospital's informal environment and then enter a real culture-building process. Before senior management can orchestrate culture binding, they must know what people in their hospital are really thinking and believing in the cultural network. First knowing, then skilled working of the network, is the only way to get the job done. Before refocusing common purposes, a leader must know what exists by touching the perceptions of his or her people at all levels.

To what degree does your hospital have a culture of pride in and between departments, an environment, which operates through an integrated high performance management system? Is your culture an environment of empowerment? An empowering climate means high bottom-line performance, profit, and increased chances for survival during economic setbacks.

Like a body fever, hospital organizations develop symptoms that all is not well and that a different diagnosis is needed. Senior management needs to know within the hospital's culture what must be addressed and where are the problems needing immediate attention before considerations of treatment and intervention. The effective leader does not have the operating philosophy of ready–fire–aim in trying to turn around a corporate culture. Answers to questions, based on research data, must be available before formulating a business plan of internal change. A sound business plan starts with knowledge of the existing culture and its images. The climate must be understood before a change strategy is implemented. Basic issues and values must be traced through all hospital levels for consistency among all levels, otherwise inconsistency will result.

TAKING CHARGE

Congratulations are again in order; be proud of your career rise to the top. A commencement is just that—a commencement, a beginning. But how to begin? What issues should you address? How do you really find out what is happening and not happening around here? Where and what are the skeletons that you need to know about? What tender land mines rest under the various surfaces here? What do you need to know about marketing against your competitors? Where and what are your marketing opportunities?

Action Recommendation 1: Start in the basement and invest time talking with the hourly personnel; they know what is going on.

Action Recommendation 2: Start with the night and P.M. shift personnel—both hourly and nonsupervisory personnel. They can give you valuable insights.

Action Recommendation 3: Start with private conversations with your vice president of human resources and director of marketing; both need your listening ear and confidence.

Action Recommendation 4: While time consuming, visit 5 to 10 percent of the patients on all units. Every week of your executive life make a point to visit with patients in their rooms to the tune of 1 to 2 percent of the census. They know and see what is and is not going on.

Action Recommendation 5: For the first 100 to 200 weeks, invest time with the physicians in their lounge, not in your office. Listen and make notes, do not argue.

Action Recommendation 6: Have "fireside chats" with groups of 9 to 15 patient care coordinators or unit manager nurses across all shifts. Be sensitive to their most hectic and hassled times.

Action Recommendation 7: Meet with 2 to 3 board of trustee members at a time, but be sure all know that you will meet with all of them; no one will be missed or avoided.

Action Recommendation 8: Schedule private meetings with each director or vice president that reports to you. Ask questions, questions, questions and more questions and listen.

Action Recommendation 9: Do not change anything in the first eight weeks.

Data, discussion and diagnosis must precede organizational intervention. Before you can be an empowering leader and empower others—resulting in an empowered healthcare system—you must be an expert in asking questions. Listen to not only what your staff members are saying through their vested interests and perceptions, but also listen to what they are not saying. This is called listening with the third ear. Are they avoiding certain topics and situations? Where do you find contradictions of information? Never listen to just one side; listen to both sides and perceptions of problems. But, what should you ask?

Questions To Be Answered

1. In the eyes of your patients and doctors, what is the hospital doing or providing with effectiveness and what should it do and provide more of to assure the continuity of the business relationships?

2. In the eyes of your doctors and patients, what is not being done, which can provide an intervention edge for your competitors with the loss of your present level of revenue?

3. By all doctors served, what are two new ways the hospital can become more of a partner in *their* business for their profits, progress, and practices?

4. What are 15 different industries or corporations, which could use our services, but have not approached the hospital for its existing or modifiable products? Where can the hospital diversify the marketplace and consumer base?

5. As a potential worldwide-thinking corporation, what business markets could be explored (considering global expansion and penetration)? Where and how is the board limiting growth by thinking only regionally?

6. Where is the hospital spreading itself too thin by trying to be everything to everyone; what are eight earmarks of excellence on which to concentrate, concentrate, concentrate, and concentrate?

7. Where should 5 to 10 percent of the present service and products be amputated if they will become "lost leaders?" What can take their place in our product and service mix for significant increase in return on investment?

8. Focusing on the next 1,000 days, what are three things to stop doing because of ineffectiveness? What three things have become ritualized but are not getting or providing the needed effects? Where is the hospital its own worst enemy?

9. In the next 1,000 to 2,000 days, who will be the *new* competitors?

10. What are six structural barriers to efficient internal systems of business transactions?

11. What are five structural roadblocks within the corporation that are generating costs and unnecessary delays in making decisions and delivering outputs?

12. What are four operational headaches, which are constantly reoccurring, that are reducing productivity, managerial enthusiasm, and innovations?

13. What are three logistical slowdown points or points of ineffectiveness, which prevent quick turnaround time for internal inquiries and suggestions and the handling of employee and patient complaints?

14. What are final action decisions members of middle management want to make without pushing the decision higher in the organization?

15. By each senior executive and by each middle manager, where is their span of control too broad for rapid decision making?

16. In your corporate culture can you utilize an organizational psychologist to identify sources of managerial distrust, barriers to managerial collaboration, and weak group dynamics, which are retarding or restricting team trust relationships?

17. In your corporate culture, where are your employees lacking in common vision and cohesiveness to goals? (Where do they lack understanding or commitment to common visions of the corporate direction and future?)

18. In your corporate culture, where do your employees and managers perceive they are underutilized and misutilized?

19. In your corporate culture by each level in the organization, where do you overutilize participative managing (Theory Y) and where do you overutilize supervisory suppression (Theory X)?

20. In the next 100 days where do your managers and executives need focused and systematic improvement of their managing skills, knowledge, and abilities for the enriched development of their competencies?

21. What are five decisions per senior executive who reports directly to you that each will have to make without coming to you? Where do you want each of your reporting executives to stand "naked" in their own decision-making excellence?

22. Where are you spinning your own paperwork spiderwebs (with too many written communications that are too long)? Where can you amputate 30 percent of meetings held each month at all levels in the organization?

23. In your corporate culture, how can you utilize an organizational psychologist to identify employee unrest, job dissatisfaction, and employee frustrations?

24. By each department or working unit, where are you running too thin and lean wherein if you added talent there would be a significant

jump in results? Where do we have an excess of staff persons for action accountability?

25. Where are supervisors, managers, and executives not getting timely and accurate financial and coordination information to serve their accountabilities?

26. What are the areas in which you must risk to invest in new technology and different human talent to increase your competitive edge?

27. What changes can you make to guarantee the open and unimpeded flow of ideas and innovations? How can you provide free channels of ideas and opportunities?

MAKING EVERY DAY COUNT

You count, your family counts, your health counts, and your time on and off the job counts. Keep the whole you in balance and proper perspective. Executive tenure can be tenuous, marriages can become marred, retreat from your religious faith can occur and your mental well-being can suffer under stress. Keeping heart, stomach, head and all of the external emotional support systems together are the personal challenges of being a senior executive. Remember: You are your choices and your choices are you. Success is how you define it to be for you. TIME stands for **Time Is Managing Effectiveness**—your effectiveness. The ways you invest your time and your life will tell you and others where you place value and worth. Kindly accept my best best wishes!

10

Self-Assessment: How To Put This Skill into Your Personal and Professional Development Plan

J. Daniel Ford, Executive Vice President/Senior Partner,
Kieffer, Ford & Associates, Ltd., 2015 Spring Road, Oak Brook, IL 60521

Michael C. Kieffer, *President/Senior Partner, Kieffer, Ford & Associates,*
Ltd., 2015 Spring Road, Oak Brook, IL 60521

How do you begin to know yourself? Executive search consultants know that when they analyze a candidate in a personal interview, they are holding a mirror (figuratively) in front of the candidate. Search consultants facilitate a conversation that the candidate is having with himself or herself. An experienced consultant, who understands and has a strong interest in people, can do a good job of facilitating a candidate's self-assessment during the interview. One important key is to probe for an individual's understanding of his or her personal and professional life, because they are intertwined. An individual who understands this and who has ongoing self-assessment practices is generally a secure, happy, and fulfilled person. Such a person does not have a cocky or arrogant manner, but in a self-assured manner enables others to also believe in him or her.

THE IMPORTANCE OF SELF-ASSESSMENT

Every individual should pursue his or her own life's activities as though pursuing becoming the successful match for a client organization. You should know yourself in order to become comfortable with the matches that take place every day in your personal as well as the professional arena. Obviously, the process encompasses goal setting for the road map of life, including both short-term and long-term plans. Goals must be reviewed periodically and are subject to change from within and without. Beware, unless you assess your life position and direction periodically, others' actions may direct your path, and you may have little control of your own destiny. If you do not understand where you are in your own life, you increase the odds that many of the variables that play a part in your working and personal environment will determine where you are going. If you allow this to happen, you certainly deserve whatever your environment has in store for you.

The first words in Scott Peck's book, *The Road Less Traveled*, are significant here: "Life is difficult. This is a great truth, one of the greatest truths."[1] Until you recognize and accept how it fits into your own life, you always may have a negative view on where you are going. According to Peck, life is a series of matches—an individual always follows a map of a series of tensions and adjustments. This map is based on one's outlook on life and experiences, and its corrections are determined by an objective self-assessment. This determines your life direction. If you do not know where you are in your own life, you are subject primarily to the influences of your environment.

When a professional and experienced search consultant conducts an assignment with an organization, the goal is to facilitate a positive match between that organization and the candidate of choice. An experienced consultant is adept at analyzing an organization and its needs and responding with sound consultation and qualified candidates. After the organizational and position assessment, the consultant assertively pursues in the marketplace candidates who appear to match the client's needs from an experience, career, skill, values, and personality standpoint. Eventually, the consultant interviews and recommends qualified candidates to the client.

To facilitate this process, it is important for individuals to maintain an ongoing assessment of their own experience, career, values, skills, personality, and goals, among others. This is important for an individual who may be working with a search consultant as a candidate on a specific search, but is even more important for lifelong personal and professional growth. Self-assessment as well as some techniques of self-assessment are important concepts in this chapter. The discussion is pragmatic and advisory rather than theoretical.

Much of the work of search consultants is based on intuition and they care about the people with whom they interact, both after as well as during the search. They want an individual who is placed in a new position to continue to grow and develop. The individuals interviewed, those presented, and those not should benefit by their interaction with a firm's consultants. The interaction should cause individual candidates to look seriously at themselves during and after the search process. The primary goal is to motivate and encourage self-assessment.

YOUR PERSONAL BOARD OF DIRECTORS

One way to begin self-assessment is to identify a personal board of directors. This technique is introspective. Draft a list of those who have influenced your life and particularly your values. Everyone can identify the individuals on the board of directors in his or her own life. These are individuals from your personal and professional life from the past or present who influence you. These also may be individuals whose behavior you do not necessarily condone or like. The board could include your role models, mentors, heros, family, friends, and peers, among others. A most interesting thought is who would chair this board of directors?

These individuals are important to your personal assessment process. Review what their impact was on you and your values, profession, taste in music, life-style, or whatever. It virtually is impossible to examine your life without considering the input of others. These individuals comprise your network and your network changes throughout your life.

Board Members

In his thought provoking book, *You and Your Network*, Fred Smith discusses the idea of a personal board of directors and suggests some types of individuals who have helped people get the most out of life. "Quality education does not have to take place in schools, nor does it have to have a degree to be valid."[2] Some of the most thoroughly educated people have attended no institution of higher learning nor received a degree—but they have drawn from others, learned for themselves, and earned a genuine education. Successful, secure people know they have not been self-educated, they have been mentored, either in person or by reading and associating with those of superior mind, greater skills, and mature spirits. "Our best mentors are those with whom we share a common philosophy in life, knowing that what we do is an expression of our philosophy."[3] Smith also suggests that your mentors need to be respected individuals who believe in your potential. Smith makes some observations for being mentored:

- Ask your mentor to help you ask the right questions, search in the right places, and stay interested in the right answers.
- Decide what degree of excellence or perfection you want.
- Accept a subordinate learning position.

- Respect the mentor, but never idealize him or her.
- Put into effect immediately what you are learning.
- Set a discipline for relating to the mentor.
- Reward your mentor with progress and appreciation.
- Learn to ask crucial questions.
- Never threaten to give up.[4]

Smith suggests that you inform your mentors that you are a persistent person, a determined winner, and that in mentoring you, he or she is helping to build a unique individual, not imitator. There will come a time for a change in mentors, and both you and your mentor must recognize that time. A periodic identification of and communication with a mentor is an important part of the assessment process.

Another group of individuals who are important and should be part of your self-assessment are heros or those individuals that are looked up to. According to Smith

> Heroes are who we can become if we diligently pursue our ideals in the furnace of our opportunities. Heroes are those who have changed history for the better. Heroes are the personification of our ideals and our highest values. Those who have no heroes have not yet identified their highest ideals. Greatness demands an appreciation of greatness shown in others. As a person changes his heroes, so he changes the direction of his life.[5]

Heros are real, dedicated, they concentrate, and make sacrifices. Heros are committed individuals, epitomized by apostle Paul's words: "But one thing I do: Forgetting what is behind and straining toward what is ahead."[6] Many times they are remembered not for what they had, but for what they gave.

Other individuals to identify are role models whom you emulate, as you idealize heroes. With models you may personify their desirable character traits, functions, and techniques. These may be individuals who are famous or everyday people who motivate you.

Next, identify your significant peers. All of your life you encounter peer pressure and it has some, if not considerable, influence on you. Peers exist in our profession, neighborhood, organization, church, social and political settings, and in other areas and relationships. Think back to college or graduate school, your colleagues and professors then, and reflect on your emotions as they relate to changes in your life and the lives of these individuals over the years. This influence is subtle, but can affect the way you see and live your life.

There are individuals that you may identify as enemies whose behavior you do not accept or condone. In order to better understand yourself, you must understand who your enemies are and why you feel the way you do about them. You need to understand that competition and involvement in causes can create enemies. The fact that you are different from others causes enemies. Your occasional self-centeredness can produce enemies and your aggressive behavior can cause people to be harmful to you.

Two very important, not to be omitted, groups are your friends and family members. You may assume the importance of these groups, but assumptions may dilute their role. Consider the intimacies of friendship: the ability and the moral obligation that friends have to confront. They can produce jealousies, reliances, commitments, constraints; and they have a part in the sharing of successes and failures, and mutual irritations. Friends share confidence keeping, common characteristics, and time. There is dignity in true friendship, not hypocrisy or masks. Be aware of the total reservoir of friends with whom you have relationships.

Along with a higher spiritual being, your family is the ultimate measure of relationships and is one of the more critical elements of your self-assessment process. The support function and relationships among family members is a constant challenge and motivation, and one that we can never take for granted. Peck suggests that love is an action, an activity, that must be worked on constantly and involves considerable freedom and free exercise of choice: "Two people love each other only when they are quite capable of living without each other, but choose to live with each other."[7] That assertion by Peck is a challenging suggestion for the emphasis of developing self-esteem. A mature individual can use it to become a leader as well as a partner in a healthy marital relationship.

Successful executives experience and enjoy successful personal lives and relationships. Unsuccessful personal relationships and unhappy marriages present major barriers for successful leaders.

YOUR RECORD OF PERSONAL GROWTH

A key to ongoing self-assessment is keeping a journal. Buy a blank book and record your personal board of directors, and thoughts, feelings, quotes, and anything else that may be important to you. In addition to a Bible or other religious book, it may become the most important book of your life. Keeping a journal can be an awkward and cumbersome activity initially. It may be threatening to many individuals, particularly males. You may recollect that during childhood diaries generally were kept by young girls. However as you grew and matured, you realized that feelings are extremely important. Whether or not you share those feelings with other individuals, they are a major factor in determining who you are and what you become. Perhaps males should have started diaries or journals earlier. Individuals of all ages should consider using journals to record their important feelings, key lines or thoughts from speeches, inspirations from sermons, goals, objectives, strengths, weaknesses, or whatever is important to the writer. All too often a fleeting thought is forgotten. Writing down thoughts reinforces them, as well as facilitates the growth of additional ideas. Many individuals carry journals with them constantly. It is a way of capturing and retaining important ideas for future use, thereby helping you become all you can become.

An interesting sideline to journal keeping, and a long-term benefit, is its value to future generations, especially one's children. Most people have pictures, letters, video cassettes and perhaps other memories of their family and friends. However, one of the most important memories of family members may be the personal thoughts recorded in a journal, but not shared while alive. The journal may be used to record many of the same kind of things that you may discuss in a personal interview. This includes significant professional and personal experiences, strengths, weaknesses, accomplishments, management and work styles, people of significant influence, values, goals, personal interests and hobbies, religious beliefs, and health issues.

A journal can help you look at all areas of your life, including mental, physical, spiritual, and business. Remember, you need and deserve private time in order to record these genuine and sincere thoughts. Take it. Whether it be early morning, late at night, during an airline flight, while taking yourself out to lunch, it is too important to let other things take priority. Whatever you do, do not have guilty feelings because you are taking a few minutes for yourself.

The amount of time you spend on writing in your journal or other self-analysis is unimportant. It is the quality of time that counts. Spencer Johnson, author of *One Minute for Myself*, suggests deliberately taking a minute periodically every day to reflect: "What I am thinking. What I am doing. . . . How can I take good care of myself?"[8]

The opportunities are everywhere. If you are recording your thoughts in a journal when listening to a speech it many times provokes another idea from a related subject. You do not have to be regimented. It is not necessary to be on a regular schedule. It is entirely at your will and whim.

LEADERSHIP TRAITS AND SELF-ESTEEM

Seasoned consultants have learned that strong leaders have a good basic understanding of who they are as human beings as well as what natural and learned leadership skills they possess. Peck suggests, "We are incapable of loving another unless we love ourselves, just as we are incapable of teaching our children self-discipline unless we ourselves are self-disciplined."[9] The Bible suggests this also.

Leadership Traits

Napoleon Hill suggested a number of leadership characteristics in his influential book, *Think and Grow Rich*. By the way, these can serve as good journal entries when you are reviewing and updating your own leadership goals.

1. *Unwavering courage.* Such courage is based upon knowledge of self, and of one's occupation. No follower wishes to be dominated by a leader who lacks self-confidence and courage. No intelligent follower will be dominated by such a leader for long.
2. *Self-control.* People who cannot control themselves can never control others. Self-control sets a mighty example for one's followers, which the more intelligent will emulate.
3. *A keen sense of justice.* Without a sense of fairness and justice, no leader can command and retain the respect of his or her followers.
4. *Definiteness of decision.* People who waver in their decisions show that they are not sure of themselves and cannot lead others successfully.
5. *Definiteness of plans.* The successful leader must plan his or her work, and work his or her plan. A leader who moves by guesswork, without practical, definite plans, is comparable to a ship without a rudder. Sooner or later he or she will land on the rocks.
6. *The habit of doing more than paid for.* One of the penalties of leadership is the necessity of willingness, upon the part of the leader, to do more than he or she requires of his followers.
7. *A pleasing personality.* No slovenly, careless person can become a successful leader. Leadership calls for respect. Followers will not respect a leader who does not grade high on all of the factors of a pleasing appearance and personality.
8. *Sympathy and understanding.* The successful leader must be able to sympathize with his or her followers as well as understand them and their problems.

9. *Mastery of detail.* Successful leadership calls for mastery of the details of the leader's position.

10. *Willingness to assume full responsibility.* The successful leader must be willing to assume responsibility for the mistakes and the shortcomings of his or her followers. If he tries to shift this responsibility, he will not remain the leader. If a follower makes a mistake, and appears incompetent, the leader must consider that it is he or she who failed.

11. *Cooperation.* The successful leader must understand and apply the principle of cooperative effort and be able to induce followers to do the same. Leadership calls for power, and power calls for cooperation.*

There are many other traits that can be added, such as political savvy, and an understanding of regulatory legislative and environment issues, but Hill's observations have stood the test of time. A sure way to know if you have these characteristics is to maintain a constant assessment of your personality traits, abilities, and skills.

Self-Esteem

A person's self-esteem is a key part of this life-long process. It shows up as a common thread of Hill's leadership characteristics, and is a basis for and goal of continuous self-improvement. A person who feels good about himself or herself will develop good relationships with others, thereby increasing the chances of leadership successes, regardless of the criteria used. Conversely, people who do not feel good about themselves do not generally develop good relationships with others, tend to use negative energy, and greatly diminish their chances of success in leadership.

If you possess self-esteem you constantly will strive to grow and develop. It you are secure and like yourself, you will be able to assess yourself objectively in an ongoing manner: learning, sharpening, and crafting your leadership skills and abilities. Many key leaders in the health care industry, who are both the visible ones and those who do not seek the limelight, indicate by their actions that they feel good about who they are, how they got to where they are, and how they came to know themselves.

---

*From *Think & Grow Rich* by Napoleon Hill. New and Revised Edition, Copyright © 1967, 1966, 1960, 1937 by the Napoleon Hill Foundation. A Hawthorn Book. Adapted by permission of E.P. Dutton, a division of NAL Penguin Inc.

PROFESSIONAL PROCEDURES

Interviews

Personal interviews are extremely important in the self-assessment process as well as when others assess you. The discipline in and motivation for the interview are as important as the actual interview. You should never waste someone's time just to get interview practice, but you should be able to take advantage of every legitimate opportunity.

When an interview is being conducted, the search consultant is not only looking for answers to specific questions and the potential match with a client organization, but how an individual handles himself or herself in that process. Frankly, an individual can interview himself at any time he or she chooses. Traffic lights and ball games are fine, but quiet, private and free time are optimum. As mentioned at the beginning of the chapter, a formal interview is a setting in which the consultant (figuratively) is holding a mirror in front of the candidate and facilitating a conversation.

To prepare for an interview review yourself and think through all the factors involved in your particular situation—talk to yourself. Then convert your conversation to writing in your journal for a most important and long-lasting benefit. Interview yourself on subject areas important to your own growth and include the classic questions on strengths, weaknesses, accomplishments, values, temperament, management and work styles, goals, personal and professional career interests, health, family, and hobbies. Among Hill's observations, the following should be answered in a personal inventory:

1. Have I attained the objective I established for this year? (You should work with a definite yearly objective to be attained as a part of your major life goals.)
2. Have I delivered the best possible service, or could I have improved any part of this service?
3. Has the spirit of my conduct been harmonious and cooperative at all times?
4. Have I permitted the habit of procrastination to decrease my efficiency, and if so, to what extent?
5. Have I improved my personality, and if so, in what ways?
6. Have I been persistent in following my plans through to completion?
7. Have I reached decisions promptly and definitely on all occasions?
8. Have I been either overcautious, or undercautious?

9. Has my conduct toward my associates been such that it has induced them to respect me?
10. Have my opinions and decisions been based on guesswork, or accuracy of analysis and thought?
11. Have I followed the habit of budgeting my time, my expenses, and my income, and have I been conservative in these budgets?
12. How much time have I devoted to unprofitable efforts, which I might have used to better advantage?
13. Have I been guilty of any conduct, which was not approved of by my conscience?
14. Have I been unfair to anyone, and if so, in what way?
15. If I had been the purchaser of my own services for the year, would I be satisfied with my purchase?
16. Has the purchaser of my services been satisfied with the service I have rendered, and if not, why not?
17. Am I in the right vocation, and if not, why not?*

Using a journal lends itself very nicely to the idea of a periodic self-interview. You should establish a schedule for conducting such a review. It also is good practice for someone who may be interviewing for a new position. Since you never really know when that might be, it is best to be prepared and anticipate the potential interview questions.

It is important to have periodic professional interviews with someone other than yourself to help develop your comfort level. It is awkward, sometimes embarrassing, and revealing to interview an individual who has little ability to describe his or her own strengths or weaknesses. You can have practice interviews with the assistance of a family member or friend.

Professional Testing

The American College of Health Care Executives (ACHE) developed a formal system for professional self-development in 1982. The self-assessment program helps health care executives focus on a broad range of areas. Eighteen management functional areas are studied and profiled:

---

*From *Think & Grow Rich* by Napoleon Hill. New and Revised Edition, Copyright © 1967, 1966, 1960, 1937 by the Napoleon Hill Foundation. A Hawthorn Book. Adapted by permission of E.P. Dutton, a division of NAL Penguin Inc.

1. board, medical staff, and administrative accountability relations
2. comprehensive systems of services
3. education
4. financial management
5. government relations and regulations
6. human resources management
7. interorganizational relations
8. law and ethics
9. long-range planning
10. marketing
11. plant and facility management
12. preservation of assets
13. professional relations
14. public and community relations
15. quality assessment and assurance
16. research
17. strategy, planning and policy
18. systems management

ACHE workshops are conducted across the country and are designed to help the health care professional determine professional areas of strength and weakness and develop a plan for change. The profiles are developed by comparing health care executives and opinions and judgments of experts in the field. Participants receive feedback on their status as decision makers and problem solvers. The workshops, a major effort on the part of ACHE, help individuals who may not or would not do this on their own and through this structured process, contribute to their professional growth.[10]

Outplacement Counseling

Another technique that fosters self-assessment is outplacement counseling. This consulting service generally is provided an individual as a result of termination by an organization. The objective is to help the person recover from any resulting trauma; and to assess and measure his or her work experience, personality characteristics, skills, aptitudes, and strengths and weaknesses.

This process helps to guide a terminated individual toward an understanding of positions that fit his or her qualifications, and advises on locating and obtaining a new position. This consultation assessment fostered by ethical professionals is invaluable and provides pragmatic advice at a time when an individual may be at an emotional low. In-depth interviewing and testing, simulated job interviews, candid advice, and an assessment of the personal and professional aspects of the person's life serve to redirect his or her pursuits. Most people do not volunteer for termination, but should a termination occur the benefits of outplacement counseling far outweigh the perceived negatives and are a key technique for self-assessment at this juncture of life.[11]

Some search consultants view potential candidates who are working with an outplacement firm in a negative manner. This is unfair. Many times a firm has to work hard to present and sell candidates who may be unemployed. The firm has to overcome occasional negative client perspectives, but this has no relationship to outplacement assistance. A mature and discerning consultant will review the credentials and experience of these individuals just like those of employed candidates, and make arbitrary and constructive judgment calls and decisions about these individuals as part of a greater universe or pool of candidates.

It is important to consider the whole subject of career direction. The considerable changes in the health care industry, downsizing and restructuring, and the seeming oversupply of health care executives are causing many health care professionals to reassess their careers and the direction of their lives. Many individuals will vow to continue (and should) with a health care career. Others may choose to pursue other occupations. Self-assessment at this stage is critical, but do not let the emotions of the moment (e.g., a termination) overrule your judgment. Each should know his or her own personal desires, ability to manage stress, and comfort level. With the frenetic pace and change of the health care industry, many may in fact be happier in other industries and occupations. It may be a tough and revealing assessment that causes such a change, but may contribute to greater happiness over the long run. The health care industry needs people who are happy in their chosen profession and are not deterred by the barriers that appear. Be advised that even though the time between employed positions is a golden opportunity for self-assessment, interviews, resume writing and updating, and journal writing, you will do better if your assessment has been an ongoing process, not forgotten when you are at a peak or valley. There also are other professional testing organizations and agencies (some in academic environments) that administer various psychological and other tests and provide career guidance and direction that may be useful.

Resumes

Resume writing and updating is a critical periodic discipline and self-measurement that is a key part of the self-assessment process. A review of your various positions, organizations, responsibilities, and accomplishments; your academic and professional credentials; your various civic, church, community and professional involvements; and some personal and family information will help you as much, if not more, than a search consultant or prospective employer. If you work on it seriously and contemplatively, it will facilitate the growth process.

MANAGEMENT OF STRESS

One of the most significant areas to assess is your own health and ability to manage stress. You should know your own physical condition and have periodic checkups. You know what you need to do to change. A physician's advice and counsel on stress management can be helpful, but however you tackle it, stress is one of the most significant areas to monitor.

Each of us encounters many perils in our daily activities. The challenges of this changing industry are significant. The pace is frenetic. The competition is brutal. The tension is high. Management faces boards, medical staffs, employees, communities, and other publics and constituencies and regulations that are demanding and unforgiving. How do you manage the tension? To succeed, to lead, to survive, and sometimes to even live you have to know yourself. You have to understand who you are. The management of stress is critical.

Dr. Robert Eliot and Dennis Breo suggest in their book, *Is It Worth Dying For?*, that: "Stress may be the greatest single contribution to illness in the industrialized world; controlling unnecessary stress may therefore be the single most important key to preventing heart attacks."[12] Some early warning signs include:

Emotional signs

- Apathy—the "blahs," feelings of sadness, recreation that is no longer pleasurable.
- Anxiety—feelings of restlessness, agitation, insecurity, sense of worthlessness.
- Irritability—feeling hypersensitive, defensive, arrogant or argumentative, rebellious or angry.
- Mental fatigue—feeling preoccupied, having difficulty concentrating, trouble in thinking flexibly.
- Overcompensation or denial—grandiosity (exaggerating the importance of your activities to yourself and others), working too hard,

denying that you have problems, ignoring symptoms, feeling suspicious.

Behavioral signs

- Avoiding things—keeping to yourself, avoiding work, having trouble accepting responsibility, neglecting responsibility.
- Doing things to extremes—alcoholism, gambling, spending sprees, sexual promiscuity.
- Administrative problems—being late for work, poor appearance, poor personal hygiene, being accident prone.
- Legal problems—indebtedness, shoplifting, traffic tickets, inability to control violent impulses.

Physical signs

- Excessive worrying about, or denial of, illness.
- Frequent illness.
- Physical exhaustion.
- Reliance on self-medication, including over-use of drugstore remedies like aspirin.
- Ailments—headache, insomnia, appetite changes, weight gain or loss, indigestion, nausea, nervous diarrhea, constipation, and sexual problems.*

CONCLUSION

Self-assessment is a lifetime process. It cannot be a one-time, short-lived understanding and introspective look at yourself. After all, you are always changing in your relationships, positions, and surroundings. Therefore, you have to assume that you are not the same person you were ten years ago. Self-assessment is an ongoing journey—one that must be consistent, confrontative, and challenging. The fruits that are harvested are worth the time and struggle. As you think, you become. Enjoy this journey of self-assessment. Take the time; it is worth every minute. It is never too late to

---

*From *Is It Worth Dying For?* by Robert S. Elliot and Dennis L. Breo. Copyright © 1984 by Robert S. Eliot, M.D., and Dennis L. Breo. Adapted by permission of Bantam Books. All rights reserved.

start. There are no excuses for not engaging in the exercise of self-assessment.

NOTES

1. M. Scott Peck, *The Road Less Traveled* (New York, Simon & Schuster, Inc., 1978), 15.

2. Fred Smith, *You and Your Network* (Waco, Word Book, 1984), 94.

3. Ibid, 95.

4. Ibid.

5. Ibid, 68–69.

6. *Holy Bible New International Version* (Grand Rapids, Zondervan Bible Publishers, 1983), 1078.

7. Peck, *The Road Less Traveled*, 98.

8. Spencer Johnson, *One Minute For Myself*, (New York, Avon Books, 1985), 56.

9. Peck, *The Road Less Traveled*, 82–83.

10. American College of Healthcare Executives, *Health Executive Professional Assessment—Ambulatory Care (Medical Group Management) Professional Assessment—An Assessment and Development Workshop*, Brochure, (Chicago, 1988).

11. Career Decisions, Inc., *Outplacement Counseling—The Proven Method for Reducing the Trauma and Costs of Terminating Managerial Personnel*, Brochure, (Itasca, Illinois, 1988).

12. Robert Elliot and Dennis Breo, *Is It Worth Dying For?*, (New York, Bantam Books, 1984), 14–15.

11

Resumes: How To Write Them and How To Evaluate Them

Earl A. Simendinger, PhD, *Professor and Chairman, Department of Health Education and Health Sciences, Central Michigan University, Mt. Pleasant, MI 48859*

Terence F. Moore, *President, Mid-Michigan Health Care Systems, Inc., 4005 Orchard Drive, Midland, MI 48640*

INTRODUCTION

Perhaps no single document holds greater value to its author than his or her resume. It is this two- or three-page document which creatively describes the professional life of the individual. Every significant professional step taken and every important contribution made is captured in this document. It is not unusual for the resume writer to spend several hours per page on its final design. Moreover, many professionals revisit the document time after time during the year to ensure that it is current and accurate.

These same professionals spend hours trying to develop ways to separate their curriculum vitae from the hundreds of others with whom they will be compared. For example, individuals have used different sizes and colors of paper and styles of type; typed on parchment; folded the resume in half (vertically for the first page); combined multiple colors of type on one sheet; and used multiple letter styles on a single sheet.

This chapter will provide a framework for constructing a resume that you can be proud of sending, will present a strong professional image, and will set yours apart from possibly hundreds of others.

Do not forget that, in the majority of cases, a resume may only produce a telephone call, not necessarily an invitation to come in for an interview. Also, recognize that there is no one way to do a resume. Clearly, there are factors that either advance or detract from the image you want to project. The authors will suggest some of those most often found in resumes, which they have seen during the past 20 years and learned from several top search consultants.

It is important to note that there is no one answer and there is no absolutely right way or wrong way to do a resume, but there are ways to elevate its image and to increase the probability that your resume will survive the cut for further review.

THE COVER LETTER

Put as much thought into a cover letter as you put into your resume. In some respects, the cover letter actually may be more important than your resume. Remember, it is the cover letter that must spark the interest of the reader to want to flip the page and proceed to the resume. There are cases where much work has been expended on an individual's resume only to have it bypassed because of a poor cover letter.

Larry Tyler discusses cover letters in his article entitled, "Tips on Preparing Cover Letters."[1] His article recommends three paragraphs to the letter. He explains that the first paragraph should discuss the specific position for which the resume is being sent. (The authors of this chapter recommend that the specific newspaper in which the ad appeared be referred to in some way in the first paragraph.) The letter must quickly identify the position the writer is seeking, to eliminate any possible confusion and, perhaps, loss in the pile of other applications. Remember, your letter and resume will not only compete against perhaps hundreds of others submitted by well-qualified candidates for the position but, depending on whether the letter is sent to the personnel manager or the chief executive officer (CEO), could very well compete for proper handling with resumes for other job openings in the institution.

Tyler suggests that the second paragraph discuss your background and experience and demonstrate how you fit the specifications of the position described in the ad. It is this second paragraph to which considerable thought should be devoted. How you explain the quality of fit between your skills and the needs of the position could be all it takes to get you into the next pile. This paragraph also should help spark the reader's interest so that he or she will continue to read the cover letter, and generate enough interest to complete the reading.

Tyler further explains that, if applicable, this same paragraph should show how you have completed similar assignments. This demonstrates that you have direct experience related to the job needs. Tyler emphasizes, that if there are any statistics that demonstrate objective results such as increased admissions 25 percent or reduced expenses 25 percent, these quantifiable data are important, persuasive and should be included.

The third paragraph, according to Tyler, should convey the salary range you are seeking as well as geographic preferences. Also identified in his article is an important point that is often left out of cover letters—your phone number and, just as importantly, the times you most likely can be reached.

The authors suggest a short fourth paragraph of a personal nature, which conveys why you are interested in the geographic location of the hospital along with some brief personal information about yourself.

Based on the authors' experience as practicing CEOs, as well as their discussions with many of the contributors of this book, the following additional thoughts are provided to help you separate your cover letter from your competitors'.

- The cover letter should be on stationery that matches the paper on which the resume is printed or typed.
- It is also impressive to have personalized stationery, again using the same type of paper for both resume and cover letter, as opposed to using hospital stationery.
- Remember that the purpose of the letter is only to entice the reader to go further, to review the attached resume, and make a telephone call. The purpose is not to get the job. Too often, the cover letter and resume miss the mark by trying too hard to get the job versus receiving a telephone call or a request for further information.
- Although form letters may be a rapid way to help determine jobs that may be available in a large area, the customized letter focused on a particular position for a specific hospital will receive a greater response.
- It is important to obtain feedback to your letter. Have several people review the letter and make suggestions to you. Remember, this is the first impression the prospective employer will have of you. The well-organized, neat letter that sets you apart from others can only increase the probability that your resume will be read.
- Some job seekers have increased the presentability of their letters and resumes by using the same type style on both cover letter and resume.
- Preprinted resumes may convey the wrong message. No employer wants to feel that she or he is part of a blitz campaign.
- The cover letter should be no more than one page and should not be too cramped on that page. The two- or three-page cover letter will tire the reader and could easily prevent him or her from proceeding to your resume, which is the primary focus of the contact.

Exhibit 11-1 contains a typical advertisement for an administrative position. Exhibit 11-2 is a sample cover letter, which demonstrates some of the items discussed in the preceding paragraphs.

THE RESUME

Many authors of resumes use the document not only to land the call, but to get the job. It cannot be overemphasized—the only purpose of the resume is to stimulate the interest of the personnel manager or other reader who may forward it to the administrator. Your resume needs to hold a level of interest high enough to have someone call you. If the level of interest is only high enough to separate your resume out for further review as compared to others, it will have accomplished the first part of the job. Of course, the second part is to further stimulate the reader's interest to conduct a telephone interview or, better yet, to invite you to come to the organization for an interview. It is important to keep in mind that, just as in advertising, if too much information is squeezed into a single document, the effectiveness is lost. Overcrowding creates the wrong impression and could very well prevent a perfect match from occurring.

Exhibit 11-1 Example of a Typical Ad

EXECUTIVE VICE PRESIDENT/CHIEF OPERATING OFFICER

Progressive, full service community hospital in northern New York State has an immediate opening for an Executive Vice President/Chief Operating Officer.

The hospital is a 426-bed complex, with 222 acute care beds, 204 long-term care beds, and a wide range of outpatient programs and services. It is located in an area of great natural beauty, just a short drive away from the 1,000 Islands, Canada, and the Adirondack Mountains.

The successful candidate must possess a master's degree in hospital administration or related discipline, and seven to ten years of progressively responsible administrative and supervisory experience in hospitalwide medical, clinical, and support functions.

Please send resume and salary history, in confidence, to:

CHIEF EXECUTIVE OFFICER
Box 1733, Modern Healthcare
740 Rush St., Chicago, IL 60611-2590

Exhibit 11-2 Example of a Cover Letter

November 4, 1988

Chief Executive Officer
Box 1733, Modern Healthcare
740 Rush Street
Chicago, IL 60611-2590

Dear Sir or Madam:

This letter is a confidential inquiry to your ad in Modern Health Care Magazine of March 25, 1988, for an Executive Vice President/Chief Operating Officer in northern New York State.

As my attached resume explains, I have significant experience in hospitals of similar size including the operation of a 65-bed, long-term care division, the implementation and management of 14 outpatient programs, administrative responsibility for a 100,000-visit per year clinic and finally the management of support departments. My salary is currently $65,000 per year not including benefits. The salary range I am seeking is $70-$80,000 per year with competitive benefits.

My wife's family, and my own, live in upper New York State and we would like to return from Ohio to our home state.

At this preliminary point, I would appreciate this inquiry being kept strictly confidential until there is a mutual feeling of a potential fit. It also would be appreciated that references not be directly or indirectly contacted until we reach an appropriate point in the process. At that time, I will be happy to provide a full and complete list of direct supervisors, board members, physicians, and subordinates I have worked with over my 10-year career.

In the meantime, if you would like to get in touch with me, I may be reached in my office (216) 555-6969 (direct line) between 8:00 A.M. and 5:00 P.M. or my home number (216) 555-3214 after 7:00 P.M., Central Standard Time.

Thank you for your time and consideration.

Sincerely,

William B. Bills
Senior Vice President
Ivory Hospital

Attachment

The Resume Is You

No single document is perhaps more important or more representative of the individual writer than his or her resume. It therefore is important that the document reflect the individual as he or she really is. The authors of this chapter have read hundreds of resumes during the course of their careers. Evaluations and predictions about the writers of the resumes were quite accurate, although the judgments were based solely on the manner in which the resume was put together. Some of these predictions included being on time, presentable dress, level of organization, ability to carry on a conversation, and skill level in answering interview questions. In many ways, by studying the resume almost anyone can be fairly accurate in these predictions.

Therefore, it is important to ensure that your resume does, in fact, represent you; much time, thought and energy should be devoted to this point. It is important to remember that there is perhaps no single document that you will construct, which will affect the course of your life more than a well-prepared, well thought-out resume.

Contents of the Resume

The First Page

The first page of the resume is the next most important page outside of the cover letter. The first page of the resume must impress the reader by its very appearance. There are many ways to do this through organization, type style, and quality of paper. At the top of the first page, most agree that the resume should provide the complete name, home address, home phone number with area code as well as a business office phone with area code. Surprisingly, it is not unusual to find the telephone numbers excluded from the resume. This, of course, makes it difficult to get in touch with the candidate and could result in the loss of an opportunity. Ideally, along with the telephone numbers, the candidate should include the hours he or she may be reached at either number.

A small amount of personal information (height, weight, health, marital status, and number of children) typically is included at the beginning point of this first page. The complete business address usually is included under the name as well. The display of this basic beginning data should be well organized and not too crammed. It is appropriate to include on the resume, beside the person's name, any academic degrees earned. It also is appropriate if you have obtained a fellowship in the American College of Healthcare Executives to include FACHE.

The next piece of information is always one of controversy. Should one start with the position held or is this the place where the educational data should be placed? Again, there is no one good answer and it depends on where you are in your career and the amount of education you have obtained. One top executive recruiter believes that if a person has an exceptionally strong educational background, this should be provided to catch the reader's interest. Weaker or less impressive academic degrees may be more appropriately placed on the second or third page.

When providing your educational background, clearly state, in bold or in capitals, the specific degree earned such as Master's in Hospital Administration, in addition to the program where the degree was earned and the dates attended. It also is important to include (and this is very often left out) the areas of academic concentration, if any, in the earning of the degree. This particular piece of information can cause the resume to be investigated further if the area of academic concentration happens to fit with a need of the organization. Having one or two areas of concentration may increase the probability of a match.

The complete name of the undergraduate degree earned, location, years attended, major and minor also should be included under the educational category. One often asked question is, "Should the individual include one's academic performance, the grade point average?" Clearly, if a person graduated with honors or received any academic awards, this should be included. If a person achieved a 3.4 or better out of a 4.0 grade point average, it may be helpful to include.

There is information that some resume writers typically include under this category that is inappropriate. Continuing education courses, specific individual classes in a general or nonrelevant area and courses or programs one is planning to attend should not be identified.

The description of the individual's most recent position, aside from the education, could be the second most important piece of information on this page. Start with your current exact title and the date started, the name of the organization (highlighted), its complete address with some basic information about the institution (i.e., nonprofit, general medical/surgical, community hospital). The description is important to include so that the reader has a quick idea about the size and type of institution with which you are associated. The number of beds always should be included in this particular bar of information.

The rest of the page should describe the results of your time there. List using bullets the most specific accomplishments. Use action words to describe what you did and use no more than one or two lines for each. The description should start with action words like "organized," "responsible for," "developed," "implemented," and "designed and implemented" to demonstrate to the reader that you are an action, results-oriented person.

Different Formats

Some administrators have up to four different formats for their resumes. This is unusual, but think about the following. It is important when constructing the resume that you consider the reader. If you write a resume for a board, the organization and content will be somewhat different than if you write the resume for the hospital's CEO, or chief operating officer (COO). If the reader happens to be the manager of a health maintenance organization (HMO) or preferred provider organization (PPO), the items emphasized and discussed in the resume need to be different than those that would appear in a classic assistant hospital administrator's resume.

Another format may be used if you are writing a general resume for review by an executive search firm or several different types of prospective employers, including CEOs, COOs, and boards. The point is no one resume format really satisfies all readers. Clearly, there is no easy way to complete one document that will fully stimulate the interest of all types of readers. The individual who is truly trying to tap all possible opportunities in the best possible way needs to keep in mind that there are many different types of readers and there may be unique ways to organize and write certain resumes for certain positions.

On one hand, a preprinted resume which is well organized will catch the reader's eye and certainly leave a good impression. On the other hand, a preprinted resume may convey, as suggested earlier, that the reader is part of a "shotgun" effort that may have been going on for some time. Again, who will be reading the resume dictates what may produce the best results.

Gimmicks

There are many gimmicks, including the use of parchment paper, different color type, multiple type styles, video cassettes, audio cassettes, and a clear acrylic sheet of paper with embossed wording. Gimmicks usually turn off the reader, and if it is necessary to include them in a resume to get the reader's attention, one may make the bridge that such gimmicks also may have to be utilized for the individual to be successful in his or her job. The general consensus of administrators and executive search consultants surveyed is that gimmickry is a turn off and its use is a highly risky step, which could very well prevent an otherwise qualified person from being evaluated.

Length of the Resume

Although the authors of this chapter recommend two, or possibly even three different formats for a resume, there certainly is varying opinion as to the proper length of a resume. Most CEOs and executive search consultants agree that there should be at least two resumes. The first should be a one-page executive summary covering the professional history of the job seeker. This should include the same information at the top—name, address, and phone numbers. It should include titles, positions held, dates of those positions, location of the hospital, and perhaps, a one-line description of the type of hospital (i.e., general, medical, surgical, inner-city, community, or 400-bed facility). There should be a summary of the individual's educational experience, a section covering the professional organizations and levels of leadership participation, and one or two ending lines of a personal nature. Exhibit 11-3 provides models for consideration.

The Two-Page Resume

The second type of resume that most would agree on is the two-page document. Many say a resume should not go more than two pages and, at the most, three. However, if the job is a CEO position and the person has a 20-year career to describe, four or even five pages are not out of line if such a resume is being requested and evaluated by a search committee. However, this lengthy resume is too long to be sent to executive search firms. Also, remember that if a candidate is being recommended for a particular opportunity, the person should suggest to the search consultant that a more detailed resume is available if he or she would like to have more complete information.

Should you choose to construct a two-page resume, you may have enough space to include personal information such as activities and interests. Whether or not personal information should be included in a resume is an area of some discussion and disagreement among executive search people as well as hospital administrators. The authors, as practicing CEOs, believe that it is nice to have a small, two- or three-line section at the end of the resume that provides a little personal information on the job seeker. Such information may trigger the interest of the employer and it is often used to get the interview started on more of an informal basis. Again, the all important ground rule is, "Who is the reader?"

The second page of a resume must look as good as the first and demonstrate the same kind of impression that the cover letter and the first page carries. The items that traditionally are found on the second page of a two-page resume describe the second half of one's career. As stated before, the resume should detail the first ten years of the resume writer's career.

Exhibit 11-3 Example of a Resume

BILL E. WILL

513 Sunshine Court   Date of Birth: 9/22/48
Ann Arbor, MI 48106   Excellent Health
Telephone: (512) 555-1212—Office   5 feet, 11 inches—160 pounds
Telephone: (512) 555-3859—Home   Married

WORK EXPERIENCE
July, 1980–
May, 1982

UNIVERSITY OF MICHIGAN HOSPITALS, Ann Arbor, MI
Administrative Fellow. Engaged in a two-year management training program; responsibilities included working in the departments of clinical administration, fiscal affairs, management engineering and data processing, human resources, nursing and agency relations.

June–
August, 1979

ST. LUKE'S ROOSEVELT HOSPITAL CENTER, New York, NY
Administrative Resident. Observed the merging of medical and administrative services in a two-site, 1,300-bed medical center; gathered and presented the financial and utilization data necessary for the design of a major financial action plan; and prepared a detailed analysis of the medical staff appointments procedure.

June–
August, 1979

MONTEFIORE HOSPITAL AND MEDICAL CENTER, New York, NY
Administrative Intern. Served as administrator on call and prepared a contingency plan for an employee strike. Also served as the executive coordinator for the department of rehabilitation medicine for two months.

EDUCATION

CORNELL UNIVERSITY
Graduate, School of Business and Public Administration
Master of Business Administration, May, 1980
Sloan Program for Hospital and Health Services Admin.

INDIANA UNIVERSITY
B.S., Magna Cum Laude, March, 1986
Major: Health Planning and Administration.
Commissioned 2nd lieutenant, U.S. Army, upon graduation.

MILITARY SERVICE
June, 1976–
June, 1978

Served from 2nd lieutenant to 1st lieutenant, U.S. Army Infantry. Stationed Fort Benning, Georgia, as training officer for officer candidate school.

ACHIEVEMENTS

Member of Phi Eta Sigma and Phi Kappa Phi Honorary Fraternities; Dean's list all four years of college—graduated with a 3.78 cumulative GPA; received university academic scholarships in sophomore and senior years.

**ACTIVITIES/
INTERESTS**

President of the Association of Student Health Planners and Administrators while at University of Indiana; member of the American Hospital Association. Worked in an alpine resort for three months while traveling in Europe, April–September, 1976. Enjoy jogging and reading military history.

REFERENCES

Furnished upon request.

However, condense any time before 10 years. Jobs before the ten-year period should show the title, location and provide the data in the same format as on the first page. The condensed part, however, only explains those major accomplishments which were achieved at each of those facilities. This portion should be abbreviated and perhaps identify only the top three or four most significant accomplishments.

If there was upward mobility with one employer, list that on the second page, but in a way so that it does not look like there were multiple positions with different employers. Exhibit 11-4 (second page) shows one example of how a person had progressed from assistant to associate to interim administrator in a way that demonstrates upward mobility, but the description does not appear like three new employers.

On the second page, traditional education should be provided in a condensed version. However, it is important to provide some specific information about degrees earned. This would include the actual name of the degree that is on a diploma, the college or university where the degree was earned, and the dates and location of the school attended. It is important that if a degree has not been earned that it be clearly stated. It is perfectly acceptable to include academic work in process, but it is clearly unacceptable to show it in a way that hints or conveys a degree has been earned when it truly has not.

Also, include on the second page selected professional affiliations in which you have participated. If there has been advancement in any of those professional organizations (i.e., from the membership to fellowship in the American College of Healthcare Executives), such advanced membership should be indicated on the page. Include civic and other outside community activities in which you participate. However, keep the list short so that it does not give the impression that you spend a lot of time on activities outside of work.

If you have published anything, it is important to include this on the second page. Depending on the available space either list specific articles in the same kind of format that you would find listed in a formal college paper or footnote format found in a book or have a one-line listing stating that publications had been made and the number. Some resume writers list the magazines in which the publications have appeared. Also, if the resume writer has made any contributions to any books or has written books, they should be listed on the second page of the resume. Again, the format should be consistent with the types mentioned earlier. Exhibit 11-4 shows a two-page resume and provides a suggested format.

The last item on the two-page resume should include at least one line that conveys that, if appropriate, the resume writer has a more detailed resume

Exhibit 11-4 Example of a Two-Page Resume

William Terence Bill, Ph.D., FACHE   DATE OF BIRTH: March 5, 1945
1600 Redondo Avenue, Apartment #18   HEALTH: Excellent
San Diego, CA 90804   HEIGHT/WEIGHT: 6 feet, 170 pounds
Telephone: (619) 494-8630 (office)
           (619) 494-5414 (home)

HOSPITAL WORK EXPERIENCE

CHIEF EXECUTIVE OFFICER—SAN DIEGO BEACH COMMUNITY HOSPITAL, 10 Termino Avenue, San Diego, CA. A 300-bed acute medical/surgical hospital part of a multihospital system. (Appt. 09/87 to present.)

Responsible for total operations of medical center with an operating budget of $60 million. Report directly to the president of the company.
- Reversed operating deficit to a profitable bottom line in four months.
- Constructed a detailed Long Range Strategic Planning process, which gained support of medical staff, trustees, and administration.
- Initiated a network of several large medical group practices around hospital to bond physicians to hospital and staff specialties.
- Advanced a joint venture effort between hospital's cardiologists and facilities.

PRESIDENT & CHIEF EXECUTIVE OFFICER—SAN FRANCISCO HOSPITAL, 87555 Market Street, San Francisco, CA. A 260-bed private medical/surgical community hospital. (05/83 to 6/87.)

Responsible for the total operation of the medical center, including: hospital, nursing school, doctors' office building, with an annual gross revenue budget of $61 million. Reported directly to the board of trustees.
- Reversed operating profitability from a deficit position of over $1,637,000 in 1983-84 to a gain from operations of $878,507 in 1984-85.
- By year-end (12/86) increased hospital's occupancy rate by 30 percent.
- Increased the number of HMO and PPO contracts from three in 1983 to fifty-nine.
- Reorganized hospital's Quality Assurance and Risk Management Program.
- Designed and implemented the hospital's first Long Range Strategic Planning Process, Public Relations Department, Marketing Department, Trustee Education Program, performance evaluation program, physician recruiting program, formal hospitalwide policy and procedure system, and position control system.
- Achieved the following new patient care programs: nineteen-bed acute voluntary inpatient psychiatric program, seventeen-bed skilled nursing care facility, short stay outpatient surgical unit, women and infant children nutrition program, and home health program.
- Designed and implemented several programs to reduce the eight-year decline in occupancy rate and CARE-LINE Program; improved use of doctors' office building and clinic facility, multiple marketing programs, patient questionnaires, general and target-specific informational brochures, use of outdoor advertising, radio and TV programs, new patient care programs, emergency room marketing program.

Exhibit 11-4 continued

VICE PRESIDENT—CLEVELAND UNIVERSITY MEDICAL CENTER, 24 Moore Road, Cleveland, OH. A 1,000-bed university/teaching facility (six specialty hospitals), affiliated with Cleveland U. (11/77 to 4/83.)

ADMINISTRATOR—UNIVERSITY CHILDREN'S HOSPITAL. A 220-bed Pediatric hospital, part of the University Hospital System.
- Direct authority and responsibility for 27 departments/divisions throughout the 6 hospital university system.
- Assisted in the revitalization and reorganization of the dermatology department composed of 5 clinicians, 10 residents and 10 staff members.
- Assisted in rebuilding the neurology department, which transformed the service from one neurologist in 1979 to 12 neurologists and 6 residents.
- Completely reorganized the Administration Department; upgraded support staff in order to improve operations and enable the department to be more responsive.
- Established several quasi matrix task force structures to facilitate more efficient problem solving in a large bureaucratic health care facility.

INTERIM ADMINISTRATOR, WILLOUGHBY COUNTY HOSPITAL, 36056 Blackwood Avenue, Willoughby, NY. A multihospital general medical/surgical nonprofit county facility (333 beds). (1/77 to 11/77)

Reported directly to the hospital board of trustees. Had direct authority and responsibility for complete operations of both health care facilities, Willoughby Unit (185 beds) and Blackwood Unit (148 beds).
- Developed several programs to significantly improve press relations.
- Developed programs which improved work relations between the hospital, board and medical staffs.
    - **ASSOCIATE ADMINISTRATOR** (11/75 to 1/77)
    - **ASSISTANT ADMINISTRATOR** (11/72 to 10/75)

ASSISTANT DIRECTOR, TERRANCE HOSPITAL, 151 Terrace Road, East Cleveland, OH. An inner-city general medical/surgical nonprofit facility (467 beds). (5/70 to 12/72)

ADMINISTRATIVE RESIDENT, THE CLINIC HOSPITAL, 34512 Torrence Avenue, Cleveland, OH. A private multiple clinical and hospital facility (1,000 beds). (9/69 to 5/70)

EDUCATION

- **Doctor of Philosophy** (Business Administration), Case Western U., Cleveland, OH, 1981.
- **Master of Industrial Engineering,** Cleveland St. U., Cleveland, OH, 1975.
- **Master of Health Care Administration,** Washington U., St. Louis, MO, 1970.
- **Bachelor of Science** (Business Administration), Ashland College, Ashland, OH, 1968.

SELECTED PROFESSIONAL AFFILIATIONS

Fellow—American College of Healthcare Executives
Member—American Institute of Industrial Engineers

Exhibit 11-4 continued

PUBLICATIONS

ARTICLES: Published over 30 articles in most health care journals.

BOOKS:

- San B. Husten & William T. Bill, *Nurse Recruitment and Retention,* Aspen Publishers, Inc., March, 1988.
- William T. Bill & Terence F. Moorley, *The Health Care Executive,* Aspen Publishers, Inc., September, 1988.
- William T. Bill & Earl A. Singer, *The Changing Hospital Executive: A Guide to Why Management Style Must Change,* Aspen Publishers, Inc., Sept., 1986.

Detailed resume and references available upon request.

---

that is available on request. Further, the same comment with regard to references should be included.

The Three-Page Resume

Basically, if you believe strongly that a three-page resume is necessary, complete one. However, realize that most executive search consultants prefer a two-page resume. They begin to become turned off by having to go to three pages. If you are going to use a three-page resume, a more detailed explanation with regard to specific accomplishments on the job is desirable. Also, more detail should be provided under the educational section giving areas of concentration as described earlier in this chapter. A three-page resume usually will have a more detailed listing of publications as well as outside civic responsibilities. There is a strong belief that, if there was military service, some explanation of where and how that time was spent should be included in the resume. Having three pages also provides space to give a little personal background on an individual, which should be kept to no more than three sentences.

Four-Page Resume

The four-page resume may be more appropriate when applying directly for a job either through The Wall Street Journal, Modern Health Care, or directly to hospitals. Also, longer resumes are usually found when applying to academic medical centers or teaching positions at colleges or universities. The four- and even five-page resumes provide the space to clearly list one's entire list of publications. Exhibit 11-5 is an example of a five-page resume.

There really is no absolute right or wrong way to write a resume. What is clear, is that you must consider the reader, his or her available time, the level of competition your resume will have with others, and the types of resumes the reader will most probably be reviewing for the position for which you are applying.

THE TOP TEN LISTS

Lists of the most important items of a resume shown in the following paragraphs, as well as the worst mistakes, were provided by some of the best health care recruiters in the United States. Following these guidelines, in addition to giving your resume to friends for feedback, will also help ensure a good product.

A final suggestion: If a person is working in a hospital or has access to a human resource department, the individual should contact the Human Resources Director and look at the resumes that come into the institution over several weeks. By reviewing submitted resumes over a period of time, you will pick up many good ideas on how to structure your new resume.

In the development of this chapter, each of the contributors to this book was contacted and asked to identify the areas they believed were the 10 most important points to include when writing a resume. It is important to keep in mind the hundreds, and possibly thousands, of resumes that are reviewed by these individuals each year. The following list represents, in priority order, a summary of what these contributors feel are the top ten. (Some consolidation of these items was made by the editors to prevent duplication.)

Ten Points To Include in a Resume

1. Listing of Professional Data. List professional accomplishments, experience, education, and functions. Delineate your level of responsibility in each job well. Show how you made a difference. Provide dates and locations of schools.
2. Accurate Personal Data. Name, home and office address, and phone numbers should be the first items on the resume and accurate.
3. Organization and Length. Have an easy-to-read format. Be succinct, and describe yourself in 30 seconds. Length should be short, two pages or three at the very most.

Exhibit 11-5 Example of a Five-Page Resume

JOHN DOE, M.A., FACHE
14 Westheimer Way
Houston, TX 77203
TELEPHONE: (712) 554-1254 (OFFICE)
                        (712) 446-3566 (HOME)

DATE OF BIRTH: MARCH 5, 1945
HEALTH: EXCELLENT
HEIGHT/WEIGHT: 6 feet, 170 pounds

HOSPITAL WORK EXPERIENCE

PRESIDENT & CHIEF EXECUTIVE OFFICER—RIDGEWAY HOSPITAL—
3653 JACINTO, HOUSTON, TX 77222, A 260-BED, PRIVATE, MEDICAL/SURGICAL,
METHODIST COMMUNITY HOSPITAL. MAY 1983 TO PRESENT.

Responsible for the total operation of facility including medical center, nursing school, and doctors' office building. Annual gross revenue budget of $51 million. Report directly to the board of trustees.

- Reversed operating profitability of the hospital from a deficit position of over $1,637,000 in 1983-84 to a gain from operations of over $878,507 in 1984–85.
- By year-end (Dec. 1986), increased hospital's occupancy rate 30 percent.
- Increased the number of hospital HMO/PPO contracts from 3 in 1983 to 59 in 1987, including a Texas Health Plan and Blue Cross Prudent Buyer Contract.
- Initiated and successfully obtained a change in the Houston City Planning Code to allow Ridgeway Hospital exclusively to display penthouse level signs to adequately identify and market the facility; the only exception to a citywide ban on elevated building signs since 1976.
- Organized the necessary political effort to change the city's tax supported ambulance system to include only Houston hospitals, and increased hospital emergency department visits by 20 percent.
- Organized the necessary political action to reduce significantly the totally unfunded disproportionate number (43 percent) of the city's indigent patients (M.I.A.s) diverted directly to Ridgeway when the city/county hospital lacked the service capability.
- Reorganized and implemented a new Hospital Quality Assurance & Risk Management Program.
- Designed and implemented the hospital's first: long-range strategic planning process, Public Relations Department, Marketing Department, Trustee Education Program, performance evaluation system (for all employees), image enhancement program, physician recruiting program, formal hospitalwide policy and procedures system, and position control system.
- Resigned from Affiliated Hospitals of Houston, (eight Houston hospitals joined for the purpose of multi-employer bargaining) resulting in the negotiated settlement of three union contracts more beneficial to Ridgeway Hospital.
- Introduced and implemented the following new patient care programs: 19-bed acute outpatient surgical unit, women and infant children nutrition program and home health program.
- Developed and implemented the following hospitalwide remodeling projects: Radiology, Psychiatric Unit, Skilled Nursing Facility, 43-bed, 9th floor Medical/Surgical Unit, Main Lobby, Short Stay Unit, Employee Cafeteria, and Emergency Services Area.

Exhibit 11-5 continued

VICE PRESIDENT—DAVENPORT HOSPITALS OF ATLANTA, 4088 ABBY ROAD, ATLANTA, GA 44106. A PRIVATE UNIVERSITY TEACHING MULTIHOSPITAL FACILITY (1,000 beds). NOV. 1977 TO MAY 1983.

- **ADMINISTRATOR**—BOWIE BABIES AND CHILDREN'S HOSPITAL. A 220-BED SPECIALTY PEDIATRIC HOSPITAL. Worked with the BB&C board composed of thirty-three women.
- Direct authority and responsibility for 27 departments or divisions universitywide.
- Assisted in the revitalization and reorganization of the Dermatology Department composed of 5 clinicians, 10 residents and 10 staff members.
- Assisted in the rebuilding of the Neurology Department, which transformed the service from one neurologist in 1979 to 12 neurologists, 6 residents and 16 staff members.
- Completely reorganized the Administration Department. Upgraded support staff in order to improve operations and enable the department to be more responsive to the needs of the institution.
- Established several quasi matrix task force structures to facilitate more efficient problem solving in a large bureaucratic health care facility.

ADMINISTRATOR—PIKE CO. MEMORIAL HOSPITALS, 8200 EVANS AVE., WILLOWS, CA 94302. A MULTIHOSPITAL GENERAL MEDICAL/SURGICAL NONPROFIT, COUNTY FACILITY (333 beds), INTERIM TERM JAN. TO NOV. 1977

- Reported directly to the hospital board of trustees as their chief executive officer. Administrator's position offered but I declined.
- Total responsibility for complete operations of both health care facilities. Willoughby Unit—185 beds/Painesville Unit—148 beds.
- Developed several programs to significantly improve press relations.
- Developed programs, which improved work relations between the hospital board and medical staffs.

ASSOCIATE ADMINISTRATOR—OCTOBER 1975 TO JANUARY 1977

- Operating responsibility for the west facility (185 beds).
- Responsibility for both hospitals in the administrator's absence.
- Assisted in the planning, design, and construction of a $3 million expansion program including total replacement of Radiology, Emergency Center, and Outpatient Departments.
- Direct line authority and responsibility for all professional departments.

ASSISTANT ADMINISTRATOR—DECEMBER 1972 TO OCTOBER 1975

- Direct line authority and responsibility for all support departments.
- Organized a department operational and financial performance evaluation program.
- Developed several programs to improve the vertical and horizontal communication process.

ASSISTANT DIRECTOR—HURON HILLS HOSPITALS, 1035 VENTURA WAY, CONCORD, CA 94112. A GENERAL MEDICAL/SURGICAL NONPROFIT PRIVATE INNER-CITY FACILITY (467 beds). MAY 1970 TO DEC. 1972.

Exhibit 11-5 continued

- Assumed direct authority and responsibility for half of the hospital's departments.
- Developed and implemented a complete departmental operational and financial performance evaluation program for assigned departments.

EDUCATION

MASTER OF BUSINESS ADMINISTRATION—STANFORD UNIVERSITY, Hern Graduate College of Business Administration, Palo Alto, CA; completed evenings and weekends while working full time. Concentration: Analytical Management, Qualitative Methods, Statistics, and Systems Analysis (3.8/4.0 accum.)—December 1972– December 1975.

MASTER OF HEALTH CARE ADMINISTRATION—SAN FRANCISCO STATE UNIVERSITY, School of Medicine Graduate Program in Health Care Administration, San Francisco, CA. Areas of concentration: Hospital Organization, Operations, Systems and Financial Management—September 1968–June 1970.

BACHELOR OF SCIENCE—BUSINESS ADMINISTRATION—RICE UNIVERSITY, Houston, TX. Areas of concentration: Management Sciences, Economics, Accounting, and Biological Science—September 1964–June 1968.

FACULTY APPOINTMENTS

1986/present **ADJUNCT FACULTY**—University of Houston
1975/1983 **ADJUNCT ASSOCIATE PROFESSOR**—GEORGIA STATE UNIVERSITY, College of Business Administration
- Coordinator (informal): Graduate Hospital Administration Program 1980 to 1983
- Course Responsibility—BA 440-Hospital Organization and Administration for Technical Managers. Provide 13-week course to graduate hospital administration students & MBA students each fall semester.
1976/1979 **INSTRUCTOR**—San Francisco State University, College of Business Administration, Graduate Department of Business Administration Evening Course Responsibility:
- BA 579 Hospital Accounting Systems
- BA 486 Hospital Management
- BA 402 Systems Analysis of Health Care Facilities

PROFESSIONAL/ACADEMIC/COMMUNITY ACTIVITIES

Fellow　　—American College of Healthcare Executives
Member　—American Institute of Industrial Engineers
Member　—Editorial Review Board, Journal of the American Medical Association
Member　—Editorial Review Board, Journal of Clinical Engineering
Member　—National Fellowship Review Board, Achievement Program of the American Society for Hospital Marketing and Public Relations of the American Hospital Association

Exhibit 11-5 continued

Member   —Editorial Advisory Board, Hospital Legal Form Manual, Aspen Systems
              Corporation
Member   —International Registry of Organization Development Professionals
Facilitator—Willows Society for the Blind, trained a weekly group of sight impaired
              clients, 1979–1980
Founder   —First President, Health Care Administrators Association of California,
              1973–1974
Trustee   —American Lung Association of Alameda County, California, 1973–1974
Member   —Exchange Club of Atlanta, 1978–1979
Member   —Atlanta Chamber of Commerce, Community Publications Commission,
              1978–1982

SELECTED PUBLICATIONS

ARTICLES

- Thomas Brooks and John Doe, "Degrees of Education: Letters," *Modern Healthcare,*
July 1975.
- Thomas Brooks and John Doe, "Continuing Education for Hospital Admin-
istrators," *Michigan Hospitals,* September 1975.
- Eugenia Zamperre and John Doe, "Evaluation as a Two-Way Street," *Supervisor
Nurse,* June 1976.
- John Doe, William R. Brown, and James Hamilton, "Keeping Up with New Roles
within the Health Care System," *Health Care Management Review* (Harvard School of
Public Health), Fall 1976.
- Eugenia Zamperre and John Doe, editor Barbara Ellis, "Decentralized Laundry
Service: An Often Overlooked Alternative," *Hospitals* May 1, 1977.
- John Doe, William R. Brown, Helen Tom, and James Hom, "The Case for the In-
House Clinical Engineer," *Dimensions in Health Service,* May 1977.
- John Doe, William R. Brown, Helen Tom, and James Hom, "Administrative
Dilemma—The Need for an In-House Clinical Engineer," *Hospital Topics,* May/June
1977.
- John Doe, Helen Tom, William R. Brown and Louise A. Tuzi, "A Mathematical Model
to Determine Facility Needs for a Radiology Department," *Hospital Engineering*
(England), January/February 1978, *Industrial Management,* May/June 1978.
- William R. Brown and James Doe, "The Matrix Organization: Its Significance to
Nursing," *Nursing Administration Quarterly,* Winter 1979.
- John Doe, Helen Tom, and Vicki Gilbert, "Flexible Staffing," *Supervisor Nurse,* March
1979.
- John Doe, Helen Tom, David Natale, and Doohi Lee, "Contributions and Conse-
quences of Clinical Engineering," *Engineering in Medicine,* October 1982.
- John Doe, Helen Tom, and John D. Aram, "Dilemma, Contradiction and Negative
Incentive: The Management Job of the Hospital Administrator," *Hospital Topics,*
vol. 60, November/December 1982.
- John Doe, "How to Make Decisions That Pay Off," *Hospital and Health Services
Department,* A Book Review, November/December 1982.
- Kevin R. Monroe and John Doe, "Organizational Burnout: Is Your Hospital on Fire?"
Dimensions, December 1982.

Exhibit 11-5 continued

- John Doe, James Hom, and Sharon L. Lyon, "How a University Teaching Hospital Implements CPR Training for its Medical Staff," *Hospitals,* December 1982 and *The Hospital Medical Staff,* Vol. 12, January 1983.
- John Doe and Kevin Rilley Monroe, "The Formation and Destruction of Physician/ Administrative Cooperation," *Hospital Forum,* March/April 1983.
- John Doe, Michael E. Carver, and Leslie M. Wood, "Developing a Strategy for Managing the Hospital's Growing Technology," *Journal of Clinical Engineering,* April/ June 1983.

BOOKS
- John Doe, *The Effective Hospital Administrator,* Aspen Publishers, Inc., September 1986.
- John Doe and Albert Hall, *Health Care: A Look Toward the Future*, Aspen Publishers Inc., 1984.
- John Doe and Albert Hall, *Principles and Practices of Clinical Engineering,* ("Health Delivery System"—Chapter 1 and "Economics of Health Care"—Chapter 3) John G. Webster and Albert M. Cook (eds.), Englewood Cliffs, New Jersey: Prentice-Hall, Inc., 1979.
- John Doe, *The Development and Destruction of Cooperation in Health Care Systems,* approximately a 250-page manuscript, 30 percent complete.

RECENT PRESENTATIONS—1980 TO PRESENT
- John Doe and Albert Hall, "How To Make Decisions That Pay Off," *Foundation of the American College of Healthcare Executives;* Southwestern Conference, Dallas, TX, November 17–20, 1986.
- John Doe, "Power and Leadership," presentation made at *The Association of Western Hospitals;* Megamanaging: Leadership Development in a Competitive Era, San Diego, CA September 3–5, 1986.
- John Doe and Kevin James, "Planning Your Career," presentation made at *Ohio State University,* Program in Hospital Administration, Columbus, OH January 22, 1986.
- John Doe and Keven R. Monroe, "Hospital Burnout, Symptoms and Prevention," presentation made at *The American College of Healthcare Executives,* Annual National Professional Convention, Chicago, Illinois, February 1985.
- John Doe and Keven R. Monroe, "Organizational Burnout of Hospitals: Why It Happens and What to Do About It," *The Association of Southern Hospitals,* Annual Convention, New Orleans, LA, October 1985.
- John Doe and William Pasmore, "Conflict Resolution in Group Practice/HMO Medical Management," *A Conference of Medical Directors of the Group Health Association of America,* San Antonio, TX, November 1982.
- John Doe, "Disproportionate Provider Forum: California Disproportionate Providers: Responsibility and Perspectives—Building the Coalition," *California Association of Public Hospitals,* San Francisco, CA, October 1986.

ACCOMPLISHMENTS

- Founder and First President of the Health Care Administrators Association of Northern California that includes 150 members.
- One of six Founding Fathers and Senior Executive Officers. Sigma Nu Fraternity, Rice University.

Exhibit 11-5 continued

- Who's Who Among Students in American Colleges and Universities—1968
- Certificate of Community Recognition, WJW Radio (Atlanta) 1977

PERSONAL

Interests include jogging, tennis, snow and water skiing and most outdoor sports.

REFERENCES

Available upon request only, please.

4. Community Involvement. List civic activities, leadership positions outside of hospital, honors, certifications, and publications.
5. Organization. List positions in reverse, chronological order and keep record clear.
6. Statistical Data. Provide statistical information on accomplishments.
7. Image. Use standard size stationery, typeset or original copies, put name on each page.
8. Contact Information. Provide information to make it easy for the recruiter to contact the client during business hours.
9. Grammar. A grammatically correct, well-organized resume gives a good impression and is your marketing tool. Therefore, check your grammar and spelling.
10. Cover Letter. Provide a cover letter and include your reason for leaving, desired alternative positions, type of organization you are seeking, geography or state preferences, exact position to which aspiring, current compensation, and location restriction.

The remaining list includes other important items suggested by the contributors of this book.

- Specify position titles carefully, include dates, organization, city, state.
- Include personal data, such as marital status; spouse's occupation; number of children and dates (limited).
- Include a brief statement of goals and objectives.
- Focus the resume on past ten-year experience and summarize thereafter.
- Identify employer by name and location.
- Be aware that it's a dynamic document; it should change as does the person.

- Must show career growth.
- Must be insightful about one's self.
- Describe each organization—size and scale.
- List personal interests and hobbies.
- Include references.
- Provide facts which are illegal to ask for—gender, age, religion, and family status.
- Make functional skills clear.
- List objectives.
- Provide military data.

Top Ten Mistakes Seen in Resumes

Conversely, the same contributors were asked to identify the top ten mistakes that they have seen on resumes throughout their careers. The following is a summary of those items in priority order.

1. Length: too long, wordy, more than two pages, or too short.
2. Accuracy: have time gaps in listing of experience; incomplete facts (i.e., degrees have not been earned); or inaccurate information (i.e., about family status and state of employment).
3. Appearance: grammatical errors; typos; biographical data incorrect (i.e., phone number); use of "I did this," "I did that;" and arrogance in writing. Sloppy appearance, colored paper, fancy or poor printing, and unprofessional appearance.
4. Accomplishments: lacks statistical/objective data on one's accomplishments, unclear objective. Boasting of accomplishments, puffery, presumptuousness is obvious; or does not include job accomplishments.
5. Cover letter: a form cover letter or one which is inappropriate, impersonal, or starts, "Dear Recruiter." Lacks careful craftsmanship and is not pertinent, not factual, and not brief.
6. Gimmicks: Use of 8½- × 14-inch paper, faddish works, bullets, formatting, color paper, and folding.
7. Completeness: too general or irrelevant information about duties, poorly defined responsibility of positions held, list name of organization but leave off location, and unclear employment history.
8. Ease in locating and contacting: hard to locate candidate during the day; leaves off home address and/or phone number.

9. Organization: out of order, confusing format, and difficult to read.
10. Progression/clarity: showing job changes with one employer such that it appears to have been multiple employers.

The remaining list were other mistakes suggested by the contributors of this book. A resume is considered inferior if it

- includes a complete list of references (all data) with no caution about making contacts where the person is employed
- provides unverifiable references
- provides letters of endorsement with resume
- comes packed in folder or cumbersome binder
- does not include most important items listed earlier
- excessively emphasizes community involvement
- lists a job objective
- includes a picture
- has insufficient white space
- lacks brief profile on organization
- includes two or more variations to same person

SUMMARY

We have never met an executive who was not secretly proud of his or her resume, but we have never seen a resume that could not be improved. Although a resume will not obtain a position for someone, it is usually essential as a first step, which leads to the interview. Professionals make a serious error if they do not keep their resume up-to-date and heed the advice outlined in this chapter.

NOTE

1. Larry J. Tyler, "Tips on Preparing Cover Letters," *Personnel Management,* Reprint from *Southern Hospital Magazine,* November-December 1983.

12

Attention To How You Are Perceived: Appearance, Style, Body Language, and Preparation

J. Larry Tyler, President, Tyler & Company,
9040 Roswell Road, Atlanta, GA 30350

> "Oh would some power the talent give us
> To see ourselves as others see us.
> It would from many a blunder free us
> and foolish notion . . ."
>
> *Robert Burns*

PERCEPTIONS ARE IMPORTANT

The interview and employment process often has been characterized as a beauty contest. Contestants parade before the panel of judges strutting to the music showing their best features while occasionally being asked shallow questions to which they respond with their most creative answers. The only thing missing is the swim suit competition. This can be a lousy way to select executive talent but it's the common and accepted way because of the lack of objective measurement techniques. Recruiters put all of the candidates through the same processes, ask them the same questions, and see how they respond. The one that messes up the least gets the job.

Perceptions also are influenced by the lack of adequate interviewer experience. The candidate is at the mercy of inexperienced interviewers who may never get into the "meaty" questions, thus really never understanding the candidate, and his or her motivations and abilities. The shallow interviewer usually will make decisions based entirely on perceptions. The answers to the questions may not be correct or intelligent, but if they are quick and bold, then perhaps the perception of a decisive leader will carry the day. In order to deal with the employment process, you must understand perceptions and how to use them to your best advantage.

What a wonderful idea, to know how others see you, especially on an interview. Knowing how you are perceived, you can work to improve those areas where you are weak. But perceptions are not always correct when revealed in light of the facts. Therefore you, as a candidate, need to be able to mold perceptions into favorable conclusions. Influencing perceptions especially is important if you are to be seen as the ideal candidate for the job. This chapter deals with perceptions and how to mold them.

APPEARANCE AND DRESS

The initial impression of a candidate is an extremely important one, thus appearance and dress take on an enhanced importance in the interview process. John Malloy's book, *Dress for Success*,[1] has for years been the substantive authoritative support for executive dress. Some quick tips follow for those who have neither the time nor attention span to read the book:

Male Appearance and Dress Tips

- Navy blue suits or subtle "banker's pinstripes" are best. Do not wear checks, plaids, or sport coats. Certain sections of the country such as south Florida or southern California may have a "laid back" style, but that style is best adopted after you get on board. On an interview, your dress should be as conservative as a mortgage banker's.
- White or light blue shirts are acceptable. Button downs are preferable. Do not wear a bow tie on the interview. Wear a red, burgundy or yellow long tie; striped, club or paisley.
- Be sure your shoes are polished. Loafers or laceups are fine.
- Haircuts are extremely important. Get a haircut a couple of days before your interview.
- A neatly trimmed mustache is acceptable, but a beard is a turnoff.
- The mixing and blending of plaid, stripes, and patterns can be an art unto itself and is influenced by the current reflection of style. Even if the current vogue is to mix plaids together, don't. It is better to be conservative than fashionable in the health care industry.
- Limit the amount of jewelry. This is not the Olympics, so don't "go for the gold." Chains, bracelets, diamond rings, and engraved cuff links are ostentatious for an interview setting. Save them for another place and time.

- Suspenders currently are in vogue and depending on the person, may be a minor negative. If you are older or overweight, don't wear suspenders. They connote fashion and are best left to a younger, slimmer set.

Female Appearance and Dress Tips

- It is best to wear a suit on an interview, although a dress with a coat is acceptable. Do not wear a dress only or a skirt with a blouse; always have a jacket.
- A white or light blue blouse is fine. Deviation into other colors also is acceptable for women; however, a conservative appearance is important.
- Floppy bow ties are "out." A simple, single strand of pearls is "in."
- Closed-toe pumps and natural hose are recommended. Colored hose are a negative.
- Purses should not be oversized or overstuffed.

In the area of appearance, sometimes people have "blind" spots, areas where they think they look good when, in reality, they are not up to standards. In order to determine where you have blind spots, select two or three people you trust, whose opinion you value, and whose standards of dress and appearance are very high. Ask them for their candid advice by posing the question, "Will you help me by giving me your objective opinion on my appearance and dress? I am preparing for some interviews. I promise that I will accept your opinion as constructive and in my best interest." Take the feedback you get and use it to help influence how others perceive you.

It seems so simple to follow the above guidelines, yet candidates ignore them too often. Before you go into the interview, duck into the restroom and check your appearance in the mirror. Flash a smile at yourself and then go "knock 'em dead!"

STYLE IN THE INTERVIEW PROCESS

What the Interviewer Perceives

In the "beauty contest" employment process, interviewing style is very important and has a direct relationship on how you are perceived. There are six ways to show you have style: (1) be a good listener, (2) maintain eye contact, (3) be enthusiastic, (4) be open, (5) be yourself, and (6) use appropriate body language.

Be a good listener. Candidates who are good listeners do well on interviews. They are able to understand the interviewer and interject positive comments where necessary. Sometimes candidates get very nervous and try to sell too hard. When they start selling hard, they may never give the interviewer the opportunity to ask questions or to cut off the discussion of a particular point. The candidate keeps on talking while the interviewer is sitting there and thinking, "Why is this person selling so hard? Is there a weakness in the candidate's mind regarding this point? Maybe he is selling hard to overcome it." A number of candidates "shoot themselves in the foot" by not listening. In one case a client said "The longer he talked, the more shallow his knowledge seemed to be." The candidate rambled on and on, with anecdote after anecdote. The client did not get his questions answered and the candidate was eliminated. In the movie, *Being There*, Peter Sellers plays a slightly retarded gardener who becomes the confidant of the President of the United States and an industrial magnate by listening intently and occasionally saying, "I understand, Ben." The message—listen attentively—is clear.

Maintain eye contact. Look the interviewer in the eye most of the time. Avoid at all costs the following two extremes: (1) never looking at the interviewer and (2) staring at the interviewer. The natural conclusions are that a candidate who doesn't look you in the eye is lying and the candidate who stares at you is weird.

Be enthusiastic. Nobody wants to interview a "negative naysayer." Stay away from "down" topics or from describing how bad your current situation is. Don't disparage your current boss or your coworkers. Don't be cocky or arrogant. Remember, enthusiasm almost always appears on interview rating sheets. Make sure your enthusiasm grade is an "A."

Sometimes interviews get intense. People fire questions at you left and right. Some of these questions may hit raw nerves or sore spots. It is important to remember to smile. This indicates your pleasant demeanor and keeps you from letting those hard questions decrease your enthusiasm.

Be open, but cautious. Candidates often ask how open they should be on the interview. You should be open and honest in all of your answers, answering questions in a friendly and nonthreatened manner. But, always be on guard. Some interviewers are very experienced at putting candidates at ease. Candidates can get so at ease that they begin treating the interviewer as an intimate friend, telling him or her details of their lives in a way which might be inappropriate for an initial interview. The conversation becomes casual and not professional. The candidate relaxes and his or her answers are not as sharp. It is best for the candidate to be cautious and alert to the questions and the direction of the interview.

Be yourself. Be cautious, not to lose track of the objective of this whole process. What is the objective? Is it to get a job offer? Probably not. Is the objective to get an offer for a job that you want? Maybe. The real objective is to get a job offer for a job that is a good match—it matches your desires and your skills and you match the organization's needs. If there is not a match, either party may become disenchanted. If you are not careful, you may let your desire for a position outrun your judgment, thus causing you to answer questions according to what the interviewer wants to hear instead of what is true in your mind and heart. The result can be a bad match, which ultimately will fall apart. In today's competitive health care environment, your career cannot stand too many bad matches. All philosophical issues, i.e., management styles, attitudes toward employers, objectives, and mission, must be discussed objectively. Never accommodate the interviewer on philosophical issues.

Use appropriate body language. As a candidate you not only must display appropriate body language, you must be able to perceive body language, which may indicate how the interview is going and how you are being judged. Body language in the interview should be dealt with from two perspectives: your perspective as the candidate and the interviewer's perspective. Your use of body language will influence how you are perceived. The interviewer's body language will give you tips as to how you are being perceived. Your handshake is a powerful indicator. One of the first impressions formed comes from the handshake. Most people through the years have learned to shake hands well enough to get by. There seems to be only two exceptions: (1) the limp-wristed handshaker and (2) the "what's my role" handshake.

The limp-wristed handshaker may position his or her hand properly, but has no power in his or her hand, letting the other person exert the power and give direction. The limp-wristed handshaker indicates a lack of decisiveness and assertiveness in the mind of the other person.

The male–female "what's my role?" handshake also is not beneficial. Sometimes women are guilty of this handshake or have it perpetrated on them. In this handshake, the man does not grasp her hand and shake palm to palm. He grabs her fingers (or perhaps she only extends her fingers) and he holds them as if he was holding a delicate and fragile object. This should be avoided as it indicates a lack of assertiveness and the inability of the woman to compete on an equal basis. Women should not allow this handshake to be used against them.

What You Perceive

A number of books have been written on perceiving the interviewer's interest through body language. Not all people give visual signs as to how they are feeling, but some do. Here are body signs that indicate how you are being perceived. For example, if the interviewer is fidgety, playing with a desk object, or tapping his or her fingers, boredom has set in. Turn the tables quickly. Ask an open ended question to get the interviewer involved. Ask a personal question such as, "What lessons have you learned, which you can share with me on being a successful administrator?"

If the interviewer folds his or her arms, frowns, crosses his or her legs, or draws away from you, anger or defensiveness is present. You probably have said something the interviewer disagrees with. If you know what it is, then get the interviewer to share his or her perspective. Nod affirmatively and say, "I understand." If you don't know what the disagreement is, find some common ground and common agreement quickly. A bold candidate might say, "I get the feeling I may have said something, which you took exception to. Perhaps you could tell me what it was because I would be interested in your perspective on the issue."

If the interviewer gives no eye contact, seems in a hurry, or seems to be thinking, the interviewer is distracted and has something else on his or her mind. You are now in battle with an unseen enemy. If you have a clue as to the distraction, get the interviewer to talk about it or ask an open-ended question to get the interviewer to think about something else.

If the interviewer smiles, nods affirmatively, leans forward with legs and arms are uncrossed, you are being accepted. Keep it up. And give the same body language to the interviewer. This is the way it ought to be.

PREPARATION: A CATALYST TOWARD POSITIVE PERCEPTIONS

"Be prepared" . . . Boy Scout motto

If there is anything, which can give a positive perception, it is preparation for the interview. Information is power. Knowing something about the interviewer and the institution ahead of time is an extraordinary way to swing an interview your way. This is because of two reasons: (1) You will ask and answer questions with more insight, and (2) the other candidates probably will not prepare. You will stand out on your own merits and others will look unprepared. Most candidates do not prepare well for the interview, therefore if you have even minimum preparation, you will come out ahead.

One job searcher related a story about his interview for a very prestigious and exciting position. Prior to the interview he journeyed to the state capital and reviewed the hospital's most recent certificate of need (CON) application for a sizeable project. From this interview he learned a significant amount of information from which he gleaned questions to ask on his interview. Needless to say, when he interviewed at the hospital, his questions showed considerable insight. He interviewed the hospital instead of being interviewed himself. After it was all over, the other candidates were distant horses, far back behind this front-runner. Was he smarter or more dynamic than the others? Maybe, but he definitely was better prepared.

Gathering Information on the Employer

A mistake many candidates make is showing up cold for an interview and expecting the client to provide all of the information about the organization, board, and position. Unfortunately, many institutions cannot even produce job descriptions for their positions much less any other information necessary to make a decision. It behooves the candidate to do his or her own preparation and information gathering. Luckily, the health care field is attuned to disseminating information about various organizations. Facts, statistics, and information can be gleaned from a variety of publications such as

- American Hospital Association Guide
- Clark's Directory
- Annual reports
- Membership listings of various groups
- CON filings
- Magazine articles
- State hospital associations
- Metropolitan Hospital Associations

In many cases, informational packages on the hospital can be requested from the personnel department, the public relations department, or from administration when the interview is being scheduled. Information about the community can be obtained from the Chamber of Commerce or from such books as *Places Rated*.[2]

Information on individuals in health care can be obtained easily. If a person is a member of the American College of Healthcare Executives, his or her entire professional experience will be listed in the ACHE Directory. Other publications such as *Who's Who in Healthcare*[3] may provide an excellent opportunity to gather information on individuals. Your information getting also can be aided by the networking which is so prevalent in the industry. Health care is permeated by layer upon layer of networks. Networks are formed by:

- school alumni groups (i.e., a Masters in Health Administration (MHA) program)
- professional associations (Healthcare Financial Management Association (HFMA), American College of Healthcare Executives (ACHE))
- Local or national associations or alliances (state hospital associations, Voluntary Hospitals of America, SunHealth)
- individuals referred by contacting referrals from the above groups

Contacting your network can give you insight into the organization and its management. The "scuttlebutt" will be of tremendous value to you. In many cases candidates have saved their careers by acting on information that was not readily available to the general populace.

Gathering Information on Yourself

Part of your preparation for the interview should involve understanding yourself, your strengths and weaknesses, and preparing to answer questions. Have you ever been on an interview and been asked an insightful question that you had never been asked before? You may have stuttered, then given a half-coherent answer off the top of your head. On the way back to your office, you thought about the question and came up with the perfect answer. You said to yourself, "If only I had the opportunity to answer that question again, this is what I'd say!" Preparing yourself for the interview should involve preparing to answer all kinds of questions about yourself.

Exhibit 12-1 is a sample list of a request and questions that could be asked on an interview. Rehearse how you might answer them. Although this list is comprehensive, a creative interviewer will probably come up with some questions that are personal favorites and for which you cannot prepare. Usually there appears to be no correct or absolute answers to these questions. The interviewer usually is testing for thought process and your reaction to the question. In this situation, your self-confidence gained from preparation for the interview will carry the day. There are a few questions which can be tricky and for which you might need some guidance.

Exhibit 12-1 Structured Interview Format

Prepared by the staff of Tyler & Company

I. Personal Background
A. Tell me about your background.
B. Where are you from?
C. Outside interests?
D. Academic achievements?
E. What is your current financial situation? Any problems or litigation?
F. How is your health?

II. Work Experience
A. Tell me about your work experience.
   1. What were your duties?
   2. What did you like or dislike about each job?
   3. Specific achievements (list)?
   4. Why did you leave each job?
   5. What has been the biggest disappointment in your career?

III. Personality and Interpersonal Skills
A. How would you describe yourself as others (subordinates) see you?
B. Most important aspects of your life?
C. How do you get along with people?
D. What type of characteristics do you like in other people?
E. What type of people rub you the wrong way?
F. How do you react when someone criticizes your work?
G. How do you handle interpersonal disagreements?
H. Why did you choose this field of work?
I. What do you consider to be your strengths? Weaknesses?
J. Do you consider yourself organized? Creative? Careful? Disciplined? A hard worker? Why or why not?
K. What causes stress for you? How do you handle it?
L. How well do you express yourself before groups? In writing? Can you furnish examples of your reports?

IV. Supervision and Management Style
A. Describe your management style? (Or your selling, planning, etc., style?)
B. What are the two most important points or considerations to remember when managing, dealing with, or handling people?
C. Characteristics a good supervisor should have?
D. How could your last supervisor have been better? (Fair and consistent, respect and dignity)
E. How would you describe your relationship with other departments? Review by department.
F. What financial reports must you generate that help you manage your department?
G. When faced with a difficult management problem, whom do you consult for a resolution of the problem?
H. Rate yourself in the following areas: Planning? Organizing? Controlling? Motivating?

Exhibit 12-1 continued

V. Job Expectations
  A. Why are you leaving your present job?
    1. What are its negatives?
    2. Does your supervisor know you are looking for a change?
  B. What are you looking for in a job?
    1. Ideal job?
    2. Future goals?
  C. What appeals to you about our position?
  D. What can you do for us?
  E. Current salary?
  F. Salary requirements?
  G. Time frame for making a change?
  H. Are you considering other job opportunities?
  I. Geographical preference?
  J. Have you discussed relocation with your family members? What was their response?
  K. Does your spouse work? What profession?

Source: Reprinted with permission of Tyler & Company, Atlanta, Georgia.

---

1. *Tell me about your background.* This request is meant to get some of the initial information out of the way. Where are you from? How did you get where you are? What are your values? A 15-minute soliloquy should suffice. Do not make this any longer or you will risk losing the attention of the interviewer.
2. *What are your strengths?* Four or five strengths are sufficient. It would help if your strengths matched issues that are important in the job. For example, the last person in the position may have had problems in dealing with employees, yet this is one of your strengths. On the opposite side of the coin, if one of your strengths is in oral presentations and oral presentations are not needed, you just "wasted a bullet."
3. *What are your weaknesses?* If there is any one question you had best be prepared to answer, this is it. Your choices are two-fold. One is to answer with actual weaknesses, which you have overcome, i.e., "I have had problems in giving speeches before large audiences; however, I took the Speakeasy Course and now I have earned a number of compliments on my speeches." Another way is to answer with a weakness which really is a strength, i.e., "I work too hard and don't play enough." This question is one that is often asked. The answers

sometimes are humorous. One candidate, when asked her major weakness, said, "I have a weakness for chocolate!"

It helps to have a "dry run" interview before a real interview. This is best accomplished with a video tape. This is a favorite exercise of outplacement firms because it can give verbal and visual feedback to the candidate. Candidates have said that of all the preparation they did, this was the most helpful. Get a friend or professional to interview you asking the questions in Exhibit 12-1. Observe your speech pattern and body language. Make notes on your enthusiasm level and eye contact. And listen to yourself. Are you convincing? Are you sincere? The video tape will help you immensely as you try to change the way you are perceived.

CONCLUSION

In the interview process, perceptions are reality. To get the job, you must be perceived as the very best candidate for the job. If you are perceived to be the best, then you are the best (whether you really are or not). The ability to influence perceptions is extremely important for candidates. You can influence perception by preparing properly, understanding styles, reading body language, and paying attention to your appearance. Remember this when invited for your next interview.

NOTES

1. John Malloy, *Dress for Success* (New York, P.H. Wyden, 1975).
2. Richard Boyer and David Savageau, *Places Rated*, Second Edition (Rand McNally, 1981).
3. Elliott A. Sainer, editor, *Who's Who in Healthcare*, second ed. (Aspen Publishers, Inc., 1982).

SUGGESTED READING

Half, Robert, *The Robert Half Way to Get Hired in Today's Job Market*: Bantam Books, 1983.

Nelson, Richard Bolles, *What Color is Your Parachute?*: Ten Speed Press, 1986.

Tyler, J. Larry, "Tips on Being Interviewed," *Hospital Purchasing Management*, April 1985.

13

The Interview Process from the Hospital's and the Candidate's Perspective

John R. Clark, PhD, Manager, Health Care Executive Search Management Consulting Services, Coopers & Lybrand, 203 N. LaSalle Street, Chicago, IL 60601

THE HOSPITAL'S PERSPECTIVE

Preparing to Interview

The first step in preparing to interview candidates is to establish objective comparison measures. Most people believe that they will know the right candidate when they see him or her. However, that is simply not true. You must identify objective measures so that you can distinguish the best candidate from the others who also have excellent interpersonal skills, general management ability, and strong success records.

These measures usually involve behaviors that are critical to future success. You identify them by determining what problems in the hospital are in need of fixing. For example, if you have difficulty gaining support and cooperation of medical staff, then, the critical behavior is demonstrated experience in establishing joint ventures with physicians. You can ask the candidate specific questions about experience in this area and verify the answers through reference checks.

A second step is to develop realistic job performance specifications. Matching the right size people to the right size jobs is a continual problem in management selection. Management is full of large people stuck in small jobs that are beneath their skills or interest. Many hospitals have adopted the common sports approach of always recruiting the best possible athlete (executive) in the erroneous belief that the best athlete (executive) will provide the greatest overall benefit to the team (hospital). That may work in sports, but in management what typically occurs is that an executive who has been recruited into a job that has less content and less action than expected becomes bored and uninterested. He or she is underused and begins to look for the next career move.

Therefore, you need to consider carefully exactly what will be expected in the job and what sort of person is likely to fulfill those expectations. For example, assume that you want to hire a chief financial officer for a hospital that is running smoothly, is financially strong, has appropriate financial controls, and has a functioning management information system. In this situation hiring a financial executive with an MBA from a prestigious business school and experience in a very progressive corporate group may be a feather in your cap, but would be a very poor selection.

To structure reasonable performance expectations for the new executive, identify the four or five most important and realistic activities. Realistic means measurable, attainable, and within the new executive's control. Realistic job performance expectations for a chief executive officer (CEO) include increasing joint venture activities with medical staff, upgrading management information reporting systems, increasing productivity in the hospital, and reducing nursing staff vacancies. Unrealistic job performance requirements (e.g., to increase morale) are too general and cannot be measured.

Step three is to assemble a search committee. The benefits of assembling a search committee, rather than handling the entire process yourself, usually outweigh the disadvantages. The major disadvantage of a search committee is that it complicates the interview process by involving the calendars of more busy people. It also will increase indirect costs by a small amount. You will need to invest time in the process to counsel committee members on the objective measures, job performance specifications, and the precise role and fit within the hospital, and to gain agreement on appropriate selection criteria.

The major advantage of assembling a search committee is that it is an excellent management development tool. Time invested in defining objectives and criteria improves the quality of the decision-making process. Members learn about the hiring process, interview a range of candidates, and gain a better understanding of how executives have performed in similar situations in other organizations. They also develop a better understanding of the range of available talent. Using a committee can greatly enhance the acceptance of the new executive because each committee member has psychological ownership in the decision and a vested interest in the new executive's success. One caution: selection committees tend to work best when they are small. Three to five people is a practical committee size. The selection process becomes unwieldy with more than five members. It also is best when the number is odd so that there cannot be a tie vote.

Step four is hiring an executive search consultant. The role of the search consultant is to focus attention on the search process. The search consultant usually interviews each committee member individually to develop agreement on job specifications. He or she informs the committee of current market conditions for candidates of the type they are seeking and briefs them on the best background and skills for the position, based on knowledge of the market. The search consultant also conveys the candidate's perspective of the job and the hospital to help members determine whether the scope and level of the job match the level of executive they would like to recruit.

The search consultant frequently manages the process when the candidates interview before the board. He or she helps ensure that the candidate explores all the issues before the hospital and that board members probe all relevant areas of the candidate's knowledge and experience. "If your search consultant doesn't add value in several areas—the quality of candidates, efficiencies in time, ability to objectively evaluate technical skills, ability to "close" the desired candidate, and ultimately the success of the new CEO—then you've retained the wrong consultant," says Bob Murphy, Partner-in-Charge of Executive Search at Coopers & Lybrand.

Avoiding the Most Common Interviewing Mistakes

The most common mistakes employers make when interviewing candidates are failing to prepare for the interviews, treating candidates discourteously, and breaching confidentiality. Candidates often complain that interviewers are not prepared or qualified. The interviewers had no information on job specifications, or on what was expected of the new executive. Interviews then became a social rather than a business exchange. In this situation, the candidate receives a negative impression of the hospital and the hospital does not gather the information necessary to make an informed decision.

Discourtesies range from excessive waiting time, missed appointments, interruptions, and failure to promptly reimburse travel expenses to including too many or the wrong people on the interview schedule. Candidates typically resent being interviewed by a prospective subordinate. Poor conditions are another discourtesy. For example, a busy restaurant or an airport do not provide good conditions for a quality interview. It also lacks confidentiality.

The worst mistake an employer can make is breaching the confidentiality of the candidate's visit. There is an overwhelming temptation to make an informal preliminary reference check with a colleague who knows the candidate well or to mention the interview to a good friend at an association meeting. Do not yield to this temptation. Because the health care network works with the speed of light, your breach of confidentiality can result in the candidate's organization's knowing about the interview. The result could be your losing the candidate, the candidate losing his or her job, and your having unnecessary legal exposure.

John King, President and CEO of Evangelical Health Systems in Chicago, warns, "The end of the interview process is as important as the beginning. You'll see many candidates and choose only one. So if you say "no" courteously and have a candid discussion, candidates can become friends who sing your praises in the community."

Selling the Opportunity

The demand for health care executives skilled in dealing with the current competitive market conditions greatly exceeds the supply. Therefore, selling the opportunity to candidates is critical to successful recruiting.

Identifying the Selling Features of the Job

The first step in selling the opportunity to candidates is to identify those features of the job that outstanding candidates would find attractive. There are three areas of motivation for today's health care executives.

1. *Professional growth.* The desire for professional growth motivates the candidate to work hard for the reward of increasing his or her personal skills, knowledge, and professional capabilities. You can offer opportunities for professional growth in a state-of-the-art technical system, the most current techniques in specialized clinical areas, or a new strategy such as a vertically integrated provider system. Also, the opportunity to work with a seasoned executive who is known as a trainer of executives is a powerful incentive. A potential mentor relationship appeals to the best and brightest candidate's desire for professional growth.
2. *Recognition for achievement.* Some executives are achievement-oriented and will respond well to a bonus compensation system or other type of positive reinforcement. In addition, the opportunity to gain professional visibility within a hospital system, or a region, or within the industry, will be attractive to many. "A total compensation plan— base, bonus, benefits and perks—should fit the candidate just as you want the candidate to fit the job," says Mike Lew, Partner–Executive Compensation at Coopers & Lybrand.
3. *Making an impact.* Many executives are motivated by the freedom to take action and to put their personal stamp on the results. Strong

candidates will be attracted when the solution to the problem will have their name attached, when it will be known that Jane pulled this merger together or Tom was the guy who constructed a plan with the medical staff that enabled the hospital to stay in business.

The important focus in packaging information is to tell the whole story. Candidates expect to hear the good news along with the bad news and will find an attitude of open disclosure very inviting. "Candidates should see problems as opportunities," says Jerry Cambron, President and CEO of St. Thomas Hospital, Akron, Ohio. "Don't hide anything."

Understanding the Candidate's View

The candidate's view of hospital management has changed substantially in the past decade. It has shifted from avoiding harm and averting trouble by managing defensively, to identifying and seizing opportunities wherever they can be found. However, these aggressive executives often want more balance in their private lives.

The current breed of executives is less interested in glory and prestige and more interested in challenge. They want to work for hospitals where management has a strong power base and where their contribution is going to make the significant difference between success and failure. They are aggressive and are willing to undertake significant risk to obtain the expected high reward.

Therefore, an organization with an illustrious medical staff, a notable medical research tradition, or a widely recognized medical education program has less appeal than before. What appeals to today's health care executive is an opportunity to motivate employees to higher levels of performance and productivity, to implement innovative financial controls and productivity techniques, and to adapt the organization to appeal to new customers.

Today's health care executives want to balance family and recreation with career opportunities and professional advancement. With hospitals merging, closing, and reorganizing, they also want to accept challenges only at hospitals they believe will be winners in the long run. They consider location, life-style, and amenities, as well as how the position will affect their career options.

Choosing a Candidate

Conducting the Interview

In the face-to-face interview you should gather enough information to determine whether the candidate has the skills to do the job and would fit well within the organization, and which of several candidates is likely to be the most successful. It's assumed that more than one person will be interviewing. Each interviewer should focus on one or two areas. Sharing information from different perspectives and on different issues will help ensure that you have the right data to evaluate candidates.

To ascertain skills, obtain a complete work history so that you can identify past experiences that are likely to match current problems that you are trying to solve. To determine "fit," ask about how the candidate manages and makes decisions and compare answers with the prevailing style at your hospital. To identify the standout candidate in the group, probe for extra knowledge or extra skill using work samples, a technical interview, or case studies.

As you interview, you can probe a candidate's concrete experience handling one of the key challenges you face. For example, if one of your challenges is joint venturing with your medical staff, ask detailed questions about exactly how he or she handled a joint venturing experience. Determine the precise level of involvement and responsibility. Did this executive negotiate the contracts, obtain the financing, and structure the terms of the business relationship? Did he or she generate the policy guidelines that made that activity possible? Or was the candidate merely present when those activities were occurring? Once you have determined whether this candidate caused the joint venturing activity, worked as part of a team that made it occur, or observed the actions of others, you can make a reasonable guess about how well he or she will handle your joint venturing.

You can learn a lot about a candidate through a "second opinion" technical interview, conducted by a professional who has held the position for which you are recruiting. "We use this technique to sort out the candidates who really know their stuff from those who know the right words," says Bill Young, a former hospital CEO who is now a health care consulting partner with Coopers & Lybrand. This especially is true when board members do not have day-to-day knowledge of the organization.

If you're still unsure about skills or about who's best for the job, you or your consultant can present case studies that highlight challenges you are facing. Give the candidate adequate time to prepare recommendations and an approach to solving your problem. Case studies give you the opportunity to observe the candidate's problem solving processes, grasp of the details and issues, and depth of knowledge. Equally as important, if you handle the case study technique formally, you also can get a first-hand view of his or her presentation skills. This can be a useful indicator of how the candidate will deal with the board and how he or she will handle presentations to outside groups.

Checking References

Checking references can provide valuable insight into a candidate's ability to handle the job and to get along with your board and staff. However, many organizations are becoming more sensitive to the legal ramifications of what they disclose about current or past employees. As a policy, they disclose only names, dates of employment, and most recent salary. If you believe there may be sensitive personal areas that you would like to inquire about, we suggest that you check first with legal counsel before asking the questions.

THE CANDIDATE'S PERSPECTIVE

Preparing for the Interview

You are responsible for learning everything you can about your prospective employer. You will need full information to help determine whether the position is likely to be a good fit. Therefore, it is wise to tap every possible information source at the hospital and elsewhere before, during and after the interview to answer these questions:

- *What is the board's structure and role?* You should know how the board of trustees is structured and elected so you can determine how much input the CEO can have in the nominating process. Is the board's role strategic planning and policy making or management? How active are board members in the day-to-day operations of the hospital? It is not always easy to get an honest appraisal. Board members can see themselves as making policy but then they get involved in operational details like wage increases for dietary personnel.

- *What are the board politics?* According to Gus Donhowe, President and CEO of Fairview Hospital & Health Systems of Minneapolis, a candidate needs to know which members of the board can influence the vote of other members. "Often a most influential member of the board is not a current officer. Look into other ties among members that can affect their behavior as trustees." For example, in one case the chairman of the hospital board was an attorney whose major client was a company owned by another board member, who was not an officer. The chairman sought approval of every decision from this other board member.

Learn about members' professional backgrounds and spheres of influence. What kind of contacts do they have in the area? What is their particular view of the hospital? Do they represent a major employer or a governmental body or are they willing volunteers who care about the hospital?

- *How are board–medical staff relations?* "Do they see themselves cooperating with the doctors or fighting with the doctors?" asks John C. Fitch, President and CEO of Wyandotte Hospital & Medical Center in Wyandotte, Michigan. "If the board has taken an adversary position with the physicians, the CEO knows he has to take swift action." The candidate needs to determine the board's attitude towards the medical staff. Do board members understand their fiduciary responsibility and their legal responsibilities for medical delivery? If so, how has the board handled a malpractice or other physician related problem? How much input does the medical staff give to the board on strategic planning and general policy issues?

  Do the officers of the medical staff have real authority and have they taken action on medical staff problems? What is the medical staff's attitude towards group practice, prepaid health care, or alternate delivery patterns? How has the medical staff monitored the performance of its members? Have members adequately monitored the quality of care and taken action upon cases of unacceptable care?

- *What is the history of the hospital's leadership?* It is important that you determine whether the hospital historically has been driven by medical staff, management, or board, and whether there has been cooperation or conflict among board members, managers, and medical staff.

  Balance usually is important. Without it, you'll be unable to make things happen. For example, in one case a situation existed where the medical director reported directly to the board. The clinical departments were all managed by physicians and even the patient care services group had to have a physician's approval for their actions. The hospital administration managed only the hotel and business office functions of the hospital. Here the CEO had virtually no power and influence.

- *What is the nature of the employee group?* You need to determine the strength and responsiveness of the employees. Are they high seniority people who have been running a stable business or low seniority people who have seen considerable turnover? High seniority employee groups can have overwhelming resistance to change, believing that "administrators come and go, but we are here forever."

- *What is the prevailing management style?* Was the previous CEO's management style directive or participative? How does it compare with your style? The more different they are, the more challenges you will face. A newly placed CEO followed a very directive manager who had built a staff incapable of initiating and taking responsibility for actions. With a participative style, the new CEO has a long and arduous task of teaching, counseling, and upgrading the staff's management skills.

- *What is the culture of the organization?* If the culture has changed recently or if there has been a recent merger of differing cultures, you'll need to consider how effective management will be. For example, the new CEO of a newly merged hospital group found that the two groups had significantly different cultures. One had employees locally born and trained, who displayed unquestioning loyalty to their hospital and had enjoyed years of stability under a very centralized management. The other hospital's employees were not locals. They were well credentialled, highly educated, and enjoyed the freedom of a very participative management climate. Therefore, the two groups mixed as well as oil and water and it became the CEO's job to make the merger work.

Your sources of information are limitless. You can seek information from public sources such as state or regional hospital associations, from colleagues, the hospital's current or former employees, and of course from the hospital itself. If the hospital does not give you an information package, it is appropriate to ask for copies of:

- the organizational chart
- the most recent long-range plan
- the last three annual reports, financial statements for the past six months, and the last three auditor's management letters
- the most recent Joint Commission on Accreditation of Healthcare Organizations (JCAHO) survey
- a list of HMO, PPO contracts
- the medical staff bylaws
- the minutes of the last six board meetings, the last six medical/executive committee meetings, and the last three joint conference committee meetings
- the last six issues of the employee newsletter
- the Chamber of Commerce materials on the city and region

State or regional hospital associations can give you competitive market data, performance statistics and salary surveys. Salary surveys can reveal a hospital's self-image. Low salaries might indicate a hospital where there has been little turnover, little recent hiring, or an uncompetitive management staff. Low salaries also can indicate that the hospital sees itself as a high prestige organization that pays its executives and managers in prestige rather than money. High salaries can indicate that the hospital is in a building mode and hiring top management talent at premium market prices, or that the hospital overpays managers because it believes it cannot attract quality managers for the going rate.

Deciding What To Tell Your Current Employer

A ticklish question is what and when to tell your current employer about your involvement in the interview process. Do you say something the moment you begin to interview or do you wait until you have an offer in hand? In the first case you would rely on your boss's acceptance and willingness to let you pursue the opportunity. In the second case you would have to cover your absences and maintain the confidentiality throughout the process. Each strategy has its advantages and its costs.

Many health care executives take pride in helping associates in their career paths. If you believe that your current boss values your contribution, has displayed a nurturing attitude, and has a record of training executives for growth opportunities elsewhere, early disclosure could bring you valuable counseling and guidance. Early disclosure may be dangerous, however, if you have incorrectly analyzed your relationship with your boss or if your performance has not been satisfactory. You can find that the organization bypasses you—you no longer receive memos, you are not invited to meetings, and the organization functions as if you weren't there. Or you can find that you are asked to leave.

If you do decide that honesty is the best policy but get a cold shoulder, it's time to make an objective appraisal of your ability to read people. Your career might best be served by steering clear of situations where your success depends on your ability to read others. How well you know your boss is the key determinant of whether announcing your decision to pursue other jobs is going to rope you out of your organization or open doors in new ones.

Relating to the Executive Search Consultant

The role of the executive search consultant is to match jobs and executives. He or she keeps the selection process on a businesslike timetable and makes sure that both parties have complete and accurate information about the other.

The consultant must understand fully the hospital's business condition, politics, structure and other issues that affect the executive position he or she is recruiting for. He or she also must identify, contact, evaluate, and present likely candidates for that position, people who have already done the job elsewhere or show the ability to handle it. The consultant must know candidates' skills and experience strengths and weaknesses. The hospital, not the consultant, makes the selection decision.

The search consultant has been effective when there are no surprises on either side. He or she gives full disclosure to the candidate of the hospital's true situation, including information on finances, operations, competition, internal politics, prevailing management style, and culture. You can expect a description of life as it really is in this hospital.

The consultant assures the hospital that you are interviewing for a job that is appropriate for your skills, experience, and interests and is one in which you will find satisfaction and have the highest probability of success. He or she gives details of your achievements and frustrations, and explains clearly why you are a good match for this particular job.

You should ask the consultant virtually everything you want to know about the position, the hospital, the location, and the politics. You can ask the consultant about:

- what you will be expected to do;
- what major achievement will be expected in the first year or two;
- how decisions are made and who makes them;
- the history of the position and what has happened to the incumbent and executives who held this position;
- details of the search process and the schedule of events; and
- how many candidates the hospital is interviewing.

After your hospital interview, it is important to get feedback from the consultant on how you were perceived by the prospective employer.

It is seldom a good idea to ask the search consultant what kind of a person the search committee is looking for and then try to portray your skills and personality in a way that you think is going to increase your appeal. This is a risky strategy because if you guess wrong on what the hospital wants, you could be eliminated unnecessarily from a good opportunity. If you guess right, get an offer and take the job, you are likely to revert to normal at some time and become incompatible with the executive team. It's best to be yourself.

It also is inappropriate to ask the consultant about other candidates— who they are, where they come from, or how well they did. The consultant and the hospital are always careful to respect the confidentiality of all candidates.

Interviewing at the Hospital

It is always difficult to determine how well you will like the job and the hospital. Here are tough questions to help you determine how your style and preferences, values and behaviors will fit with the culture of the hospital.

- *How do you reward people?* With money, bonuses or additional perks like company cars or outside club memberships? Is the reward for meeting standards continuing to get a paycheck?
- *What behaviors are acceptable?* Is it acceptable to get to the bottom of a problem by digging and confronting people to ferret out the facts wherever they are? Or is it critical to maintain harmonious relations among team members and medical staff members? What has happened in the past to executives who have behaved in those ways? You will need to determine if your usual behaviors will fit with the hospital's style.
- *What is the extent of medical staff input into decision making?* Do the physicians make the decisions and the management team comply? Does management seek and consider physicians' input in the decision-making process? Are physicians excluded from that process? By learning where the decision-making power base is, you will know how comfortable you will be working in the hospital.
- *What is the extent of union activity?* Learning about the extent of union activity can provide important clues about past management– employee relations and how much latitude managers have in decision making.

    If there is a high level of union activity you need to know why. Is it because previous administrative policies caused employees to seek union representation to gain a balance with management? Or, is it because the hospital is in a city where strong union representation is a way of life? If there is little or no union activity, you need to determine if the reason is a lack of union aggressiveness or a high level of employee satisfaction with management policies and practices.

- *How many levels of approval does a department head need to hire a person or purchase equipment?* You will find out whether the hospital's management style fits your own. Do managers have freedom to make decisions and take actions for their departments or is there strong centralized control? If you like flexibility and decentralization, you may find a hospital with a well-ordered chain of command and several levels of approval stifling. If on the other hand you prefer centralization and the hospital is decentralized, you will face a difficult task of tightening controls and increasing structure.

- *How many board members have responsibility for a budget or for an employee group greater than that of the hospital?* Few issues affect a CEO's authority more directly than board members' perspectives. A board member who is responsible for a division or company that is larger than the hospital is likely to find discussions of strategic direction and competitive strategies to be rewarding and productive. A board member who is a professional without general management responsibilities or an individual whose perspective is based on a personal household may have difficulty relating to a multimillion dollar budget and a large employee group. This board member is more likely to be interested in operations and the routine day-to-day events that he or she can understand.

- *What is the CEO's dollar sign-off limit without specific board approval?* Are expenditures of over $500 whether it was on a regularly budgeted item or not off limits? Is spending $1 million subject to quarterly review? If you are accustomed to considerable freedom and are interviewing with a board that wants to debate tiny expenditures, you can predict a struggle with the board for authority.

- *What caused the last 25 employee departures?* This information gives you insight into the corporate culture, value systems, and management styles. If there is an exodus of employees departing for other hospitals in the area, there may be major problems in the organization causing people to flee. If there are only retirements, there may be problems of productivity and the demands for employee performance. If there is a pattern of recent terminations for cause, you will need to dig deeply to identify serious problems.

- *Is there a particular social grouping that you would be expected to join?* How well you will fit is affected as much by social as by job factors. If you enjoy your privacy and prefer to spend your free time at home with your family, you may be uncomfortable in an organization where you are expected to spend time after hours at the country club or civic organization. If you are a fast moving and fast talking easterner considering a hospital in the more leisurely Midwest, you need to be sure to assess how well you will be accepted into the community. Be sure to check social expectations as carefully as you check job requirements.

If you question the long-term viability of the hospital, you should ask penetrating questions in the interview process about the board's orientation, responsibility, and focus.

- The board's long-term versus short-term orientation. "I check a board's focus on today's problems or tomorrow's opportunities," says Glenn Shively, Coopers & Lybrand's national health care industry chairman. "Are they facing and acting on major components of long-term survival or are they preoccupied with other issues? Are they dealing with issues of joint investment with the medical staff? Are they monitoring market share and assessing patient needs in their service area?"
- The board members' operational responsibilities. "Are they really digging into issues of productivity, fiscal responsibility and clinical responsibility?" asks Bob Pellar, health care consulting partner for Coopers & Lybrand.
- A board's outward versus inward focus. Robert S. Bonney, EVP, Research Medical Center, Kansas City, states, "A board that is not focusing on developing a feeder network from the surrounding region may be missing a key element to their survival. Do they look to the marketplace and the competition or to the internal organization? Are they innovative or traditional?"

It is very important to recognize when your appraisal of a hospital's viability is different from the board's so that you can assess your ability to make changes. For example, a large community hospital had four candidates reject the offer to become CEO. The candidates believed that the hospital's long-term survival depended on building new linkages with other hospitals and with contract purchasers while the board stood on their past record of success as an independent organization. The board finally relented and today the hospital is a successful and thriving member of a hospital chain. But if your vision of the future of this organization is not consistent with the current management or board's view, you have to question your ability to fit smoothly in the organization.

Selling Yourself

Candidates often find that they simply do not have much time to sell themselves in the interview process. The time went by too quickly. The prospective employer did not ask the key questions that would have permitted them to display knowledge.

To sell yourself effectively, follow these three steps: (1) prepare yourself thoroughly; (2) present your answers in an executive style (well documented with examples); and (3) ask deliberate questions that are designed to open up a topic of conversation that permits you to display your knowledge.

Prepare yourself. Do extensive homework before setting foot in the hospital. (See the section Preparing for the Interview.) You need to determine in advance what its needs are—whether the major problems or opportunities lie in medical staff relations, finance, operations, clinic issues, construction, or marketing issues. You can acquire this information by thoroughly questioning the search consultant or by using any other source you have at your disposal.

A second part of your preparation is making an inventory of your experiences and skills. Sort through your list of experiences and pick out the ones that relate directly to the issues you have just identified. For example, if the major issue is medical staff relations, think through all of your past medical staff activities. Actually write them down. Make a short list of ten situations where you resolved medical staff conflict. This is called psychological rehearsal. You will have short, concise, and impressive anecdotes to display your knowledge and accomplishments in an area of particular interest to the prospective employer.

Present the information in an appealing manner. It has been demonstrated that an interviewer forms a strong opinion of a candidate within the first two or three minutes. Once formed, the initial opinion will usually prevail to the end of the interview. So it is important to address the key issues or problems you've identified at the beginning of the interview if possible.

The prospective employer hopes to find in you well-developed executive decision-making ability. So put your examples in a decision-making format. Briefly describe the nature of a problem, the factors that led you to identify the problem, the alternatives you considered and the pros and cons of each. Then tell how you chose the alternative, how you implemented it, and what the outcome was. If you include a before and after comparison, the interviewer can more easily gauge the magnitude of your accomplishments.

Ask questions carefully. The purpose of asking questions is to steer the conversation into an area you know is important to the interviewer for which you have a ready list of well-rehearsed examples that you would like to talk about. For example, as you complete your discussion of medical staff relations problems, you can ask "How is your nurse-staffing situation?" This is the likely question if you know that the hospital has a large number of nursing staff openings and has not been successful in nurse recruiting and internal job adjustments. As the interviewer responds, you can describe your relevant experience.

You also can ask questions to let the interviewer talk. For example, ask the interviewer about his or her recently published article or about his or her association activities to give him or her the chance to feel good by talking about accomplishments. It will also give the message that you have done your homework.

Handling a Past Termination

Terminations are becoming more frequent and more accepted in the general business community and in the health care industry as well. Terminations frequently are caused by acquisitions, divestitures, and rapidly shifting business and market conditions. More often today they are not related to an executive's on-the-job performance or ability to continue to be a strong performer in the industry. Therefore, a termination in your past is now much more likely to be viewed as just another event in an executive career.

The most effective way to deal with a past termination is to face the issue squarely. Say: "Yes, I did get terminated and here is what happened" and then explain precisely what occurred. You can assume that the prospective employer will carefully doublecheck the circumstances of a termination in your career. So, relate your story accurately. Any inconsistencies that may be found during reference checking will certainly reduce your credibility.

The other necessity in dealing with a past termination is self-appraisal. While there may have been some factors beyond your control, some deficiencies in your performance may have contributed to the termination. Now is the time to honestly appraise your deficiencies, to accurately assess the working conditions, and to honestly identify where the mismatch occurred so that you can avoid getting into a similar situation again. For example, if one reason for your termination was that the hospital expected financial achievements when your strengths are in human relations, you may want to be wary of seeking a new job where the budgeting system is the most pressing need.

Handling the Interviewer Who Can't Interview

When you encounter interviewers who have no interviewing skills or interviewers who only want to sell the job to you, seize the situation for your best advantage. Where the employer is well meaning but does not know the correct questions to ask, you can ask leading questions to which you know the answers. You will give yourself the opportunity to display the experiences and skills that you want the employer to hear about. The well-prepared candidate will always have the advantage with unskilled interviewers of steering the conversation by asking leading questions. You may even be able to control the discussion completely.

14

What To Do between Job Searches

Terence F. Moore, President, Mid-Michigan Health Care Systems, Inc.,
4005 Orchard Drive, Midland, MI 48640

Earl A. Simendinger, PhD, Professor and Chairman, Department of Health
Education and Health Sciences, Central Michigan University, Mt. Pleasant,
MI 48859

One of the primary responsibilities of an employed executive, a duty to himself or herself, is to prepare for the next job search. For an executive to do less is irresponsible. Executives who fail to utilize the time when they are employed to strengthen their ability to obtain another, hopefully better, job make a serious career error. Unfortunately, there are a large number of executives who treat employment as an end rather than a means and they pass the time or spend their time rather than invest their time. They are similar to college students who believe that by simply attending classes and receiving a degree, they will be successful.

College is similar to a long train ride; the student buys a ticket (pays the tuition) and "rides" for a semester. Then the student repeats the same scenario again and again. Eventually, it may be two years or four years, the student steps off the train exactly where he or she got on. The "train" does not take the student anywhere, and all the student has are new skills and the means to get on another train (graduate school or a job). Health care executives who are employed are in a similar situation—eventually, they too will be asked to leave the train or will elect to move. When that time comes their professional preparation, in addition to their regular job performance, will be vitally important to their future success.

This chapter is based on the premise that some time during an executive's career he or she will have to move. If you have an assurance that you will not have to move from one institution to another throughout your career, you can ignore the recommendations outlined in this chapter. Certainly, numerous executives have gone to the top of Fortune 500 companies who have not had to focus on doing anything other than the job at hand as well as some political activities. But, this is somewhat rare in the health care industry given the high turnover in chief executive officer (CEO) positions. Assume that you will have to move someday—either voluntarily or involuntarily. Prepare for that move professionally, psychologically, and physically as a Marine trains for amphibious landings.

LEVELS OF PROFESSIONAL BURNOUT

A considerable amount of time has been spent analyzing why organizations burn out. Part of that analysis indicated that executives also fall into several levels of personal burnout.[1] The most severe form of personal burnout, or what may be termed third degree burnout, is an illness associated with the pressures of a job. Sometimes this is manifested in the form of a myocardial infarction, sometimes it is a complete mental breakdown. Both the organization and the individual suffer severely when third degree burnout occurs.

The most severe form of third degree burnout is suicide. A 45-year-old CEO of a large hospital was told that his position would be phased out during the next six months. He was distraught and unable to cope with the situation. Two weeks later his family found him next to the revolver he used to shoot himself.

Levinson has described a situation in which an executive committed suicide because he perceived his superiors had lost confidence in him (they had not).[2] The executive felt no self-actualization because he had depended upon the approval of others to satisfy his superego and had failed to receive a promotion. The vacation his superiors said he deserved only compounded the problem because he had so much idle time, which added to his guilt and feelings of uselessness. Eventually, his self-esteem was severely eroded.

The second most severe form of personal burnout is the accelerated physiological and psychological deterioration of an individual or second degree burnout. Most of the factors causing this degree of burnout can be controlled by the individual health habits. Unfortunately, those executives whose rates of speed are greater than their physical and mental capabilities often find their abilities irreversibly impaired. These "barnburners" may contribute handsomely to an organization when they are well, but when they burn out physically or mentally or both they become liabilities not only to themselves but to their organizations. These people often are busy storing nuts for a winter that they might not live to see. It is a great sadness to see the number of health care executives in the so-called golden years of their careers who look like burned out buildings.

The mildest form of personal burnout and the one that deserves the most attention can be termed first degree burnout. This is a particularly insidious form and can best be described as the failure to keep up to date. Mark

Silber, a contributor to this book, often says: "Professionals are in a great horse race—a race between obsolescence and retirement—and the best they can hope for is a photo finish."[3] Many executives appear to be spectators to such a race.

The failure to keep up to date usually is accompanied by a sense of complacency. When the material needs of an executive are being met he or she often becomes complacent and lulled into a false sense of security. There is tremendous ego satisfaction in being at or near the top of an organization and having employees laugh at your jokes, seek your advice, and agree with you on almost any issue. It is easy to "wrap the organization chart around you" and not work to continually hone your leadership and managerial knowledge and skills outside of your immediate job duties. Vacations and association meetings in resorts can add to the belief that life is indeed sweet. Gradually, the executives who become complacent lose touch with reality and even themselves. Based on the authors' professional contacts, there was a time when 80 percent of all health care executives were in some form of first degree burnout; however, the shake out of ineffective health care executives that has occurred in recent years has probably reduced that level to around 40 percent. Exhibit 14-1 summarizes the three levels of personal burnout.

After they are terminated, executives usually have a clearer understanding of reality. An executive who lost his job as the CEO of a hospital said: "One of the big revelations to me was that I had always thought that

---

Exhibit 14-1 "Degrees" of Personal Burnout

1st Degree Burnout	Failure to keep up-to-date Complacency Gradual loss of reality
2nd Degree Burnout	Accelerated physical deterioration • Loss of sleep • Loss of energy • Weight Gain Graduated indifference to work situation
3rd Degree Burnout	Major physical and/or psychological breakdown • Heart attack • Ulcer • Mental Illness

Source: Reprinted from *Organizational Burnout in Health Care Facilities: Strategies for Prevention and Change* by E.A. Simendinger and T.F. Moore, p. 55, Aspen Publishers, Inc., © 1985.

employees sought my advice and counsel because they respected my opinion. I have since found that they could care less about my opinions and counsel now that I am not a CEO."

Another executive experienced a similar situation. He was one of the most powerful health care executives in the United States. After he was fired, he conducted a seminar at a large regional conference and only two people attended. He had done nothing to build his expertise outside of his immediate organization and no one really cared about what he thought. To reduce the possibility of complacency and stagnation, health care executives should engage in numerous activities outside their immediate job duties.

OUTSIDE PROFESSIONAL ACTIVITIES

Competition is too tough to allow executives the luxury of only carrying out the responsibilities of their position as adequate preparation for their next career move. When the time comes to move they will find their resume in a pile with 300 others and they will not be able to compete with those who have labored to prepare themselves for their next career move. Figure 14-1 illustrates the importance of spending a portion of time on activities other than your immediate work situation if you are to prepare adequately for career advancement. The authors assume that an executive is working hard at his or her respective job assignments and, therefore, do not expand on that subject. However, the other professional activities, which merit the time and attention of the employed health care executive, will be explored. Executives should spend between 10 and 15 percent of the amount of time they actually work involved in other professional activities. In other words, if an executive works sixty hours per week, he or she should invest between six and nine hours doing the activities described in this chapter.

Continue Your Education

When Warren Bennis, a well-known author and lecturer, studied 90 leaders across the United States, he discovered that every one of them had an ongoing interest in continuing education. They constantly were reading, taking formal courses, or just trying to improve their knowledge. "They were enthusiastic learners, open to new experiences, seeking new challenges, and treating mistakes as opportunities for self-improvement."[4] Health care executives should be motivated similarly.

Figure 14-1 Use of Employed Executive's Time

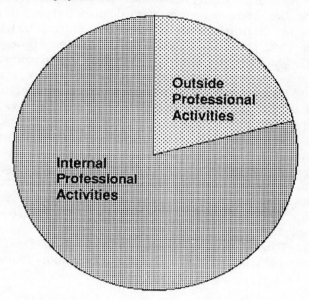

It is amusing to see graduates of various accredited programs in hospital administration or masters in business administration programs who believe that once they graduate they have "arrived" and need not put themselves through any further educational discipline. They remind some observers of the freshman college student who wears his high school varsity jacket with the little medals pinned on it around campus during the first few weeks of college.

What a tragedy that many executives spend a concentrated period in academic study and then concentrate only on work. Education is a lifelong process and formal classes that are taken while an executive is working full-time can be a rigorous, but rewarding experience.[5]

A number of health care executives have beaten their competition, not because of an outstanding work performance, but because they went to school nights and obtained a law degree, a Ph.D., DBA, master's or second master's beyond their current level of training. One young health care executive went to work for an administrator and it became apparent that the administrator was an insecure autocrat who would not do anything to help the young executive advance. The young executive worked hard on the job and went to law school at night. In four years he obtained a law degree and became the CEO of another 300-bed hospital.

It is not absolutely necessary that health care executives continue to take course work after receiving their master's degrees, but the authors recommend that they do. Importantly, if you do take formal course work be certain that it will eventually lead to a degree. Another strategy is to take course work, which will strengthen a gap or weakness in your resume. For example, if an executive has had very little training in marketing, he or she could take additional graduate work in marketing. If finance is a weakness, the person should take additional course work in finance. Occasionally, executives refrain from taking courses because they are uncertain that they will be able to complete the program. Do not let that uncertainty dissuade you—begin.

Other, less formal courses and seminars also can be helpful. Choose those which will help you strengthen your professional abilities, not just because they happen to be in the city your spouse wishes to visit or near a ski slope. Some of the executive training programs of between one week and six weeks that are taught at prestigious universities such as Harvard are excellent. The American College of Healthcare Executives (ACHE) and Aspen Systems also offer a wide range of excellent short courses.

Participate in Professional Associations

One of the best ways to meet other health care professionals is to participate actively in professional associations. Regional and local hospital councils, state hospital associations, the American Hospital Association, and American College of Healthcare Executives all offer opportunities to meet others and hone your leadership skills in a board or committee structure. This type of activity can also have the advantage of giving the professional additional visibility.

Work with a Professional Partner

If you want to maximize your efforts outside your immediate work setting, find another health care executive who has ambitions similar to yours and form a strong professional relationship. Such a relationship is synergistic and can more than double your output. Your partner also can give you objective feedback and support through difficult times and particularly during times of defeat. Based on the authors' experience, it is difficult to overemphasize the value of such a relationship.

Market Yourself

One of the traits of failing executives cited in a previous chapter is their failure to become known—to market themselves. Often, when you only keep your "nose to the grindstone," you get a flat nose. Self-marketing is not showing off, it is a wise investment in time, for as so many people have said, "It is not who you know that is important, but who knows you." The following are a few activities that increase your professional profile.[6]

Write Articles

Our advice is similar to the advice about entering additional education programs—begin. Do not start with prestigious journals such as the *Harvard Business Review*. There are a number of other professional journals, which need well thought out material from practicing health care executives. When you have published enough articles, write, co-author or edit a book. It takes time, but it can be a worthwhile discipline because it enables you to develop indepth expertise in some field. It may take one or two years to develop a book, but most executives can do it if they have an idea and pursue it.

Do not become depressed if your articles are rejected. The authors know several professionals who have published dozens of articles and several books and still have 50 percent of their material rejected. Also, do not expect your colleagues to write you congratulatory notes when they see your name in print. One well-known health care consultant who wrote a book that sold more than 180,000 copies said that he only received five letters and four of them were to note that there was an incomplete sentence on one page. (It is a worthwhile activity to write authors complimentary letters or seek their expertise. Very few health care executives take the time to do this.)

Teach Courses and Give Lectures

Teaching at a nearby college or university can be a great learning experience and it looks good on a resume. It also can perfect your verbal skills. If you cannot teach a course, at least seek professional speaking engagements. State hospital associations, American College of Healthcare Executives, and other professional societies often are willing to give health care executives the opportunity to present programs.

For some reason, many executives believe that it takes someone with a special talent to present such programs and, therefore, they spend their careers attending these programs as spectators rather than orators. The only major difference between most speakers and their audiences (other than a speaker must work harder than the audience) is that the speaker is out in front. Being out in front is the key to leadership so get out in front.

Volunteer for Leadership Positions in the Community

This may be less important in a large community than it is in a medium size or small community. Nonetheless, this type of activity can be rewarding to the junior executive. Junior executives have received the attention of board members by being involved in leadership positions in community organizations. In one instance, a major factor in an executive's rise to the top of one of the major hospitals in the United States was his leadership activity in a church that also had a number of board members as parishioners. When the executive is involved in community boards he or she should attempt to be an officer on such boards. It takes about the same amount of time to be the treasurer, secretary, or even president of many community boards as it does to simply serve as a board member. This type of training can be invaluable to a junior executive who has very little board experience.

Senior executives have sometimes commented that serving as a board member of various civic organizations provided them with a different perspective about their own boards and what a CEO should or should not be doing for board members.

Maintain Your Health

The stress on health care executives is acute. They must deal daily with a large number of well-educated professionals over whom they often have very little authority. Their workday often begins with a 7:00 A.M. meeting and ends with some social obligation lasting until 11:00 P.M. Moreover, CEOs become the "bull's eye" for community members, employees, physicians, regulators, volunteers, or anyone who wishes to take a "shot" at the health care system. There is not much that health care executives can do to change this situation, but they can change the self-destructive health habits many have.

If health care executives could only do one activity in addition to their regular job duties, it should be maintaining their health. Too many senior executives and even some junior executives are unwittingly shortening their careers and their lives by ignoring their physical and mental well-being. Being fit means being able to work, and health care executives must be fit enough to make it to retirement.

Is your physical condition worse than it was a year or two ago? If so, you are headed in the wrong direction. You do not have to be able to run five miles, but you should be able to handle stressful, prolonged work activities. Smart executives put a priority on their physical health. Attempt to get some exercise every day.

In addition to a regimen of routine exercise, health care executives should: get an annual physical check up; cease smoking or not start; reduce alcohol intake levels; and develop proper diet, work, and sleep habits. If you win every battle but lose your health, you have lost the "war" and thousands of health care executives are losing this war.

Maintaining a Job Search Folder

Health care executives frequently are terminated and do not have their resumes up to date or the material at hand to construct one. It is important to maintain a folder, at work, or preferably, at home, in which all information pertaining to your next expected or unexpected search is placed. An integral part of such a folder is this book. In addition, include: your most recent resume and cover letter, articles about job searches, the outline of a job search plan, as well as other relevant, miscellaneous information.

If you are not going to keep your resume up to date, as was suggested in a previous chapter, then at least make a habit of putting any information which should be added to your resume in your job search folder on an ongoing basis. Additional responsibility, promotions, new outside activities, committee appointments, and publications should all be included. This material makes it easy to upgrade a resume if one is needed.

The other information to include in the folder is a listing of all of the people that may have worked with you that have networked during your recent past such as classmates, professors, former employers, fellow committee members, and even casual acquaintances. In addition, a listing of the more than 100 executive search firms that handle health care executive searches in the United States would be helpful. (More than twenty-five of these top firms are listed in Appendix A in this book.) It also would be helpful to compile a list of the questions most frequently asked on interviews. You can develop your own list of questions by talking with friends and from your own past interviews. Conversely, a list of questions that you believe are appropriate to ask should be developed. Candidates sometimes lose out to their competition because they do not ask the right questions, not because they do not answer questions correctly.

Network

It is easy for a health care executive to become isolated. Even in a community with several hospitals it is easy to be isolated because of the competitive nature of the health care industry. Therefore, it is wise for health care executives to spend a portion of their time outside the facility. When they do, they should make a concerted effort to network with other professionals. Often executives go to seminars and do not take the time to get to know the other attendees. An important part of any seminar is getting to know the other attendees and enabling them to know you. It is also worthwhile to forward a letter to the speaker following such a seminar, commenting on the presentation.

Time at professional association meetings should be maximized. The smart executives do not spend time by themselves at the swimming pool or sightseeing during a professional meeting. They spend it getting to know as many colleagues as they can and enabling their colleagues, in turn, to get to know them.

It is difficult to know how many executives obtain jobs because of their professional network or how many receive it by formal executive searches or some other means. There are many instances where executives would have been unemployed for a much greater period of time than they were if they had not had contacts in other hospitals. Some of the top health care positions in the United States have been filled by searches that did not go beyond the hospital's board contacting several executives who had developed excellent reputations and were known by the former CEO or board members.

Build Cash Reserves

The better an executive's financial position, the better he or she can weather a period of unemployment. The ideal way for employees to save funds for such an emergency was once through tax-deferred annuities, but the requirement that these funds not be taken out until age 59 may affect the use of this instrument. However, there is a hardship clause which allows some executives to use these funds in times of unemployment, but with some penalty. This requirement becomes effective in 1989.

Another change that took place in 1986 was the elimination of tax-deferred programs, which some executives used to defer funds for an emergency. The 1986 law allows someone who was participating in a tax-deferral program to continue, at the same amount, but a person who has not been participating in one, cannot now enter into such a program. Under the old program, employees of participating institutions could put up to 100 percent of their salary into deferred compensation programs.

It is not unusual for a health care executive to be unemployed for a year or more. Therefore, the following guidelines represent the amount an executive should attempt to reserve.

- If under 35, save enough for one year's expenses.
- If between 35 and 40, save enough for two years' expenses.
- If between 45 and 50, save enough for four years' expenses.
- If between 50 and 60, save enough for five years' expenses.

A severance contract can be invaluable in protecting an executive from a financial catastrophe if he or she is terminated. Ironically, often the people who most need this type of protection are the least protected. Contracts, except for those executives at or near the top of an organization, are all too rare.

Seek Other Alternatives

Another option is to develop some side business or skill, which will enable you to earn a living while looking for another position. This is difficult to do, although numerous health care executives enter into other types of work when they retire.

Still another strategy worth pursuing is to educate your spouse to be prepared to carry part of the family's financial burden should you become unemployed. As distasteful as this may be to many executives, it is much easier on the family, including the spouse, if the executive is laid off and the spouse is gainfully employed. If the spouse is already trained in some marketable field, it is a worthwhile investment to keep the license or any other requirement for practice current.

The executive's spouse sometimes is less prepared to handle an executive's involuntary move than the executive. The spouse can either add to the trauma of unemployment, or help alleviate some of its emotional and financial effects.

CONCLUSION

Every autumn, many states have a deer hunting season. And every autumn there are a large number of year-and-a-half-old deer running around, living out in the open and just having a good time. The first time a high-powered rifle is fired and a deer sees the deer next to it explode or a bullet whistles past, the deer's life is changed forever. It understands that it is a hunted animal and it acts accordingly. Like the hunted animal, a health care executive who has had his or her superior "shot out from over them" or has been fired understands the need not only for vigilance, but for continual preparation.

To prepare for your next job move requires a well thought out work plan, but, more importantly, it requires discipline and perseverance. The most common refrain is, "But, I do not have the time." You have the same amount of time as those who rise to the top. Everyone has the same twenty-four hours in a day and 365 days in a year. When you are actively searching for a job, especially if you are unemployed, you will not have the luxury of doing the activities outlined in this chapter.

If you are passing time or spending time, you cannot expect to compete with those who are planning and working toward their next career move. Life is not a dress rehearsal. Like the old story about the race between the tortoise and the hare, the tortoise, who methodically plodded toward the goal, won the race. It is essential that you invest your time, preferably some every day, while you are employed, to prepare for your next job search.

NOTES

1. Earl A. Simendinger, Ph.D. and Terence F. Moore, *Organizational Burnout in Healthcare Facilities: Strategies for Prevention and Change* (Rockville, Md: Aspen Publishers, Inc., 1985).

2. Harry Levinson, "What Killed Bob Lyons?" *Harvard Business Review* 59 (March-April 1981): 160.

3. Mark Silber, Seminar at the Midland Hospital Center, June 1982.

4. Warren Bennis and Burt Nanus, *Leaders: The Strategies for Taking Charge,* (New York: Harper and Row Publishers, Inc. 1985), p. 204.

5. Terence F. Moore and Earl A. Simendinger "Continuing Education for Healthcare Executives: After the MHA Degree," *Journal of the Michigan Hospital Association* (June 1975): 18–21.

6. Many of these activities were cited in Donald Carter, "Marketing Yourself," *Hospital Forum* (June–July 1985): 81–83.

15

Psychological Problems of Job Loss: What To Expect and How To Manage

Terry Riedinger, Director, Employee Assistance Program, The Dow Chemical Company, 47 Building, Midland, MI 48674

> I have some bitterness still but generally I'm a lot better off than I was then. Tony still has a lot of pain, even though he has another job. He will not, even to this day, speak to anyone at the company.
> —*A terminated professional*

Health care executives in today's economic climate are losing jobs with much more regularity than in the past. The temporary stress that comes with a job loss, while predictable and understandable, for some can lead to long-term bitterness, resentment, or even psychological problems. However, like the professional quoted above, reactions can vary in both intensity and outcome. For others, job loss actually becomes an opportunity to catapult themselves into new and even more fulfilling careers. What makes the difference? What determines how any one individual will deal with losing a job? The answers to these questions are complex with research showing that multidimensional factors influence the outcomes of job loss for individuals. The more job losers understand these factors the more they can control their reactions to job loss. The more health care organizations understand, the more effectively they can manage the termination process.

THE PROFESSIONAL JOB MARKET

In recent years there has been increasing interest in the area of job loss and unemployment. The number of publications dealing with termination of employment has increased by over 400 percent since 1981.[1] This increased interest matches the fact that job loss has become increasingly common for professionals since the mid-1970s. U.S. Department of Labor statistics show that in the early seventies the largest single group of

251

unemployed professionals was job losers (51 percent) as opposed to job leavers (16 percent).[2] Today, some 56 million postwar baby boomers are between the ages of twenty-six and forty and are ready to enter the already bulging managerial ranks.[3] Add to this the general rise of the college educated work force, the increase in number of women entering full-time work, and the influx of professionals from other countries, and it becomes apparent why the United States in the last ten years has been studying the unemployed professional.

Prior to the seventies there is little written about job loss, except what was done during the Depression of the thirties. This is not surprising, since from shortly after World War II until the early seventies, the United States experienced an extraordinary period of economic growth and prosperity. Unemployment in general was not a major issue and corporations' appetites for professionals and managers practically was insatiable. With such growth, the belief developed that if one worked hard enough, remained loyal to the company, and was reasonably skilled, promotions would occur regularly and long-term employment was assured.

It now is obvious that this preseventies mentality is unrealistic. Plateauing in one's career is now common and often occurs early in the career. Unfortunately, although the reality of the job market has changed dramatically, values and beliefs about careers and job security have not. This incongruity between beliefs and reality often leads today's professionals, who are plateaued or lose their jobs, to experience extreme distress when these events unfold.

WORK IN THE UNITED STATES

First of all, job loss must be distinguished from unemployment. Unemployment describes a condition of not having a job that requires the individual to adjust to a new life-style. However, being unemployed, unlike job loss, can be a voluntary choice and does not describe the crisis that develops when a job is taken away. As Ed, a young engineer put it, "When I lost my job, it was what I think would be akin to how it would feel if your wife left you. You feel so bitter. There is such a feeling of shock."

The analogy of job loss to divorce or the death of a loved one is common in early Depression-era literature on unemployment and underscores the tremendous attachment that people have to work. Work has a highly valued place in American society, satisfying some basic human needs. The power of work as a motivating force is seen in individuals who become virtual workaholics to the point that their interests are narrowed almost exclusively to work-related activities.

Work seems to satisfy needs that generally fall under three categories: (1) economic, (2) social, and (3) psychological.

- *Economic Needs*—At a basic level money is exchanged for goods and services that satisfy primary survival needs. However, economic wealth also becomes symbolic of one's success in the work place.
- *Social Needs*—As the central, nuclear family has deteriorated, work is increasingly a source of interpersonal support. Work provides regular interactions with others, a chance to be part of a group, and an opportunity to develop friendships. One only has to look at the frequent cases of lonely retirees to see the importance of work as a social need.
- *Psychological Needs*—People often base their self concept on what they do for a living and how well they do it. Work success often is the yardstick by which people measure their personal competency. Work clearly fills a psychological need.

For professionals, the job is more than a way to earn a living, it is a career which often can consume their lives both physically and socially. Studies have shown that professionals seem to gain intrinsic ego satisfaction from their work and evaluate their life satisfaction by their job satisfaction.[4] It is not uncommon to see professionals who have little leisure time activities because work to them is more rewarding.

What Is Lost in Job Loss?

Depression-era research tended to support the idea that job loss was inevitably and overwhelmingly a traumatic event. And since professionals tended to invest more of themselves in their work, losing a job meant they often experienced fear, loss of prestige in their own eyes, loss of confidence, and feelings of inferiority.[5]

Modern-day research on white collar job losers suggests that job loss is a much more complex issue. For example, studies show that the self-esteem of white collar workers is not lowered by job loss.[6] Fineman found that 42 percent of the professionals in his study felt profound rejection or failure from losing their jobs and 23 percent felt they lost something of particular value. However, 35 percent saw their job loss as an acceptable, if not positive, experience.[7] Others have found that the more prestigious the job lost, the less devastated the person seemed to be.[8]

For other professionals studied, the impact of job loss has been more negative. Higher levels of self-blame, personal recrimination, depression, and a sense of not being a part of things (i.e., anomie) have been found.[9,10] Even suicide, particularly for males, is connected primarily with the loss of a job.[11]

Job Loss in Today's Context

The picture that emerges suggests that reactions to job loss are not uniform and are contingent on various factors. Individual reactions, then, can range from seeing job loss as an opportunity for growth to perceiving it as a severe threat to personal integrity and well-being.

The current sociological and economic context of job loss helps explain these varied reactions. When compared to the Depression era, white collar workers today have much more mobility in the job market. Unemployed health care executives often can choose a variety of jobs at the same level as well as look at different geographic areas, smaller facilities, or even jobs with less responsibility. Also, the fact that promotions today occur more commonly by moving from one organization to another versus through the ranks of a single organization lessens the stigma of job loss.

Job loss today is seen more readily as a career transition or, at worse, a break in one's career path versus an end to a career. Even the language of job loss has changed. Rather than being given the ax, let go, or fired, the terminated professional often is outplaced and given career transition counseling or assistance. This improved treatment of the terminated employee matches a general trend toward less emphasis on the Protestant ethic as a primary motivator and generally more acceptance of leisure.[12]

Job Loss As a Major Life Stress

The dynamic and individualized reactions to job loss are well explained by current stress and crisis theories. These view various life hazards such as job loss, divorce, or death of a loved one, as traditional periods that present an individual with both "an opportunity for personality growth and with the danger of increased vulnerability to mental disorder."[13] Losing one's job becomes a crisis when the person's basic psychological needs are threatened and the individual's usual coping techniques are not effective in removing this threat. An executive, for example, who is used to being in control of events in his or her life may find the sense of being out of control of his or her future career particularly disconcerting.

In a theoretical context, reactions to job loss are not preordained. Rather, individual reactions to the situation will determine to a large extent the outcome. Not only is the potential for a positive outcome present but individuals actually can determine their own destiny by how they deal with the crisis.

PHASES OF JOB LOSS

When forced with job loss, one can predict patterns that are likely to occur from the time the job is lost until reemployment occurs.[14–17] These predictable phases provide a guide or road map for what is likely to happen during the period after the crisis of a job loss. The old adage "If you don't know where you're going, any road will probably get you there," seems to apply. By knowing what to expect one can move through the phases smoothly and avoid major problems in adjusting to the crisis of the job loss.

A job loser is likely to encounter four phases.

Phase 1 is a period of shock and disbelief if the job loss is sudden, without warning. Kubler-Ross in her studies of dying cancer patients saw similar reactions in patients when they first found out they were terminally ill.[18] This "it can't be me attitude" often can lead to strong denial of the reality of what is happening. At this stage, people tend not to look for work immediately and avoid discussion of the fact that they're unemployed. Some even go on vacations as a way of avoiding taking on the new identity of being unemployed. For some, this denial process is a necessary way to deal with the cognitive dissonance that results when the self-image of being a strong, competent, successful professional is in clear contrast with the new self-image of being unemployed, not in control, and a failure at the job just lost. Until one can reconcile the two images, the anxiety that results may be too great to confront directly.

Other features of this stage include

- restriction of the support network to close friends and family
- tendency to become isolated, and
- general optimism about the future.

Phase 2 begins with an abrupt change in behavior marked by the person becoming fully involved in a job search. As one fired professional noted "once you start networking, working on looking for a job, you can move on. You start feeling a lot better."

There is optimism about finding work at this point with strong motivation to reestablish one's work identity. It may have been a few weeks since the crisis of losing the job occurred and the person is ready to proceed with his or her professional life. However, this window of optimism and motivation can be short-lived, lasting at most about three months. It seems to be affected by

- how well the person controls stress and copes with the identity issue
- how well the job search proceeds
- the financial position
- the support system

Other features of this phase include

- a reduction in anger and bitterness
- increased feelings of isolation from the work world
- reduction of denial as a defense, and more direct confronting of the unemployed identity
- more involvement by the spouse in the job search
- increased stress on marital relationships and increased marital problems for those who had difficulty before the job loss
- more openness with others about the situation

Phase 3 can be a second crisis if another job has not been found after several months. Anxiety and stress begin to peak as the prospect of not being able to continue one's career looms larger on the horizon. Health care executives with specialized skills or who have achieved a level where the number of jobs are limited, may discover it is difficult to find opportunities quickly.

The optimism about finding a job that was present earlier often fades at this time and is replaced by self-doubt about one's ability to compete professionally. It is common to experience intense anger as the denial is now completely eroded and the person comes face to face with bitterness toward the ex-employer and possibly themselves. This anger may be displaced toward the spouse, family, economy, government, or even God. It also may be directed inward resulting in depression, despair, helplessness, psychosomatic illnesses, or even suicidal feelings.

Other features of this stage include

- Withdrawal and isolation increase as a result of increasing self-doubt.
- Sporadic job search efforts that are focused on finding any job as a way to reduce the increasing anxiety and fear about never finding work.

- More moodiness is noted, which tends to further tax the support system at a time when the unemployed person needs maximum support.
- There is further threat to the self-image of being the breadwinner if the spouse begins working at this time.

The crisis of Phase 3 is resolved by developing a more stable, quiet, and resigned pattern of coping.

Phase 4—the "resignation and withdrawal" or "malaise and cynicism" stage—results if a job has not been found after about six months.[19,20] There is less anxiety at this time as these feelings are eclipsed by a strong sense of helplessness about the future. Of particular concern is the fact that the person starts settling into an unemployed life-style and develops reactions similar to the hard core unemployed.[21] Individuals in Phase 4 begin transforming their identity that was previously so strongly linked to their career to being unemployed. The more completely this transformation takes place, the more difficult it becomes for the person ever to return to work. The person may develop an external locus of control (i.e., they see others or events controlling their destiny). While, at some level, there is a lack of self-confidence and a loss of self-esteem, often these experiences cannot be confronted easily. The result is an externalizing of blame for what has transpired. Unfortunately, by externalizing blame, the person also gives up his or her self-determination and ability to control his or her destiny.

Job search activities, if they occur at all are low-risk endeavors. Only answering ads for just the right job, answering blind ads, or sending resumes become primary job search activities since they require little personal investment and reduce the likelihood of feeling like a failure.

The individual needs a great deal of support at this stage, but help from family and friends may be rejected. It may be necessary to reassess career goals or find other job search techniques. Sustained effort is needed at this time, but is very difficult. Even the assistance of outplacement counselors may be rejected or may end because of time limits on service provided. A sense of being isolated may develop. As Larry, a fired hospital CEO said, "It's like being at your parent's funeral, with both parents gone and having someone with both parents still alive try to say they understand. They really can't understand what it's like. You can really feel alone."

RISK FACTORS

Not everyone who loses a job progresses through every job loss phase. Not everyone works through them at the same rate and not everyone experiences as many negative aspects as others. What causes some to adapt and others to have difficulty? There are many factors that determine the answer to this question.

Schlossberg in her studies of how people react to life transitions focuses on three areas:

1. characteristics of the particular transition
2. characteristics of the support system before and after the transition
3. characteristics of the individual[22]

By using Schlossberg's model and examining the results of research on factors that influence adjustment to job loss, a list of risk factors can be developed that would warn a person about potential problems in being unemployed. Below is a list of some factors that generally are accepted as affecting adaptation to job loss.

Characteristics of the Job Loss

- The job loss is viewed as a major loss of security, self-worth, or social approval.
- The terminated person avoids confronting the feelings that result from job loss, and instead uses denial and repression as coping mechanisms.
- The loss of the job is sudden and unpredicted.
- Being unemployed is seen as permanent or long term.
- The overall stress level is high because of additional life stresses.

The Job Loser's Environment

- There is a weak or nonexistent interpersonal support network.
- The manner in which the person is terminated is unprofessional and disrespectful.
- The job loss requires a move from a geographic area that is highly desirable.

Individual Characteristics

- The job loser generally is not confident in his or her abilities or lacks self-esteem.
- The individual tends to have a pessimistic, negative outlook on life, and as a result, focuses on the worst aspects of the situation.

- Coping skills, such as problem solving, planning, communication, and conflict resolution are deficient.

- The individual's concept of himself or herself as a "good man" or "good woman" is enmeshed with the career identity.

- The person is at a life stage (i.e., middle or pre-retirement age) where job loss produces additional stresses.

- The individual's financial status is such that job loss causes substantial changes in life-style.

- The person's life has been fairly smooth with few crises of major proportion, to this point, thus providing few opportunities to practice coping with major life transitions.

COPING STRATEGIES

If understanding the phases of job loss is like reading a road map, then knowledge of coping techniques is like knowing how to drive on a variety of road conditions while on a trip. From a stress, crisis model, it is important for individuals in a job loss situation to utilize effective coping styles so that the journey will end at a destination they desire. There is a natural human tendency to reduce the amount of stress one experiences so that there is a balanced or steady state of psychological equilibrium. The danger, however, is that in the desire to relieve the stress, destructive and maladaptive coping patterns will develop and the individual will travel down the wrong road.

Stress theory also provides a structured model for examining effective strategies for coping with job loss. General techniques for coping with stress include: eliminating or effectively managing those things that create stress, developing effective coping mechanisms, and building up resistance to the impact of stress. Following this model, a list of effective coping techniques are outlined below. Successfully using them would increase the likelihood that the job loss will be experienced as an opportunity for growth, change, or even a more fulfilling life-style.

Managing the Stress of Job Loss

Confront the Negative Feelings

Anger, anxiety, fear, depression, or general feelings of loss are all predictable, normal feelings that accompany job loss. Like grieving any loss, it is important to allow these feelings to be experienced. After feelings of initial shock and numbness, the more intense feelings that are likely to emerge should be allowed to happen. Like a boxer, one must absorb the blow of the intense feelings that are suddenly present. Urges to cry, yell, scream, or talk with others should not be stifled, but instead, constructive ways of emotional expression should be sought.

Channel Feelings into Positive Actions

Feelings are a source of tremendous energy. When harnessed and focused in positive ways, they can be very helpful. For example, a certain amount of focused resentment could result in a strong desire to prove to the ex-employer that one is a competent, capable professional. There are numerous examples of famous, successful figures in society who have overcome adversity by using their failures as motivating experiences. Lee Iacocca's reactions to being fired as the CEO of Ford resulted in a remarkable phoenix-like rise in Chrysler. This is an excellent example of this principle in action.

Look Beyond Anger and Blame

Blaming others or one's self actually helps provide some rationale and structure for a situation that may seem chaotic and uncontrollable. Also, anger and blame, externalized emotions, are easier to experience than one's fears and anxieties, which focus more on the individual's own inadequacy. However, the longer one stays locked into anger and blame, the more likely one is to experience psychological problems in the future.

Talking about feelings and expressing frustration with friends, a spouse, relatives, or intimates is necessary. Even writing about feelings in a personal diary can help release feelings and deal with the negative side of job loss.

Engage in an Effective, Aggressive Job Search

Spending time looking for work provides a positive focus for negative feelings, helps fill time and break up boredom, enhances self-esteem, and allows the person to stay connected with the work world. It is important to put as much energy into looking for a new job as one put into the old job. Many job searchers report success when they continue to follow their same work routine even after being terminated. Getting up at the same time, wearing business clothes, and spending the day devoted to the job search can have many payoffs psychologically and from a career standpoint.

Get Professional Counseling if Needed

Severe depression, suicidal feelings, homicidal thoughts, alcohol and drug abuse, or severe marital problems may all be indications that the stresses of job loss are not being coped with effectively and professional help is needed. Even if the normal, predictable reactions continue or do not follow those typical of the job loss phases, help should be sought. Reputable mental health professionals could be invaluable in working through abnormal reactions.

Developing Coping Responses

Engage in Constructive Activities

Besides the job search, it is important to engage in activities that might be called ego enhancing (i.e., things one feels that one is good at or helps one feel good about one's self). Spending time with the family, engaging in hobbies, or exercising are examples. Serving on the board of a community organization can be an excellent way to remain active, enhance one's self-esteem, and provide valuable networking opportunities. The downside of this increased activity is that it can become an avoidance technique and help the person delay confronting the realities of being unemployed.

As one outplaced hospital executive noted "If I made one mistake it was that I took too much time early on to vacation, spend time with the family, and the like. I really hurt myself by not getting involved early enough in looking for a job. . . . I think I was avoiding having to get back in the saddle."

Engage in Problem Solving versus Anxiety Control

When faced with strong emotions there is a tendency to focus on controlling the emotions instead of solving the problem that created the emotions. Being frightened or anxious about finances, career opportunities, or family reactions are realistic fears. Effective problem solving would suggest that one confront each problem, one at a time, developing alternative approaches, evaluating each option, and following through on the best course of action. By confronting the problems head on, it is less likely that one will waste one's energy on fleeing the panic that can result from losing a job.

Building Resistance to the Impact of a Job Change

Develop a Support Network

The support of others is a vital part of coping effectively with a job loss. The desire to isolate and withdraw out of shame or guilt must be overcome or a destructive pattern can develop.

A support network might include a variety of people such as friends, a spouse, family and work associates, outplacement counselors, and members of the clergy. A support network is somewhat like a garden. It has in it a variety of people who can give various things but none of whom can individually satisfy all the needs of the job loser. However, if it is cultivated and nourished, the garden of support can yield a harvest of benefits.

The spouse is the most important person in the support network. The spouse can help reaffirm the job loser's sense of worth by being positive and reminding the job loser of his or her personal strengths and positive attributes. A good marital relationship can help remind the job loser that he or she still is good in a very important part of life. On a more practical level, the spouse can be an important day-to-day assistant in the job search campaign and should be encouraged to get involved.

Communication that is open and honest establishes an atmosphere that encourages the family to openly express the negative feelings associated with the job loss, since the spouse and children also become unemployed. Two-way communication allows them to express their own frustrations and be even more supportive. The job loser must learn to let the family know what his or her needs are, even if it is to be left alone. If these needs are not verbalized, the spouse can begin to feel rejected by seeing the spouse pull away from the family. This can create a vicious circle of mutual hurt, withdrawal, and even stronger feelings of personal failure for the job loser.

Retaining relationships outside the family relieves the pressure to take care of all the individual's needs from the family. While this is true for family members, at all times it becomes even more important during a job loss transition. Peers can provide discussions of professional issues and valuable networking contacts. Even talking with others who have lost their jobs can help ease the sense of being alone.

Keep Thoughts Rational and Optimistic

If the lost job had been a great part of a person's self-image, then the loss may be experienced as a loss of self-worth or even a loss of self. Realistically, though, when one loses a job, that is all that is lost. Careers are only externalizations of a part of who one is internally but they are not the sum total of the person. If one fails at a job, have they failed as a person? If so, one could reason that job losers would be less worthwhile than job retainers. There would be millions of worthless people in the United States. The likes of Lee Iacocca and Mary Cunningham (the fired Bendix executive) would also have to be included in that number as worthless failures.

While this logic is extreme, it points out the need to retain a rational assessment of one's self-worth. The most trusted members of the support network can help provide honest feedback about personal and professional strengths. Focusing on strengths, accomplishments, and successes of the past can help one keep in sight the half-full versus half-empty glass.

Be Flexible and Creative

Careers can tend to narrow one's thinking to particular work and professional concerns. Job loss is a chance to temporarily pull back from the routine of a career and think creatively about the future. It also is an opportunity to explore new horizons, to critically evaluate what has been automatically accepted, and to discard old, less useful ways of thinking or behaving. This, however, is a difficult process. One's routine provides a source of predictability and security that is not abandoned readily.

Often it is not that there is a paucity of options, but rather there are many possibilities and each option has something to offer. As a result, each is at least partially appealing. The tendency then is to postpone change until the right job or just the right opportunity comes along.

Honest self-assessment of personal and career goals is a necessary first step to making a change. Reflective questions that help stimulate creative self-assessment include the following:

- What would I do with my life if money were no object?
- What are the most important things to me in my career and personal life?
- Am I in control of my life?
- How much of my life is spent doing things that I value?
- What career options would match my personal interests and professional skills?
- What holds me back from making a change?[23]

If you find that your career has not evolved to a point that is congruent with your wants, values, or needs, then the challenge becomes to set new directions. Job loss, while always stressful and for some traumatic, also affords the fired health care executive the opportunity to set a new, more satisfying course for the future.

NOTES

1. Janina C. Latack and Janelle B. Dozier, "After the Ax Falls: Job Loss as a Career Transition," *Academy of Management Review* vol. 11, no. 2 (1986).

2. H.G. Kaufman. *Professionals in Search of Work* (New York: John Wiley & Sons, 1982).

3. Judith M. Bardwick. *The Plateauing Trap* (New York: Amacom, 1986).

4. Gigurin, J. Veroff, and S. Felt. *Americans View Their Mental Health* (New York: Basic Books, 1960).

5. Philip Eisenberg and Paul F. Lazarsfeld, "The Psychological Effects of Unemployment," *Psychological Bulletin*, 35 (1938).

6. Jean F. Hartley. "The Impact of Unemployment upon the Self-Esteem of Managers," *Journal of Occupational Psychology*, 53 (1980).

7. Stephen Fineman. *White Collar Unemployment, Impact and Stress* (Bath: John Wiley & Sons, 1983).

8. K.L. Schlozman and S. Verba, *Injury to Insult* (Cambridge, Mass: Harvard Press, 1979).

9. R.J. Estes, "Emotional Consequences of Job Loss," doctoral dissertation, University of Pennsylvania, School of Social Work, 1973.

10. Kaufman, *Professionals.*

11. W. Breed, "Five Components of a Basic Suicide Syndrome," *Life Threatening Behavior*, 2, no. 11 (1972).

12. Craig B. Little, "Technical-Professional Unemployment: Middle Class Adaptability to Personal Crisis," *The Sociological Quarterly* 17 (Spring 1976).

13. Gerald Caplan, *Principles of Preventive Psychiatry* (New York: Basic Books, Inc., 1964), 36.

14. William H. Jones, "Grief and Involuntary Career Change: Its Implications for Counseling," *The Vocational Guidance Quarterly* (March 1979).

15. Douglas Powell and Paul Driscoll, "Middle Class Professionals Face Unemployment," *Society*, 10 (1973).

16. Penny Swinburne, "The Psychological Impact of Unemployment on Managers and Professional Staff," *Journal of Occupational Psychology*, 54 (1981).

17. Kaufman, *Professionals.*

18. Elizabeth Kübler-Ross, *On Death and Dying* (New York: The Macmillan Company, 1970).

19. Kaufman, *Professionals*, 104.

20. Powell and Driscoll, "Middle Class," 23.

21. Kaufman, *Professionals.*

22. Nancy Schlossberg, "A Model for Analyzing Human Adaptation to Transition," *The Counseling Psychologist*, 9 (1981).

23. Janet Hagberg and Richard Leider, *The Inventurers* (Reading, Mass: Addison-Wesley Publishing Co., Inc., 1982).

16

Evaluating, Selecting, and Using Outplacement Firms by Organizations and Job Seekers

Miceal C. Rooney, Vice President, Professional Services, Career Decision, Inc., 500 Park Blvd., Suite 1245, Chicago, IL 60143

INTRODUCTION

Outplacement is a two-edged sword. On one edge is the job seeker who has been severed from his or her organization. On the other is the organization doing the cutting. This chapter will examine both edges.

The potential user of outplacement services may be feeling bewildered and confused. Perhaps even anxious and panicky. He or she has been working hard for an organization and has been doing exceptionally well. However, it does not seem to matter. The job no longer is satisfying and rewarding. The lustre is gone, the freshness has become stale, the excitement has disappeared, the sense of security has eroded. The executive feels it is time to look for a new position, and yet there is a sense of confusion as to how to go about doing that.

The reason for this turmoil is that the rules of the game have changed. The chairperson that hired the executive has been replaced and the new chairperson and the executive do not see eye to eye. They have different agendas and it may be only a matter of time before the chairperson and the board tell the executive to look for a new job. He or she may already have gotten the pink slip. What kind of assistance is needed? Where does one find it? How does one evaluate it?

The one responsible for providing outplacement services also may be wondering just what kind of assistance is out there. He or she has heard about outplacement firms and believes that it could be an answer to some of the sticky problems of staff reduction. However, just what the service is, and how it works, and how much it costs, and whether it is cost effective or not are questions that need to be answered.

Whether recipient or provider of outplacement services, relief is needed. Being cut or having to make the cut is an unsettling experience, and relief is sought as quickly and as painlessly as possible.

265

What do outplacement firms promise to do and what do they actually deliver? What are the criteria for evaluating, selecting, and using an outplacement firm? These are the topics of this chapter and each will be addressed separately. Each topic will be discussed both from the standpoint of the recipient and from the standpoint of the organization sponsoring the outplacement services.

EVALUATING OUTPLACEMENT FIRMS

From the Job Seeker's Standpoint

Most executives who are in need of job seeking assistance do not need assistance in how to do their jobs. They are professionals in their craft. Their training has prepared them to do a good job and their experience has refined their skills to the point where they are high-caliber producers. The assistance that they need is not in how to do a job, but in how to look for a job. The high-caliber producer frequently is a neophyte at job seeking. The purpose of outplacement is to train the executive to become a professional job seeker.

It can be assumed that virtually all job seeking executives are competing with equals. In the job market, one executive is just as skilled and as qualified as the other. The difference then, whereby one job seeker gains the edge over another, lies in something beyond expertise. It is in gaining a marketing advantage. Two equally talented CEOs, both in their mid-fifties, were looking for new jobs. One was enthusiastic and energetic. The other was somber, serious and "presidential." The former got a better job in three months. The latter took a lesser job after a one year search. The process of outplacement trains the individual in the subtleties of effective marketing and sales skills.

Of course, all outplacement firms claim to do just that. The problem is how does a person distinguish one firm from another? First of all, reputation needs to be considered. It would be wise to check with friends and acquaintances. U.S. culture has progressed (or regressed) so far that the notion of the long-term employee is a thing of the past. Nowadays, everyone knows someone who has been let go or who has left his or her job "by mutual agreement." Friends and acquaintances may not talk about it without prompting. But once they are asked for recommendations, they will share their experiences with outplacement firms. Like any business providing a service, outplacement firms need to ensure customer satisfaction. A check with the Better Business Bureau can also shed light on particular outplacement firms and their reputations.

Potential recipients of outplacement assistance should interview the outplacement firms that have been presented to them. They should ask questions and see if the answers provided are to their satisfaction. What do the firms say they will provide? Do they make promises or guarantees that seem too good to be true? If so, they probably are. The recipient should ask about confidentiality. His or her ex-organization is the sponsor and is paying for the service. What kind of and how much information goes back to it? What commitments are made to the job seeker? How long will these commitments continue? Will he or she be trained in the techniques of effective personal marketing and then be left to his or her own devices? Or will the job seeker receive ongoing assistance throughout the job search? A good outplacement firm not only trains people in the fine points of marketing their skills, but also stays with them on a regular consulting basis throughout the length of the search. What is the composition of the outplacement firm's staff? Who are the members? What are their credentials? How many are there? It is important that the staff have the professional background to be able to train the job seeker in marketing techniques. It is equally important that they have the personal characteristics to be sensitive to the job seeker's personality and individual needs. Is the staff stable? How long have they been with the firm? It may not be advisable to receive training from someone who works on a temporary or part-time basis. A job seeker may be stuck with a follow-up counselor who does not know him or her and is not aware of his or her specific needs.

A good program of follow-up consulting is critical to any effective outplacement service. After a person receives his or her initial training in interviewing skills, the early enthusiasm of acquiring this new marketing expertise begins to wane. Being unemployed is a devastating experience, and it is full of rejection. Without ongoing support from the outplacement firm, the job seeker must handle rejection alone. It is important, therefore, that regular support be provided. However, this does not mean that individual offices need to be provided for the job seeker. Though this may sound cruel and harsh, it is not. So often when an office is provided for the job seeker, the facade of going to work is maintained. It is too easy to go to the outplacement office and spend the day there, rather than aggressively beating the pavement. It is more advisable to work out of one's home. Ongoing telephone support from the outplacement consultant is sufficient, as long as that consulting is on a regular and indepth basis. Be leery of outplacement firms whose follow-up consulting consists only of brief, periodic phone calls where the only support given is, "How are you doing?" and "Keep in there. Things will turn around." and "The market's getting better."

What services are provided? Among them are resume writing, job leads, interview training, skills assessment to maximize strengths and weaknesses, ongoing telephone support, secretarial services, office use, ongoing face-to-face support, psychological assessment, and group support. Some of these are essential, and others are ancillary (some are even detrimental). Interview training, skills assessment, and ongoing support are critical components of outplacement services. Certainly resumes and cover letters are a part of the business culture; however, they are of secondary importance. Though resumes and cover letters should be provided, they should not be given primary attention. A person should be alert to outplacement firms that focus on paper. Few executives get jobs through resumes. Most executives get their jobs through person-to-person, face-to-face contact.

In downplaying resumes and cover letters, extensive mail campaigns and sophisticated secretarial services also are discouraged. What is needed is heavy telephone contact and frequent face-to-face courtesy interviewing. The only writing of significant value are thank you notes. These easily can be done at home in the evening. The impact of a simple, personal, handwritten thank you note cannot be overestimated.

From the Organization's Standpoint

The provider or sponsor of outplacement services wants to be assured that his or her needs are met when the organization contracts with an outplacement firm to aid in reducing or downsizing staff. Before evaluating an outplacement firm, a sponsor must know what his or her needs are. Does the sponsor need an outplacement firm to assist in working with one terminated individual? Or is there a group of people who need to be terminated in a downsizing effort? Is the need only once or twice a year, or is it necessary on an ongoing, regular basis? The question then becomes, "Will the outplacement firm be there when I need it?" It does a sponsor no good at all to find himself or herself needing outplacement assistance tomorrow and be told to wait until next week or the week after for help.

In evaluating an outplacement firm, the sponsor should ask the same questions that the recipient asks regarding outplacement staff make-up and stability. The provider needs to know that the outplacement firm is of a size large enough to be able to deliver its services consistently. By nature, the timing of staff reductions and terminations tends to be erratic. The sponsor needs to be comfortable in knowing that whenever there is a need, the outplacement firm will be there.

Costs also must be addressed. Since the industry average for outplacement is about 15 percent of the recipient's current compensation, the question is not then, "How much does it cost?" but "Will my organization receive a benefit equal to the cost incurred?" A measure of this is to assess the results. What is the outplacement firm's record with its clients? What is the average length of time that the job seekers take in getting a new job? Are the new positions satisfactory? Is the sponsor's ex-employee happy in his or her new job? Is the ex-employee focusing in on the new job and forgetting about the previous one, and not intent on bad-mouthing (much less suing) his or her old employer? What kind of feedback does the outplacement firm give to the sponsor? Though the individual recipient of the outplacement service has a right to confidentiality, the sponsor who pays for the service also has a right to some feedback on the services rendered. Is the outplacement firm able to maintain those two distinct relationships? Are they able to maintain a professional relationship with the job seeker, and still be able to document for the sponsoring organization the fact that its money was well spent?

For the sake of convenience, location of the outplacement firm in the same metropolitan area as the sponsor is desirable. However, it is not necessary. With today's ease of business travel and long-distance communications, it is not a problem for a client to fly to an outplacement firm's headquarters. In fact, it may even be preferable to do so. When an outplacement firm has full-service field offices scattered around the country, two problems can arise. One is that quality control may not be maintained. There can be good offices and not-so-good offices. Consistency cannot be guaranteed. The second problem is the appearance of partiality. If the outplacement firm is located near the sponsoring organization, the recipient of the service may not view the outplacement firm as an impartial consultant. He or she may view it as being too close to the company that fired him or her. This could lessen objectivity, rapport, and trust—qualities that are important in providing good outplacement assistance.

A final area that the sponsoring organization should consider in evaluating outplacement firms is the role differentiation of the outplacement staff. Is the professional training staff distinct from the marketing staff? Or do the consultants wear both hats? Needless to say, if the consulting staff depends on sales commissions for its livelihood, shortcuts in training are conceivable. Conversely, when the training staff is salaried, the sense of professional commitment to the executive job seeker is assured more easily.

SELECTING AN OUTPLACEMENT FIRM

From the Job Seeker's Standpoint

Once the evaluation process has been completed, selection of an outplacement firm tends to be a relatively simple matter. After the individual executive has interviewed the various firms and found out what each of them has to offer, he or she decides which can respond to his or her needs. The executive then can decide which of the firms best meets his or her objectives.

Beyond objective evaluation though, there is the intangible indicator of gut-level feeling. When an executive enters into a commitment with a consulting firm, he or she wants to have a sense of comfort with that organization. It is important then for the individual to trust gut-level feelings regarding both the outplacement firm and its consulting staff. Does the individual executive feel comfortable with the assigned consultant? If not, can he or she change consultants? Elements of this comfortable feeling include a sense of two-way communication and a sense of care and concern.

Regarding two-way communication, the individual should feel that what he or she has to say to the consultant is being heard. Though a strong element of the outplacement process is the training component, there also is a counseling aspect to the relationship. Does the consultant listen when the job seeker is expressing concerns and fears, and plans and aspirations? Related to the job seeker's sharing of these feelings, is the consultant's sense of care and concern. Is the consultant professionally competent in being able to understand a job seeker who is hurting? Does the consultant have a sense of empathy whereby he or she can tune into what the unemployed executive is experiencing?

In selecting an outplacement firm, the executive job seeker needs to consider cost. This does not mean, "How much will it cost the job seeker?" Outplacement services should not cost the job seeker anything. The fees always should be paid by the sponsoring organization. An unemployed job seeker has no business spending 15 percent of his or her annual compensation on outplacement services. This is not to say that the outplacement service does not have that value. The problem is that if a job seeker were to pay for outplacement services, it would be too easy for that job seeker to forget that he or she has only purchased training and consulting services. It would be too easy for the job seeker to feel that he or she had purchased a new job. No one can buy a job. Though the unemployed executive intellectually knows that, the job search itself is so distasteful that the job seeker will gravitate toward any excuse, which lessens the impact of the rejection inherent in job hunting. If he or she were to pay 15 percent of his or her compensation the executive easily could say, "Well, look what I paid you. Where's my job?" Any outplacement firm that charges an individual job seeker a fee should be looked at very closely.

From the Organization's Standpoint

Selecting an outplacement firm should be done with deliberation. The cost element needs to be considered. What are the total costs? Does the standard 15 percent fee include ongoing consulting? How are expenses handled? Are there hidden costs? Is the fee based on salary alone or on salary plus bonuses? The sponsoring organization also needs to know if the outplacement firm specializes exclusively in individual training. The sponsor's needs may be at one time individual outplacement services and, at other times, small or large group outplacement services. Can the outplacement firm handle each of these situations? If not, in which does it have expertise? Perhaps the sponsoring organization should consider using one outplacement firm for individual and another firm or two for group trainings.

Are there other services that the outplacement firm can provide? Though one may be leery of a company that sells anything and everything, there are adjunct services to outplacement that can be beneficial. These would include executive assessment, management succession, preretirement counseling, and employee assistance. A sensitive organization frequently can get a feel for pre-existing needs. For example, nine months before a planned termination, a problem executive could be provided a management/psychological assessment. The advantage of this, from the sponsor's standpoint, can be the possible alleviation of the future need to terminate. From the participant's standpoint, the advantage of an assessment is greater self-knowledge. It can prepare the problem executive for the possible changes to come. One can see in this approach a sponsor's commitment to humane human resource management.

Another consideration in selecting an outplacement firm is the establishment of an ongoing consulting relationship. Those charged with managing human resource departments or managing companies as chief executive officers are aware that staffing problems of one kind or another are always going to crop up. With an ongoing relationship with an outplacement firm, the organization has at its disposal a variety of resources, and also a sounding board to ease the friction that staffing changes produce.

USING AN OUTPLACEMENT FIRM

From the Job Seeker's Standpoint

In utilizing an outplacement firm, it is important for the individual participant to fully understand the process. It is too easy to mistake outplacement for placement. It is too easy for an executive who is not working to feel that the outplacement firm's role is to find him or her a job. This is not the case. No one can find a job for someone else. No one can buy a job for someone else. The purpose of outplacement services is to assist the executive in being able to find the job himself or herself. The purpose of outplacement services is to train the job seeker in the techniques of effective self-marketing. The job search is a difficult one, and it is filled with rejection and dejection. These feelings cannot be taken away. What can be removed is ignorance of the search process. A good outplacement firm is able to not only train an individual in marketing techniques but also motivate that individual to maintain a strong, aggressive job search stance.

The individual needs to realize that being hired is not a logical decision. An executive's level of expertise is, by and large, not the deciding factor in getting a new job. Not that expertise is not needed. Quite the contrary. An individual must be talented to perform well in a job. The point though is that every job seeking executive is competing with other executives at or near his or her own level of competence. Expertise is a given. The reason a person gets hired is because the decision maker in the organization likes the person he or she is interviewing.

And so, the main thrust of an outplacement program is to instill in the job seeker the effective techniques of job seeking. These include, first and foremost, a marketing of competence and compatibility. Both must be marketed. One without the other will not do. A person who is competent but has no personality will not get very far. On the other hand, a very friendly person who is not skilled does not stand much chance of succeeding over the long term. The job seeker must project the fact that he or she is professionally at the top of his or her peer group and, personally, that he or she will fit in well with the organization. The outplacement process focuses on making sure that this is comprehended, believed, and acted upon. Though this may sound simplistic, it is a lesson that many find difficult. The effective outplacement firm is able to train and motivate its clients in these essentials. Marginal outplacement firms focus on resumes and cover letters and mail campaigns.

Beyond an understanding of the outplacement process, the individual participant needs to have a commitment to the process. Without that commitment an individual cannot succeed in getting a new position in a timely manner. With such a commitment though, the individual can cut his or her job search time in half. It is assumed that when one is talking about looking for a new job, one means a job that is equal to or better than the previous position. Elements that compose equal to or better than include not only monetary reward, but also professional stimulation, personal satisfaction, geographic preference, and an enhanced life-style.

There are two parts to the outplacement process: the training function at the beginning of the outplacement process and the follow-up component. The training segment should take relatively little time. There is no need for a training program to last a month or two. The elements needed for an effective job search can be presented and grasped within one week's time. Even an in-depth psychological assessment—which is quite beneficial and which few outplacement firms provide—can be effectively incorporated in the initial training segment. After the training, the job search begins. The individual needs to be aggressively marketing himself or herself, "working the telephone" and "beating the pavement." Outplacement programs that provide unnecessarily lengthy training sessions appear to rely upon the placebo effect of comfort and reassurance. The job search is not comfortable. As mentioned previously, strong consulting support must be provided. A problem that the executive faces in the job search is continual rejection. Until the day a new position is accepted, every prior attempt is a rejection. No one likes to be rejected, and the unemployed executive finds that even doubly painful. Supportive follow-up counseling can alleviate some of this pain by letting the job seeker know that rejection is a normal part of an effective job campaign.

In utilizing an outplacement firm, an executive needs to recognize limitations that may be present. Sad to say, the business world still is a prejudiced one. The executive who is older or who is a member of a minority group or who has a handicap will face discrimination. Though that makes the job search more difficult, it does not make it impossible. A good outplacement firm helps the executive manage these situations. Though adjustments may be necessary, discrimination is not insurmountable. The nebulous qualities of attitude, stamina, and assertiveness are critical to this process. Through outplacement training, a job seeking executive refines and strengthens these qualities.

To balance the negative tone of the prior paragraphs, it is worth noting that the executive who avails himself or herself of outplacement assistance becomes a far better job seeker than his or her competitor. When it comes down to the final decision of one candidate over another, the executive who has received outplacement help tends to stand head and shoulders above his or her peers. In using outplacement assistance, the individual learns how to tap into the so-called "hidden" job market. Easily 80 percent of available positions are never published. They do not show up in the newspaper want ads or in the recruiters' listings. They are filled by word of mouth and personal contact. Since the thrust of outplacement stresses the spoken word over the written word and also stresses personal contact and networking, the outplacement client finds himself or herself way ahead of other job seekers in the job chase.

From the Organization's Standpoint

The utilization of outplacement has both benefits and cautions. As a caution, it is important for the sponsor to listen carefully to the tactical advice that the outplacement firm is giving. The issues that the outplacement firm addresses are issues with which the outplacement firm is quite familiar. Outplacement consultants deal with terminations on a regular basis and are well versed in all the nuances of termination do's and don'ts. By listening to the outplacement consultant's advice, an organization can save a lot of time, effort, and money. The time element can be seen in that a termination should be swift. There is no need to prolong the termination process, once the decision has been made. Regarding the effort expended, the outplacement firm has experience in advising sponsors how best to orchestrate the termination, whether it is on an individual basis or it is a group layoff. Regarding the saving of money, the outplacement firm can advise a sponsor on effective severance arrangements. Certainly no employer wants to gain a reputation as being harsh or vindictive in his or her termination policies. However, that does not mean he or she should go to the opposite extreme and provide unnecessary severance payments. Not only is this costly for the organization, but it also can be detrimental to the recipient.

Consider the not atypical case of an executive client who received a one-year severance. The arrangement was that the executive receive a year's severance monthly until he or she got a new job and then his or her severance would be cut. Look at the outcome. Since the job search was so distasteful, and since there was monthly income, the executive did not look seriously for a job for the first ten months. Only when the severance was coming to an end did he or she dedicate himself or herself in earnest to getting another position. The result was that the executive had been done a disservice with the one-year severance. A better arrangement would have been to give the executive six months severance pay in a lump sum. With that arrangement, it would have been to the executive's advantage to get a new position as soon as possible. Money is a good motivator. After the six-month period was up, and if the executive still did not have a position, then an extension could have been considered on a month-by-month basis. The organization's concern for its ex-employee would still have been maintained, yet in a cost-efficient manner.

A sponsoring organization also can utilize adjunct services that the outplacement firm may offer, such as management consulting and executive assessment. With a number of services available to the sponsoring organization, those responsible for decision making have at their fingertips the assistance needed to handle a variety of human resource situations.

Some sponsoring organizations may be considering an inhouse outplacement component. It would appear that the advantages of such an arrangement are outnumbered by the disadvantages. On the plus side, of course, is the fact that an inhouse outplacement function always is available when needed. However, the main problem with an inhouse function is the identification of that service with the organization. Since the nature of outplacement is addressing sticky human resource staffing problems, it would appear more advisable to use an outside firm that does not have any vested interest in the sponsor.

CONCLUSION

It is important for both sponsoring organizations and individual recipients of outplacement services to be cautious and thorough when assessing their outplacement needs. Since the stakes are so high, (for the individual recipient it is his or her future, and for the sponsoring organization it is a sizable investment in funds) an unwise decision could have harmful effects. Though the decision to contract with an outplacement firm often is a hasty one, preparations for that decision can be made with deliberation. Before the need arises, sponsoring organizations should assess and interview a variety of outplacement firms. In this way, sponsors are able to see exactly what the firms offer and see whether or not the services are in line with their potential needs. With such preplanning, the often quick decision to use an outplacement firm need not be an unwise decision.

17

The Use of Hospital Associations and Other Associations by Organizations and Job Seekers

Charlotte Beck, Manager, Placement Services, Michigan Hospital Association Service Corporation, 6215 W. St. Joseph Highway, Lansing, MI 48917

Hospital associations and other professional organizations may play a key role in helping a job seeker find a position. The listings contained in this chapter provide the reader with a better understanding of how the state hospital association and the American Hospital Association (AHA) can provide assistance in executive placement.

The majority of state hospital associations do not have an executive placement service, however, most do have a type of networking system. Networking sources include monthly or weekly newsletters with a synopsis of candidates for area administrators, word-of-mouth referrals by hospital association executives to chief executive officers (CEOs), chief operating officers (COOs), and board members, and use of a resume file bank, where resumes are kept on file from one month to an indefinite period of time. Upon request, most associations also will provide job seekers with a list of hospitals in their particular state. A job seeker may then contact hospitals directly regarding job availability or resume referral. The most important factor in obtaining assistance from a particular association is to target the geographical area of interest. Once the area is determined, the association may be a valuable resource.

The hospital associations that do provide executive placement services have had great success and are a valuable tool to the health care professional seeking a position. The Michigan Hospital Association Professional Placement Service is in its tenth year of success while the Texas Hospital Association has expanded and has been providing services for eight years. Other associations have formed joint ventures with executive placement firms and provide placement services (see Appendix 17-A).

Health care professionals can find the state association a valuable resource if used in the proper context. The listing of associations contained in Appendix 17-A is the only one of its kind published in the United States. It is current, as of 1988, and lists all 50 states and Puerto Rico.

Hospital associations and professional organizations play an important role in completing the job search. The resources available through these organizations can help job seekers select the right health care job opportunities.

AHA boasts 15 professional societies, all providing some form of assistance to the health care professional seeking a job. At the very minimum, an informal resume file bank is available to the candidate. Each professional society differs, but several have monthly or bimonthly newsletters listing available positions throughout the United States. A list of individual AHA professional societies is provided in Exhibit 17-1.

State hospital associations and other professional associations can be an important resource in a multifaceted job search or search for executive talent. The information contained in this chapter can serve as a key component in a search for an executive or for a job search.

Exhibit 17-1 American Hospital Association Professional Societies

American Academy of Hospital Attorneys
American Organization of Nurse Executives
American Society of Director of Volunteer Services
American Society of Healthcare Education and Training
American Society for Hospital Central Services Personnel
American Society for Hospital Engineering
American Society for Hospital Food Service Administrators
American Society for Hospital Marketing and Public Relations
American Society for Hospital Materials Management
American Society for Hospital Personnel Administration
American Society for Hospital Risk Management
Hospital Management Systems Society
National Society of Patient Representatives
Society for Hospital Planning and Marketing
Society for Hospital Social Work Directors

Please direct all inquiries to:
    American Hospital Association
    840 North Lake Shore Drive
    Chicago, IL 60611
    (313) 280-6111

Hospital Associations

Alabama Hospital Association
500 North East Boulevard
P.O. Box 17059, East Station
Montgomery, AL 36193
(205) 272-8781

Accepts resumes.
Sends a monthly newsletter to
  CEOs and Personnel Directors
  with a short synopsis of new
  resumes by code number.
Interested CEOs call if interested
  in a particular code number;
  resumes sent to interested
  clients.
Resumes kept on file indefinitely.

Health Association of Alaska
319 Seward Street
Juneau, AK 99801
(907) 586-1790

Accepts resumes on an informal
  basis.

Arizona Hospital Association
2411 W. 14th Street, Suite 410
Tempe, AZ 85281
(602) 968-1083

Accepts resumes on an informal
  basis.

Arkansas Hospital Association
1501 N. University Avenue
Prospect Bldg., Suite 400
Little Rock, AR 72207
(501) 664-7870

Joint venture with executive
  search consultants.
*Direct all resumes to the attention
  of:*
  Garofolo, Curtiss, & Co. at the
  Arkansas Hospital Association.

Note: This list was compiled and researched by Charlotte Beck, Manager, Placement Services, Michigan Hospital Association Service Corporation, 6215 W. St. Joseph Highway, Lansing, MI 48917, (517) 323-3443, ext. 429.

California Association of Hospitals & Health Systems
1023 12th Street
P.O. Box 1100
Sacramento, CA 95805
(916) 443-7401

Does not accept resumes; no type of resume file bank or placement service.

Colorado Hospital Association
2140 South Holly Street
Denver, CO 80202
(303) 758-1630

Accepts resumes; kept on file for 90 days.
List of Colorado hospitals available to applicants interested in relocating.

Connecticut Hospital Association
110 Barnes Road
P.O. Box 90
Wallingford, CT 06492
(203) 265-7611

Accepts resumes.
Publishes monthly newsletter called *Job Seekers* giving a short synopsis of new resumes by code number.
Interested CEOs call if interested in a particular code number; resumes sent to clients.
Resumes kept on file indefinitely.

Association of Delaware Hospitals
Bank of Delaware Building
P.O. Box 471
Dover, DE 19901
(302) 674-2853

Joint venture with executive search consultants.
Direct all resumes to the attention of:
Garofolo, Curtiss & Co.
326 W. Lancaster Avenue
Ardmore, PA 19003
(215) 896-5080

District of Columbia Hospital Association
1250 Eye Street, N.W.
Suite 700
Washington, DC 20005
(202) 682-1581

Direct all resumes to:
Hospital Council of the National Capitol Area.
Resumes will be circulated to proper facilities depending upon positions available.

Florida Hospital Association
307 Park Lake Circle
P.O. Box 6905
Orlando, FL 32853
(305) 841-6230

Accepts resumes on an informal basis.

Southern Florida Hospital Association
8245 NW 53rd Street
Suite 200
Miami, FL 33166
(305) 591-8020

Accepts resumes; kept on file for approximately 90 days.

Georgia Hospital Association
North by Northwest Office Park
Atlanta, GA 30339
(404) 955-0324

No type of resume file bank or placement service.

Hospital Association of Hawaii
320 Ward Avenue, Suite 202
Honolulu, HI 96814
(808) 521-8961

Accepts resumes; kept on file approximately one month.

Idaho Hospital Association
6520 Norwood Drive
P.O. Box 7482
Boise, ID 83707
(208) 377-2211

Accepts resumes; kept on file indefinitely.
Have weekly publication with synopsis of new resumes (sent to CEOs).

Illinois Hospital Association at the Center for Health Affairs
1151 East Warrenville Road
Naperville, IL 60540
(312) 367-9370

Accepts resumes for CEO positions only.
Direct all resumes to the attention of:
Garofolo, Curtiss, & Co. at the Illinois Hospital Association.

Indiana Hospital Association
One American Square
P.O. Box 82063
Indianapolis, IN 46282
(317) 633-4870

Accepts resumes for CEO positions only.
Resumes kept on file indefinitely.

The Iowa Hospital Association, Inc.
100 East Grand Avenue
Des Moines, IA 50309
(515) 288-1965

Accepts resumes.
Weekly mailing to administrators with a synopsis of resumes.
Resumes kept on file indefinitely.

Kansas Hospital Association
1263 Topeka Avenue
P.O. Box 2308
Topeka, KS 66601
(913) 233-7436

Accepts resumes.
Resumes are summarized as they are received.
Weekly mailing with memo attached with synopsis of several candidates.
Resumes kept on file indefinitely.

Kentucky Hospital Association
1302 Clear Spring Trace
P.O. Box 24163
Louisville, KY 40224
(502) 426-6220

Accepts resumes.
Publishes quarterly magazine *Kentucky Hospitals*; candidates may advertise their qualifications or credentials in the classified section for a fee.

Louisiana Hospital Association
9521 Brookline Avenue
P.O. Box 80720
Baton Rouge, LA 70898-0720
(504) 928-0026

Accepts resumes.
Publishes monthly newsletter *Impact Employment* with a synopsis of resumes by code number.
Resumes kept on file indefinitely.

Maine Hospital Association
151 Capitol Street
Augusta, ME 04330
(207) 622-4794

Resumes kept on file for approximately three months.

The Maryland Hospital Association, Inc.
1301 York Road
Lutherville, MD 21093-6087
(301) 321-6200

Accepts resumes.
Upon receiving resumes, letters are sent out to candidates asking whether they choose to keep their resumes confidential or if they can be summarized in a newsletter.
Approximately every six weeks, a summary of new resumes are sent to CEOs listing:
- name of applicant
- education
- position person is seeking
- current status

Resumes are kept on file indefinitely.

Massachusetts Hospital Association
Five New England Executive Park
Burlington, MA 01803
(617) 272-8000

Accepts resumes.
Letter sent after receiving resume with form to return.
Monthly publication with synopsis of resumes.
Resumes kept on file indefinitely.

Michigan Hospital Association
6215 W. St. Joseph Highway
Lansing, MI 48917
(517) 323-3443

Professional placement service.
Service fills administrative positions (directors, assistant directors, vice presidents, and CEOs) in health care facilities.
Works on contingency fee basis with Michigan hospitals.
Free service to candidates.
Letter sent out receiving resume with supplement to fill out and return.
Formal filing system of resumes (currently being computerized).
As positions become available, candidates are notified with specifics of opening.
Resumes kept on file indefinitely with status update sent periodically.
Additionally, a joint venture with executive search consultants: Garofolo, Curtiss, & Co. at the Michigan Hospital Association.

Minnesota Hospital Association
Health Associations Center
2221 University Ave. S.E.
Suite 425
Minneapolis, MN 55414
(612) 331-5571

No type of resume file bank or placement service.

Mississippi Hospital Association
4880 McWillie Circle
P.O. Box 16444
Jackson, MS 39236-0444
(601) 982-3251

Accepts resumes.
Weekly synopsis of resumes listed by code number received by administrators.
Resumes kept on file indefinitely.

Missouri Hospital Association
4713 Highway 60 West
P.O. Box 600
Jefferson City, MO 65102
(314) 893-3700

Accepts resumes; kept on file for three months (status update then sent to applicant).
Plans to expand service in the near future.

Montana Hospital Association
P.O. Box 5119
Helene, MT 59601
(406) 442-1911

Accepts resumes; kept on file indefinitely.

Nebraska Hospital Association
1335 L Street
P.O. Box 94833
Lincoln, NE 68509
(402) 476-0141

Accepts resumes; kept on file indefinitely.

Nevada Hospital Association
4600 Kietzke Lane
Suite H-184
Reno, NV 89502
(702) 827-0184

Accepts resumes; kept on file indefinitely.

New Hampshire Hospital Association
125 Airport Road
Concord, NH 03301-5388
(603) 225-0900

Joint venture with executive search consultants.
Direct all resumes to:
Garofolo, Curtiss, & Co. at the New Hampshire Hospital Association.

New Jersey Hospital Association
Center for Health Affairs
746-760 Alexander Rd., CN-1
Princeton, NJ 08543-0001
(609) 275-4000

Accepts resumes; kept on file indefinitely.

New Mexico Hospital Association
5200 Cooper, N.E.
P.O. Box 8735
Albuquerque, NM 87108
(505) 265-3686

Accepts resumes; reviewed by president; kept on file indefinitely.

Hospital Association of New York
Center for Health Initiatives
74 North Pearl Street
Albany, NY 12207
(518) 434-7600

Accepts resumes; kept on file indefinitely.

North Carolina Hospital Association
P.O. Box 10937
112 Cox Avenue
Raleigh, NC 27605
(919) 832-9550

Accepts resumes; kept on file for approximately 90 days.

North Dakota Hospital Association
Suite 307-315
312 First Bank of North Dakota Bldg.
401 DeMers, P.O. Box 669
Grand Forks, ND 58206-0669
(701) 772-4129

Accepts resumes; kept on file indefinitely.

Greater Cleveland Hospital Association
1226 Huron Road
Cleveland, OH 44115
(216) 696-6900

Accepts resumes on an informal basis.
Monthly bulletin sent to members.

Ohio Hospital Association
21 West Broad Street
Columbus, OH 43215-4101
(614) 221-7614

Accepts resumes; kept on file for approximately six months.
OHA placement bulletin published bimonthly with various positions open throughout state.
Additionally, a joint venture with executive search consultants: Garofolo, Curtiss, & Co. at the Ohio Hospital Association.

Oklahoma Hospital Association
777 Northwest Grand Boulevard
Suite 112
Oklahoma City, OK 73118
(405) 843-9587

Accepts resumes.
Outline of resumes compiled
    weekly.
Attaches resume summary to
    mailing by category and code
    number every other week; this is
    run for three consecutive
    mailings.
Computerized system.
Keeps resumes on file for
    approximately six months.
Has good response from smaller
    hospitals.

Oregon Association of Hospitals
4000 Kruse Way Place
Building 2, Suite 100
Lake Oswego, OR 97034
(503) 636-2204

Recommended that interested
    candidates call first.
Accepts resumes on an informal
    basis.

**Hospital Association of
    Pennsylvania**
P.O. Box 608
Camp Hill, PA 17011
(717) 763-7053

Joint venture with executive
    search consultants.
Direct all resumes to:
    Garofolo, Curtiss, & Co. at the
    Hospital Association of
    Pennsylvania.

**Puerto Rico Hospital
    Association**
Officina 101
Villa Nevarez Professional Center
Centro Commercial Villa Nevarez
Rio Piedras, PR 00927
(809) 764-0290
(809) 764-7819

Accepts resumes; kept on file
    indefinitely.

**Hospital Association of Rhode
    Island**
P.O. Box 9627
Providence, RI 02940
(401) 421-7100

Accepts resumes; kept on file
    indefinitely.
Periodically send summary of
    resumes to CEOs.

South Carolina Hospital Association
101 Medical Circle
P.O. Box 6009
West Columbia, SC 29171-6009
(803) 796-3080

Accepts resumes; kept on file indefinitely.

South Dakota Hospital Association
3708 Brooks Place, Suite 1
Sioux Falls, SD 57106
(605) 361-2281

Accepts resumes; kept on file for approximately six months.
Every other week a newsletter is sent out with a synopsis of resume and code number.

Tennessee Hospital Association
500 Interstate Blvd., South
Nashville, TN 37210
(615) 256-8240

Joint venture with executive search consultants.
Direct all resumes to the attention of:
Garofolo, Curtiss, & Co. at the Tennessee Hospital Association.

Texas Hospital Association
P.O. Box 15587
6225 U.S. Highway 290 East
Austin, TX 78761
(512) 465-1000

Formal placement service.
As resumes are received, letter with application form is sent to candidate.
Once application is returned, it is reviewed and summarized.
Personnel Review is published monthly with a summary of candidates' qualifications.
Resumes are kept on file indefinitely.
A status update is sent out every 60 days.
This is a free service to candidates and hospitals. (A percentage of members' dues are allocated to placement and health career services.)
Additionally, a joint venture with executive search consultants: Garofolo, Curtiss, & Co. at the Texas Hospital Association.

Utah Hospital Association
515 South Seventh East
Suite 2-F
Salt Lake City, UT 84102
(801) 364-1515

Accepts resumes on an informal basis.
Synopsis of resume (with code number) is periodically sent to all hospitals and corporate offices.
Resumes kept on file indefinitely.

Vermont Hospital Association
148 Main Street
Montpelier, VT 05602
(802) 223-3461

Accepts resumes on an informal basis; kept on file for approximately one year.

Virginia Hospital Association
P.O. Box
Richmond, VA 23294
(804) 747-8600

Accepts resumes; kept on file approximately six months.

Washington State Hospital Association
190 Queen Anne Ave., North
Seattle, WA 98109
(206) 281-7211

Accepts resumes; kept on file indefinitely.

West Virginia Hospital Association
3422 Pennsylvania Avenue
Charleston, WV 25302
(304) 345-9842

Accepts resumes; kept on file indefinitely.

Wisconsin Hospital Association
5721 Odana Road
Madison, WI 53719-1289
(608) 274-1820

Accepts resumes.
Summarizes and codes resumes as received.
Publishes summaries in a monthly bulletin to member hospitals for a period of three consecutive months.
New resumes are designated by an asterisk in mailing.
Resumes kept on file indefinitely.

Wyoming Hospital Association
2015 South Greeley Highway
P.O. Box 3390
Cheyenne, WY 82003
(307) 632-9344

Accepts resumes on an informal basis.

Appendix A

Contributing Authors and Associated Search Firms

CEJKA, Susan, President
CEJKA & COMPANY
222 S. Central, Suite 400
St. Louis, MO 63105

CLARK, John, Ph.D., Manager
COOPERS & LYBRAND
203 N. La Salle Street
Chicago, IL 60601

CAVER, Michael D., Partner
HEIDRICK & STRUGGLES, INC.
125 S. Wacker Drive
Chicago, IL 60606

KIEFFER, Michael C., President
FORD, J. Daniel, Executive Vice President
KIEFFER, FORD & ASSOCIATES, LTD.
2015 Spring Road
Oak Brook, IL 60521

HEUERMAN, James S., Managing Vice President/Sr. Partner
Health Care Division
KORN/FERRY INTERNATIONAL
600 Montgomery Street
San Francisco, CA 94111

SILBER, Mark, Ph.D., President
MARK SILBER ASSOCIATES, LTD.
16776 Bernardo Center Drive
Professional Suite B-110
San Diego, CA 92128

TYLER, J. Larry, President
TYLER & COMPANY
9040 Roswell Road
Atlanta, GA 30350

LLOYD, John S., President
COX, Mark M., Sr. Vice President
BOURKE, Joan, Senior Associate Executive Compensation
WITT ASSOCIATES INC.
724 Enterprise Drive
Oak Brook, IL 60521

OTHER EXECUTIVE SEARCH FIRMS WHICH SPECIALIZE IN HEALTH CARE EXECUTIVE SEARCH CONSULTING

CLAPP, Allen, President
ALLEN CLAPP & ASSOCIATES, LIMITED
676 North St. Clair, Suite 1717
Chicago, IL 60611
(312) 943-1201

LEPIMOIT, Art, President
ART LEPIMOIT & ASSOCIATES
608 Camelot Drive
East Lansing, MI 48823
(517) 332-1111

BARGER, H. Carter, President
BARGER & SARGEANT, INC.
One Bicentennial Square
Concord, NH 03301
(603) 224-7753

SNYDER, Jay K. (Ms.), Director Healthcare Division
BENSON & ASSOCIATES
6499 NW 9th Avenue, Suite 201
Fort Lauderdale, FL 33309
(305) 491-5004

BISHOP, Bill, President
BILL BISHOP ASSOCIATES
8282 Western Way Circle, Suite 207
Jacksonville, FL 32216
(904) 739-2764

NOVAK, Stan E., Senior Consultant
BILL MILLER & ASSOCIATES
11665 Avena Place, Suite 205
San Diego, CA 92128
(619) 487-2455

FLYNN, David
**BOYDEN/FLYNN, CAMPBELL, COLLINS EXECUTIVE NETWORK
OF AMERICA**
8505 Freeport Parkway, Suite 130
Irving, TX 75063
(214) 929-4149

BULLIS, Rich, President
BULLIS & COMPANY, INC.
1097 Green Street, Suite 3
San Francisco, CA 94133
(415) 885-0915

CARLSON, Paula, President
CARLSON & ASSOCIATES
11444 West Olympic Boulevard
10th Floor
Los Angeles, CA 90064
(213) 312-9546

KOSTEVA, Dave, B., Vice President
CHI SYSTEMS
130 South 1st. St.
Ann Arbor, MI 48104
(313) 761-3912

McCALLISTER, Richard, President
WILLIAM H. CLARK ASSOCIATES
200 E. Randolph
Chicago, IL 60601
(312) 565-1300

KABIALIS, Richard
COOK ASSOCIATES, INC.
212 West Kinzie Street
Chicago, IL 60610
(312) 329-0900

HARRIS, Jeffrey, President
DRUTHERS AGENCY, INC.
881 Alma Real Drive, Suite 301
Pacific Palisades, CA 90272
(213) 459-7938

SPENCER, Maryanne, Director Executive Search, West Region
ERNST & WHINNEY
515 South Flower St., Suite 2800
Los Angeles, CA 90071
(213) 621-1666

POWERS, Paul, Principle
FENWICK PARTNERS
450 Bedford St.
Lexington, MA 02173
(617) 862-3370

CLARKE, Bob, Vice President Healthcare Executive Search
THE FURST GROUP
6085 Strathmoor Drive
P.O. Box 5863
Rockford, IL 61125
(815) 229-7800

GAROFOLO, Frank A.
GAROFOLO, CURTISS & CO.
326 West Lancaster Avenue
Ardmore, PA 19003
(215) 896-5080

GARRETT, Don L., President
GARRETT ASSOCIATES INC.
950 East Pace Ferry Rd., Suite 1455
Atlanta, GA 30326
(404) 364-0001

ASHLEY, Dian, Director of Research
GOULD & McCOY, INC.
551 Madison Avenue
New York, NY 10022
(212) 688-8671

EAST, Robert G., Management Partner
GUIDRY & EAST
1110 Kingwood Drive, Suite 200
Kingwood, TX 77339
(800) 323-1434

HALSTEAD, Frederick, President
HALSTEAD & ASSOCIATES
7515 Greenville Avenue, Suite 712
Dallas, TX 75231
(214) 369-6800

O'BRIEN, Michael, President
HARPER ASSOCIATES
15659 West Ten Mile Road
Southfield, MI 48075
(313) 557-1700

MORONGALL, Gloria M.
HEALTHCARE CONNECTIONS
25 Braintree Hill Park, Suite 205
Braintree, MA 02184
(617) 848-8080

FITZGERALD, John, President
HEALTH INDUSTRY CONSULTANTS
9250 E. Costilla, Suite 600
Englewood, CO 80112
(303) 790-2009

ROBBINS, Jeffrey, President
HEALTH SEARCH
18662 MacArthur Blvd., Suite 200
Irvine, CA 92715
(714) 955-1991

HERSHER, Betsy S., President
HERSHER ASSOCIATES
3000 Dundee Road, Suite 314
North Brook, IL 60062
(312) 272-4050

LOTZ, R. James, Jr., President
INTERNATIONAL MANAGEMENT ADVISORS, INC.
767 Third Street
New York, NY 10017
(212) 758-7770

ISAACSON, John, Partner
ISAACSON, GILVAR, BOULWARE
105 Chancy Street
Boston, MA 02111
(617) 423-5566

OLDANI, Jerrold, President
JENSEN-OLDANI & ASSOCIATES, INC.
One Bellevue Center, Suite 570
411-108th Avenue NE
Bellevue, WA 98004
(206) 451-3938

SWEET, Charles W., President
KEARNEY: EXECUTIVE SEARCH
Division of A. T. Kearney, Inc.
222 South Riverside Plaza
Chicago, IL 60606
(312) 648-0111

LYNCH, Jennifer M., Partner
KINGSTON-DWIGHT ASSOCIATES
79 Milk Street, Suite 708
Boston, MA 02109
(617) 357-5008

PLEMMONS, Patrick F., Partner
LAMALIE ASSOCIATES, INC.
Tower Place
3340 Peachtree Road NE
Atlanta, GA 30026
(404) 237-6324

MacINNES, Dave, Vice President
M. B. SHATTUCK & ASSOCIATES, INC.
10 Bush Street
San Francisco, CA 94104
(415) 421-6264

PASTER, Steve, Senior Account Executive
MANAGEMENT RECRUITERS INTERNATIONAL, INC.
16530 Ventura Blvd., Suite 305
Encino, CA 91426
(818) 906-3155

VELGHE, Jim, President
MANAGEMENT SCIENCE ASSOCIATES, INC.
MSA Building
4801 Independence
Independence, MO 64055
(816) 795-1947

MEYER, Rod, President
MEYER INTERNATIONAL SEARCH
1811 Santa Rita Road, Suite 224
Pleasanton, CA 94566
(415) 846-9071

CARROLL, Richard J., President
MIDWEST MEDICAL CONSULTANTS
9001 Wesleyan Rd., Suite 315
Indianapolis, IN 46268
(317) 872-1053

MIERA, Orlando P., Managing Partner & CFO
MIERA & COHEN INTERNATIONAL
8305 Vickers
San Diego, CA 92111
(619) 279-8900

SIKES, Charles R., Vice President
MRA ASSOCIATES, INC.
1760 Exchange, Suite 235
Atlanta, GA 30339
(800) 523-1351

LINDBERG, Eric, President
MSI INTERNATIONAL
245 Peachtree Center Avenue
Atlanta, GA 30303
(800) 438-6086

RABINOWITZ, Peter A.
P.A.R. ASSOCIATES, INC.
27 State Street
Boston, MA 02109
(617) 367-0320

RESEARCH DEPARTMENT
PAUL STAFFORD ASSOCIATES, LTD.
45 Rockefeller Plaza
New York, NY 10111
(212) 765-7700

FOSTER, Dwight E., Principle In Charge of Executive Search Services
PEAT, MARWICK, MITCHELL & CO.
345 Park Avenue
New York, NY 10154
(212) 872-5522

QUIGLEY, John
QUIGLEY ASSOCIATES
345–83rd Street, Suite B
Burr Ridge, IL 60521
(312) 789-1200

DUVILL, Bill
R. E. LOWE ASSOCIATES
130 E. Wilson Bridge, Suite 100
Worthington, OH 43085
(614) 436-6650

DINGMAN, Bruce, Vice President
ROBERT W. DINGMAN COMPANY, INC.
32131 West Lindero Canyon Road
Westlake Village, CA 91361
(818) 991-5950

GRANT, Robert
ROBERT GRANT & ASSOCIATES
50 California St.
San Francisco, CA
(415) 981-7424

ROBISON, John H. IV, Associate
ROBISON & McAULAY
3100 NCNB Plaza
Charlotte, NC 28280
(704) 376-0059

GIFFORD, Dick, Managing Director
RUSSELL REYNOLDS ASSOCIATES, INC.
200 South Wacker Dr., Suite 3600
Chicago, IL 60606
(312) 993-6969

FORNINO, Rita, Department Manager, Health Care Services
SEARCH WEST
353 Sacramento Street, Suite 1316
San Francisco, CA 94111
(415) 788-1770

FERNEBORG, John R., Partner
SMITH, GOERSS & FERNEBORG, INC.
Ecker Square - Suite 600
25 Ecker Street
San Francisco, CA 94105
(415) 543-4181

SMITH, Toni, Managing Director, Health Care Practice
SPENCER STUART & ASSOCIATES
401 North Michigan Avenue
Chicago, IL 60611
(312) 822-0080

STEWART, Steve, President
S. K. STEWART & ASSOCIATES
The Executive Building
P. O. Box 40110
Cincinnati, OH 45240
(513) 771-2250

RATH, Connie
S.R.I.
301 South 68th Street
Lincoln, NE 68510
(402) 489-0351

HIGGINS, John B., Director
ARTHUR YOUNG EXECUTIVE RESOURCE CONSULTANTS
One IBM Plaza
Chicago, IL 60611
(312) 645-3000

ZIVIC, Jan, President
THE ZIVIC GROUP
555 Montgomery
San Francisco, CA
(415) 421-2325

Appendix B___
Association of Outplacement Consulting Firms

Headquarters and Branch Locations of Current Membership

United States
California

Drake Beam Morin, Inc.
18300 Von Karman Avenue
Suite 1050
Irvine, CA 92715
(714) 553-8404

The Ellermeyer Company[1]
17802 Sky Park Circle
Suite 200
Irvine, CA 92714
(714) 250-9541

The Ellermeyer Company
3415 Sepulveda Boulevard
Los Angeles, CA 90034
(213) 391-8291

Career Transition Group[1]
12100 Wilshire Boulevard
Suite 670
Los Angeles, CA 90025
(213) 820-4992

Drake Beam Morin, Inc.
Crocker Center
333 South Grand Avenue
Suite 470
Los Angeles, CA 90071
(213) 680-1661

The Irwin Company
6033 W. Century Boulevard
Los Angeles, CA 90045
(213) 649-1435

Jannotta/Bray, deRecat, Gallagher & Parker Associates
500 South Grand Avenue
Suite 2050
Los Angeles, CA 90071
(213) 895-7500

King, Chapman & Broussard, Inc.
Penthouse Offices
624 South Grand Avenue
Suite 2900
Los Angeles, CA 90017
(213) 614-0777

[1]**Denotes Home Office**

RMA Consulting
11444 W. Olympic Boulevard
10th Floor
Los Angeles, CA 90064
(213) 312-9516

The McCarthy Resource Associates[1]
1900 Avenue of the Stars
Suite 1400
Los Angeles, CA 90067
(213) 284-8955

Univance Outplacement Consultants[1]
2049 Century Park East
Suite 2290
Los Angeles, CA 90067
(213) 552-6969

Ward Associates-California[1]
3000 Sand Hill Road
Building 1, Suite 155
Menlo Park, CA 94025
(415) 854-7233

Career Transition Group
4040 MacArthur Boulevard
Suite 305
Newport Beach, CA 92660
(714) 476-1944

Univance Outplacement Consultants
5000 Birch Street
Suite 3000 West Tower
Newport Beach, CA 92660
(714) 476-3657

RMA Consulting
1600 Dove Street #420
Newport Beach, CA 92660
(714) 476-3030

The Irwin Company[1]
11338 Moorpark Street
Suite 203
North Hollywood, CA 91602
(818) 766-3900

Drake Beam Morin, Inc.
9171 Towne Centre Drive
Suite 355
San Diego, CA 92122
(619) 455-7131

The Ellermeyer Company
4370 La Jolla Village Drive
Suite 400
San Diego, CA 92122
(619) 546-4774

The Irwin Company
4350 La Jolla Village Drive
San Diego, CA 92122
(619) 546-4338

de Recat & Associates, Inc.[1]
150 Post Street
San Francisco, CA 94108
(415) 433-3987

Drake Beam Morin, Inc.
Four Embarcadero Center
Suite 450
San Francisco, CA 94111
(415) 986-3532

Mainstream Access, Inc.
351 California Street
San Francisco, CA 94104
(415) 398-9505

Transitions Management Group[1]
444 Market Street
Suite 333
San Francisco, CA 94111
(415) 981-0202

[1]Denotes Home Office

Robert S. Blake Associates, Inc.[1]
2055 Gateway Place
Suite 110
San Jose, CA 95110
(408) 297-7722

de Recat & Associates, Inc.
1054 Saratoga/Sunnyvale Road
San Jose, CA 95129
(408) 255-3734

Drake Beam Morin, Inc.
1731 Technology Drive
Suite 750
San Jose, CA 95110
(408) 286-2850

RMA Consulting[1]
2233 Huntington Drive
San Marino, CA 91108
(818) 795-4548

Drake Beam Morin, Inc.
100 Pringle Avenue
1 Walnut Creek Center
Suite 420
Walnut Creek, CA 94596
(415) 934-7073

Drake Beam Morin, Inc.
Warner Center Plaza
Suite 480
21600 Oxnard Street
Woodland Hills, CA 91367
(818) 710-7700

Colorado

King, Chapman & Broussard, Inc.
600 Seventeenth
Suite 1600N
Denver, CO 80202
(303) 892-6530

PMG Incorporated[1]
6000 East Evans
Building 2, Suite 400
Denver, CO 80222
(303) 759-9313

Drake Beam Morin, Inc.
6200 S. Syracuse Way
Suite 435
Englewood, CO 80111
(303) 850-9259

Connecticut

Lee Hecht Harrison, Inc.
River Bend Executive Park
77 Hartland Street
East Hartford, CT 06108
(203) 282-9800

Drake Beam Morin, Inc.
Farmington Mountain Office Park
30 Stanford Drive
Farmington, CT 06032
(203) 677-1400

J.J. Gallagher Associates
299 Farmington Avenue
Farmington, CT 06032
(203) 677-4412

The Career Development Team, Inc.
93 Cutler Road
Greenwich, CT 06830
(203) 661-0469

Drake Beam Morin, Inc.
181 Harbor Drive
Stamford, CT 06902
(203) 348-6616

J.J. Gallagher Associates
5 High Ridge Park
Stamford, CT 06905-1326
(203) 968-1555

Lee Hecht Harrison, Inc.
Six Landmark Square
Stamford, CT 06901
(203) 964-9600

Mainstream Access, Inc.
One Landmark Square
Suite 802
Stamford, CT 06901
(203) 964-0889

Swain & Swain, Inc.
10 Wright Street
Westport, CT 06880
(203) 454-2360

District of Columbia

Drake Beam Morin, Inc.
1828 L Street N.W.
Suite 600
Washington, DC 20036
(202) 466-6090

**Jannotta/Bray, de Recat,
  Gallagher & Maguire
  Associates**
1233 20th Street, N.W.
6th Floor
Washington, DC 20036
(202) 457-9586

Mainstream Access, Inc.
555 13th Street N.W.
Washington, DC 20004
(202) 347-0960

Manchester Inc.
1800 K Street, N.W.
Suite 1121
Washington, DC 20006
(202) 659-2555

Florida

Drake Beam Morin, Inc.
800 Douglas Entrance
Suite 350
Coral Gables, FL 33134
(305) 443-1955

Executive Group, Inc.
6821 Southpoint Drive North
Suite 229
Jacksonville, FL 32216
(904) 733-7100

Executive Group, Inc.
9100 South Dadeland Blvd.
Suite 508
Miami, FL 33156
(305) 661-2600

Drake Beam Morin, Inc.
2502 Rocky Pointe Road
Suite 375
Tampa, FL 33607
(813) 887-5339

Executive Group, Inc.[1]
One N. Dale Mabry Highway
Suite 990
Tampa, FL 33609
(813) 870-1230

Georgia

Drake Beam Morin, Inc.
2200 Century Parkway
Suite 220
Atlanta, GA 30345
(404) 321-1006

**King, Chapman & Broussard,
  Inc.**
900 Ashwood Parkway
Suite 200
Atlanta, GA 30338
(404) 390-3550

[1]Denotes Home Office

Illinois

The Thompson Group
2275 Half Day Road
Bannockburn, IL 60015
(312) 945-9244

**Cambridge Human Resource
  Group, Inc.**[1]
Two N. Riverside Plaza
Suite 2200
Chicago, IL 60606
(312) 454-9009

Drake Beam Morin, Inc.
55 West Monroe Street
Suite 500
Chicago, IL 60603
(312) 236-5770

Executive Assets Corp.[1]
333 West Wacker Drive
Suite 610
Chicago, IL 60606
(312) 558-9177

**Jannotta, Bray & Associates,
  Inc.**[1]
20 N. Wacker Drive
Suite 3600
Chicago, IL 60606
(312) 443-1401

Lulay & Associates, Inc.
320 N. Michigan Avenue
Chicago, IL 60601
(312) 782-0866

Mainstream Access, Inc.
224 South Michigan Avenue
Suite 425
Chicago, IL 60604
(312) 786-1808
(312) 786-1998/9014

Mulligan and Associates, Inc.[1]
20 N. Wacker Drive
Suite 2610
Chicago, IL 60606
(312) 346-9219

Sugerman Associates, Inc.[1]
150 N. Wacker Drive
Suite 2323
Chicago, IL 60606
(312) 726-1880

Drake Beam Morin, Inc.
1011 East Touhy Avenue
Suite 210
Des Plaines, IL 60018
(312) 299-2286

Lulay & Associates, Inc.[1]
477 E. Butterfield Road
#203
Lombard, IL 60148
(312) 960-0076

Hill Fitzgerald, Inc.[1]
Suite 624
Two Mid America Plaza
Oakbrook Terrace, IL 60181
(312) 954-7775

Indiana

Schonberg Associates, Inc.
650 East Carmel Drive
Carmel, Indiana 46023
(317) 843-0464

Executive Assets Corp.[1]
101 West Ohio Street
Suite 600
Indianapolis, IN 46204
(317) 684-3600

Business & Educational Associates, Inc.[1]
1316 Wabash Avenue
Michigan City, IN 46360
(219) 874-7474

Louisiana

Drake Beam Morin, Inc.
201 St. Charles Avenue
Place St. Charles
Suite 4310
New Orleans, LA 70170
(504) 582-1226

Maryland

Drake Beam Morin, Inc.
1122 Kenilworth Drive
Baltimore, MD 21204
(301) 494-0960

Mainstream Access, Inc.
1210 Woodside Parkway
Silver Spring, MD 20910
(301) 588-4212

Massachusetts

Drake Beam Morin, Inc.
1910 Prudential Tower
800 Boylston Street
Boston, MA 02199
(617) 267-2828

Stybel, Peabody & Associates[1]
6 Faneuil Hall Marketplace
Boston, MA 02109
(617) 367-5025

Troy Associates, Inc.[1]
4310 Prudential Tower
Boston, MA 02199
(617) 424-1800

MacKenna, Jandl & Associates, Inc.[1]
40 Salem Street
Lynnfield, MA 01940
(617) 246-4220

Michigan

Jannotta, Bray & Associates, Inc.
30700 Telegraph Road
Suite 2550
Birmingham, MI 48010
(313) 540-5650

Mainstream Access, Inc.
28588 Northwestern Highway
3rd Floor
Southfield, MI 48034
(313) 355-3400

Drake Beam Morin, Inc.
5505 Corporate Drive
Suite 100
Troy, MI 48098
(313) 641-5900

Minnesota

Drake Beam Morin, Inc.
8400 Normandale Lake Boulevard
Suite 470
Bloomington, MN 55437
(612) 921-8990

Compass Incorporated[1]
1200 Second Avenue South
Suite 300
Minneapolis, MN 55403
(612) 339-7387

Personnel Decisions, Inc.[1]
2000 Plaza VII Tower
45 South Seventh Street
Minneapolis, MN 55402
(612) 339-0927

[1]**Denotes Home Office**

The Thompson Group
514 Nicollet Mall
Suite 570
Minneapolis, MN 55402
(612) 340-9455

Missouri

Drake Beam Morin, Inc.
7701 Forsythe Boulevard
Suite 1295
Clayton, MO 63105
(314) 725-7441

**Human Resource Management
Corp.**
4900 Main St., Ste. 804
Bd of Trade Ctr, Country Club
  Plaza
Kansas City, MO 64112
(816) 756-1218

**Human Resource Management
Corp.**
7980 Clayton Road
Suite 200
St. Louis, MO 63117
(314) 644-5100

PMG Incorporated
1807 Park 270 Drive
Suite 220
St. Louis, MO 63146
(314) 576-2091

Swartout Associates, Inc.
11720 Borman Drive
Suite 210
St. Louis, MO 63146
(314) 997-1571

The Thompson Group
701 Emerson Road
Suite 300
St. Louis, MO 63141
(314) 977-6374

Nebraska

**Human Resource Management
Corp.**
810 North 69th Street
Omaha, NE 68132
(402) 399-8944

New Hampshire

Troy Associates, Inc.
835 Hanover Street
Manchester, NH 03103
(603) 644-7200

New Jersey

Drake Beam Morin, Inc.
334 Madison Avenue
P.O. Box 2046
Morristown, NJ 07960-2046
(201) 267-6300

Mainstream Access, Inc.
Parsippany Corporate Center
2 Sylvan Way
Parsippany, NJ 07054
(201) 267-4772

Drake Beam Morin, Inc.
685 College Road East
The Princeton Forrestal Center
Princeton, NJ 08540
(609) 799-5533

Manchester Inc.
Five Independence Way
Second Floor
Princeton, NJ 08540
(609) 520-9000

J.J. Gallagher Associates
85 Livingston Avenue
Roseland, NJ 07068
(201) 533-0390

Lee Hecht Harrison, Inc.
Park 80 West Plaza Two
Saddle Brook, NJ 07662
(201) 843-6000

New York

Windelspecht Associates, Inc.[1]
Shaker Park West
423 New Karner Road
Albany, NY 12205
(518) 456-5216

The Career Development Team,
  Inc.[1]
2112 Broadway
Room 301
New York, NY 10023
(212) 787-2247

Drake Beam Morin, Inc.[1]
100 Park Avenue
New York, NY 10017
(212) 692-7700

J.J. Gallagher Associates[1]
60 East 42nd Street
Suite 1850
New York, NY 10165
(212) 687-9688

Lee Hecht Harrison, Inc.[1]
200 Park Avenue
New York, NY 10166
(212) 557-0009

Mainstream Access, Inc.[1]
885 Third Avenue
22nd Floor
New York, NY 10022
(212) 230-2231

[1]Denotes Home Office

Mullin & Associates, Ltd.[1]
540 Madison Avenue
24th Floor
New York, NY 10022
(212) 980-4440

Swain & Swain, Inc.[1]
405 Lexington Avenue
50th Floor
New York, NY 10174
(212) 953-9100

North Carolina

Drake Beam Morin, Inc.
8720 Red Oak Boulevard
Suite 301
Charlotte, NC 28217
(704) 522-7416

Lead Associates, Inc.[1]
1509 Elizabeth Avenue
P.O. Box 35409
Charlotte, NC 28235
(704) 375-0480

Lead Associates, Inc.
408 Blandwood Avenue
Greensboro, NC 27401
(919) 274-7772

Lead Associates, Inc.
2100 Westpark Drive
Suite 202
Research Triangle Park, NC
  27713-2230
(Raleigh, Durham, Chapel Hill)
(919) 544-1869

Ohio

Schonberg Associates, Inc.[1]
1527 Madison Road
Cincinnati, OH 45206
(513) 961-6600

Drake Beam Morin, Inc.
1301 East Ninth Street
Suite 1900
Cleveland, OH 44114
(216) 621-5222

Louis Thomas Masterson &
   Company[1]
1301 East Ninth St.
Suite 1210
Cleveland, OH 44114-1824
(216) 621-2112

Patrick-Douglas Outplacement[1]
1111 Eaton Center
Cleveland, OH 44114
(216) 621-1550

Schonberg Associates, Inc.
6161 Busch Boulevard
Columbus, OH 43229
(614) 436-2022

Executive Assets Corp.
211 South Main Street
Dayton, OH 45402
(513) 449-8230

Oregon

Ward Associates—Northwest
9 Monroe Parkway
Suite 260
Lake Oswego, OR 97034
(503) 636-3886

Pennsylvania

Mainstream Access, Inc.
2045 Westgate Drive
Suite 406
Bethlehem, PA 18017
(215) 865-6633

Manchester Inc.
Walnut Hill Plaza
150 South Warner Road
King of Prussia, PA 19406
(215) 293-9100

Drake Beam Morin, Inc.
10 Penn Center
1801 Market Street
Suite 806
Philadelphia, PA 19103
(215) 564-3000

Mainstream Access, Inc.
1760 Market Street
7th Floor
Philadelphia, PA 19103
(215) 972-7000

Manchester Inc.[1]
One Independence Mall
Twelfth Floor
Philadelphia, PA 19106
(215) 351-1550

Drake Beam Morin, Inc.
600 Grant Street
Suite 1450
Pittsburgh, PA 15219
(412) 765-3410

Mainstream Access, Inc.
One Mellon Bank Center
500 Grant Avenue, Suite 2424
Pittsburgh, PA 15219
(412) 391-6633

Kranz Associates, Inc.[1]
Plymouth Meeting
Executive Campus
610 West Germantown Pike
Suite 150
Plymouth Meeting, PA 19462
(215) 825-9595

Texas

Drake Beam Morin, Inc.
Allied Bank Tower
Lock Box 210
1445 Ross Avenue
Dallas, TX 75202
(214) 855-0270

Drake Beam Morin, Inc.
5005 LBJ Freeway
Suite 900
Dallas, TX 75244
(214) 788-5302

King, Chapman & Broussard, Inc.
2323 Bryan Street
Suite 2100
Dallas, TX 75201
(214) 754-0666

Drake Beam Morin, Inc.
16945 Northchase Drive
Suite 2200
Houston, TX 77060
(713) 875-9371

Drake Beam Morin, Inc.
2525 Bay Area Boulevard
Suite 150
Houston, TX 77058
(713) 480-4311

Human Resource Management Corp.
9330 LBJ Freeway
Abrams Center, Suite 1185
Dallas, TX 75243
(214) 437-5511

King, Chapman & Broussard, Inc.[1]
110 Milam
Suite 3600
Houston, TX 77002
(713) 650-6484

Drake Beam Morin, Inc.
12500 San Pedro
Suite 695
San Antonio, TX 78216
(512) 490-1454

Virginia

The Thompson Group[1]
205 North King Street
Leesburg, VA 22075
(703) 777-3370

Washington

Executive Services Associates, Inc.[1]
515-116th N.E.
Suite 244
Bellevue, WA 98004
(206) 455-2228

Drake Beam Morin, Inc.
10900 N.E. 4th Street
Suite 800
Bellevue, WA 98004
(206) 454-7284

Ward Associates-Northwest[1]
10628 N.E. 38th Place
Suite 105
Kirkland, WA 98033
(206) 827-6876

[1]**Denotes Home Office**

Wisconsin

The Thompson Group
17700 West Capitol Drive
Brookfield, WI 53005
(414) 781-0150

Jannotta, Bray & Associates
735 N. Water Street
Suite 1128
Milwaukee, WI 53202
(414) 276-8797

Sugerman Associates, Inc.
250 East Wisconsin Ave.
Suite 1030
Milwaukee, WI 53202
(414) 291-9300

Canada

Ontario

Mainstream Access, Ltd.
1 First Canadian Place
Suite 5230
Toronto, Ontario M5X 1G3
(416) 367-3211

Mainstream Access, Inc.
1450 Hopkins Street
Suite 102
Whitby, Ontario L1N 2C3
(416) 644-4606

Western Europe

Belgium

NV Claessens SA
Louizalaan 479 B. 54
Brussels, Belgium
(02) 647 7590

Denmark

J-B Management Service Aps[1]
Julius Thomsens Gade 22
1632 Kobenhavn V, Denmark
45-1-37 41 11

The Netherlands

Raadgevend Bureau Claessens[1]
Beneluxlaan 35
3526 KK
Utrecht, The Netherlands
(0) 30-88 65 30

Appendix C
Recommended Readings

Amory, Thomas C. "Recruitment: Searching for a Search Firm." *Personnel Journal*, 62 (February 1983): 114, 116.

Ballantine, Caroline. "How to Work with a Recruiter." *Communication World*, 3 (December 1986): 32–33.

Beecher, Mathew J. "The Job Search: Tactics for Success." *FE: The Magazine for Financial Executives*, 2 (April 1986): 29–30.

_____. "What to Do When a Headhunter Calls." *Nation's Business*, 72 (October 1984): 50, 52.

Bottorff, Dana. "The Velvet Book." *New England Business*, 9 (October 19, 1987): 24–28.

Dee, William. "Evaluating a Search Firm." *Personnel Administrator*, 28 (March 1983): 41–43, 99–100.

Dorrell, John. "Anatomy of a Job Hunt." *Personnel Management (UK)*, 13 (July 1981): 31–33.

Dury, I.M. "Using an Executive Search Consultant to Find the Right Executives." *Hospital Administration Currents*, vol. 25, no. 3 (July-September 1981): 13–18.

Elmore, P.S. "Considerate Job Interviews Enhance Institution's Image." *Health-Program* vol. 65, no. 8 (September 1984): 38–39.

Ely, E.S. "How to Unmask Bogus Job Seekers." *Computer Decisions*, 17 (January 29, 1985): 100–107.

Engdahl, Lora. "The Who, What, Where, and Why of Headhunting." *Executive Financial Woman*, 2 (March/April 1987): 21–24.

Erdlen, John D. "Outplacement: How to Help Exiting Employees Tame the Job Market." *Association Management*, 34 (November 1982): 51–55.

Evans, Fred J., William A. Cohen, and Mary Pat McEnrue. "The Right Executive for the Job: An Interview with Three Top Headhunters." *Business Forum*, 11 (Summer 1986): 20–25.

Fitzgerald, James F. "Helping Departing Employees Find Another Job." *Personnel*, 64 (August 1987): 29–32.

_____. "12 Mistakes Made at Job Interviews." *Financial Executive*, 50 (February 1982): 30–34.

Hutton, Thomas J. "Increasing the Odds for Successful Searches." *Personnel Journal*, 66 (September 1987): 140–152.

Kennedy, James H. "When You Recruit an Executive Recruiter." *Marketing Times*, 30 (May/June 1983): 16–17.

McCreary, Charles. "Don't Assume Anything About Executive Search Firms." *Personnel Journal*, 64 (October 1985): 92, 94.

Nulty, Peter. "Pushed Out at 45—Now What?" *Fortune*, 115 (March 2, 1987): 26–30.

Nunan, James C. and Thomas J. Hutton. "How to Negotiate an Executive Job Offer." *Personnel Journal*, 66 (November 1987): 52–56.

Parkhouse, Gerald C. "Inside Outplacement—My Search for a Job." *Harvard Business Review*, 66 (January-February 1988): 67–73.

Phillips, Cleo and Celia Kuperszmid-Lehrman. "How to Make Your Executive Recruiter Work for You/How to Choose an Executive Recruiter." *Public Relations Journal*, 4 (April 1985): 23–24.

Polsky, Walter L. and Loretta D. Foxman. "Career Counselor: Professional Answers to Career Questions." *Personnel Journal*, 65 (December 1986): 35.

Rocco, F. and J. Faris, "Executive Recruitment. Part III—Evaluation and Selection." *Osteopathic Hospitals*, vol. 20, no. 9 (September 1976):11–13.

_____. "Executive Recruitment. Part II—The Interview: Intermediate Stage." *Osteopathic Hospitals*, vol. 20, no. 7 (July 1976): 10–13.

_____. "Executive Recruitment. Part I—The Planning Stage." *Osteopathic Hospitals*, vol. 20, no. 5 (May 1976): 13–15.

Smith, Donald and Ron Robertson. "Motivating the Terminated Executive." *Executive (Canada)* 24 (December 1982): 40–42.

Spooner, Peter. "Job Hunting." *Chief Executive (UK)*, (November 1983): 19, 22.

Stolley, Richard. "The Tales of Four Hunters." *Fortune*, 115 (March 2, 1987): 31–34.

Stoltenberg, John. "Job Hunting in the Work Jungle: The Eight Laws of the Jungle." *Working Woman*, 12 (April 1987): 95–97.

Stybel, Laurence J. "Does Outplacement Really Work?" *Business*, 33 (October/November/December 1983): 55–57.

Thompson, Jacqueline. "Anatomy of an Executive Search." *Management Review*, 75 (May 1986): 55–59.

Valentine, J.A. "In the Market for a CEO? A Shopping List of Needed Attributes Is an Important First Step." *Trustee*, vol. 39, no. 5 (May 1986): 22–23, 31.

Van Dam, Laura. "After the Fall: The Fired Executive." *New England Business*, 7 (June 17, 1985): 77–83.

Walsh, John D. "Changing Jobs? Your Best Bet: Tap the Hidden Market." *Marketing Times*, 30 (May/June 1983): 33–35.

Weinstein, Steve. "How to Capture a Headhunter's Attention." *Communication World*, 3 (January 1986): 26–27.

Index

REV:08-15 EXP:08-12 XX SIZ: 40.06

About the Editors

Earl A. Simendinger, PhD, is Professor and Chairman of the Department in Health Education and Health Sciences at Central Michigan University. Formerly he held a joint Adjunct Associate Professorship in the Schools of Medicine and Engineering at Case Western Reserve University.

He has been a practicing hospital administrator for 19 years. Former positions include the President of St. Luke's Hospital, San Francisco, California, and Vice President at University Hospitals of Cleveland, Ohio.

Dr. Simendinger holds a Doctoral Degree in Organizational Behavior from Case Western Reserve University, a Master's Degree in Health Care Administration from Washington University, St. Louis, Missouri, a Master's Degree in Industrial Engineering from Cleveland State University, and a Bachelor's Degree in Business Administration from Ashland College.

He is a Fellow of the American College of Healthcare Executives and a member of the Editorial Review Boards of both the *Journal of the American Medical Association* and *The Journal of Clinical Engineering.*

He has published over 30 articles in seventeen different health care and management journals and has co-authored *Organizational Burnout in Health Care Facilities: Strategies for Prevention and Change* (Aspen Publishers, 1985) and co-edited *The Effective Health Care Executive: A Guide to a Winning Management Style* (Aspen Publishers, 1986).

Terence F. Moore, MBA, MHA, is president and chief executive officer of Mid-Michigan Health Care Systems, Inc., Midland, Michigan, which operates Midland Hospital Center, Clare Community Hospital, Gladwin Area Hospital, two nursing homes, and seven other subsidiaries. He holds a master's degree in hospital administration from Washington University School of Medicine, St. Louis, Missouri, and BS and MBA degrees from Central Michigan University where he has done additional graduate work in economics.

Mr. Moore is a fellow of the American College of Healthcare Executives. He is a member of the boards of the Michigan Hospital Association, treasurer of the board of the Michigan Molecular Institute, and past chairman of the board of the 23-member East Central Michigan Hospital Council. In 1986 he received the Regents Award for the state of Michigan from the American College of Healthcare Executives.

He has published more than 35 articles and is the co-author of *Organizational Burnout in Health Care Facilities: Strategies for Prevention and Change* (Aspen Publishers, 1985). He is also co-editor of *The Effective Health Care Executive: A Guide to a Winning Management Style* (Aspen Publishers, 1986).

About the Contributors

Charlotte Beck, is manager of the Professional Placement Service at the Michigan Hospital Association Service Corporation, Lansing, Michigan. Her responsibilities include the operation of the placement services. She has extensive experience in recruiting, interviewing, and occupational counseling on the executive level. Ms. Beck received a bachelor's degree from Eastern Michigan University.

Joan Bourke, MM, is senior associate of Witt Associates. She joined the firm in 1969. Since 1984 she has provided executive compensation consulting services to institutions throughout the country. Assignments range from design and development of incentive compensation plans to CEO performance evaluation and counsel to the Executive Compensation Committee of the board. She also is the project director for the firm's annual executive compensation survey. Earlier she was director of administration responsible for all internal operations. She received her B.S.E. in 1963 from the DePaul University, Chicago, and M.M. (Manager of Management) degree in 1981 from Northwestern University Executive Program in Evanston.

Michael D. Caver, manages the national Health Care Practice of Heidrick and Struggles, Inc., international consultants in executive search, and is a partner and director of the firm. He received a bachelor's degree, Magna Cum Laude, from Hampden-Sydney College and was a Woodrow Wilson Fellow at Yale University. Prior to joining Heidrick and Struggles in 1979, he served as director of international personnel for Baxter Travenol Laboratories in Deerfield, Illinois.

Susan A. Cejka, CPA, is founder and president of Cejka & Company, a management consulting firm specializing in physician, administrative, and executive search based in St. Louis, Missouri. She holds a bachelor's degree in business administration from the University of Missouri-Columbia and is a licensed CPA. Cejka & Company has been ranked on the INC 500 list of fastest growing companies in America for the past two years. The firm handles over 250 search assignments annually.

John R. Clark, PhD, is manager of Health Care Executive Search Management Consulting Services for Coopers & Lybrand. He is a graduate of the University of Notre Dame. Mr. Clark also holds an MBA from Loyola University of Chicago School of Business and a Ph.D. in Industrial/Organization Psychology from Illinois Institute of Technology. He has been a speaker for numerous national and regional health care organizations.

Mark M. Cox, MBA, is vice president of Witt Associates Central Region. He joined the firm in 1979 and became a partner of the firm in 1984. He received a bachelor's degree in business from Indiana University and an MBA from the University of Dayton. He was assistant director of personnel at Miami Valley Hospital in Dayton and assistant administrator of Human Resources at Rock Island Medical Center in Rock Island, Illinois. He is a member of the American Society of Healthcare Human Resource Executives and the American Association of Healthcare Consultants.

J. Daniel Ford, MBA, is senior partner and executive vice president for Kieffer, Ford and Associates, Ltd. located in Oak Brook, Illinois. He obtained his undergraduate degree from Jamestown College (North Dakota) and an MBA specializing in hospital administration from the University of Chicago. Mr. Ford has been conducting management consulting and search assignments for senior level health care executives since 1977.

James N. Heuerman, MS, is senior partner and managing vice president of Korn/Ferry International's Health Care Division, located in San Francisco. He has a bachelor's degree in business and master's degree in hospital and health services administration from the University of Minnesota.

Michael C. Kieffer, MBA, is president and a founding partner of Kieffer, Ford & Associates, Ltd. With an undergraduate degree from Marist College and an MBA from Central Michigan University he spent seven years in hospital administration before beginning his consulting career. For the past several years, he has restricted his practice almost exclusively to CEO assignments representing every conceivable configuration including free-standing, teaching, community, multi-institutional, and religiously affiliated.

John S. Lloyd, MBA, MSPH, is president of Witt Associates Inc. He has been involved in the recruitment of hundreds of key executives in health care organizations and companies. He holds a bachelor's degree in business administration and an MBA/MSPH from the University of Missouri. He has been a speaker at numerous health care professional meetings and he is a member of the board of the Association of Executive Search Consultants.

Daniel M. Mulholland, III, JD, is partner in the law firm of Horty, Springer and Mattern, P.C., which specializes in the practice of health care law representing institutional providers such as hospitals, multihospital systems, and hospital maintenance organizations nationwide. He received bachelor's and master's degrees from Duquesne University and his Juris Doctor degree from the University of Pittsburgh School of Law.

Terry Riedinger, MA, is coordinator of the Dow Chemical Company's Employee Assistance Programs for the Michigan Division and U.S. Area Headquarters Unit. He received his bachelor's degree from Thomas More College and a master's in clinical psychology from Eastern Kentucky University. He worked as both a consultant and a psychologist for 15 years prior to assuming his present position.

Miceal Rooney, MA, is Vice President of Professional Services of Career Decision, Inc., Itasca, Illinois. He received a bachelor's and master's degree from the University of St. Mary of the Lake, Mundelein, Illinois. He oversees the consulting and testing program of its outplacement and management development services and had twelve years of counseling experience prior to joining Career Decisions, Inc.

Mark B. Silber, PhD, is president of his international Health Care Consulting firm, San Diego, California, and is the senior statesman of American College of Healthcare Executives. He received his doctorate from The Ohio State University in organizational psychology.

J. Larry Tyler, CPA, is president of Tyler & Company, Atlanta, Georgia. Mr. Tyler received a bachelor's degree in industrial management from Georgia Tech, a master's degree from Georgia State University and is a CPA. He is a member of ACHE, a member of AAHC and an advanced member of HFMA.

Peter J. Weil, PhD, is director of the Division of Research and Public Policy for the American College of Healthcare Executives. There he conducts research on health care executives' careers and industry trends. He received a bachelor's degree from the University of Chicago, a master's degree in health administration from the University of Iowa and a doctorate in sociology from the University of Chicago.